The Power of Education

Education and Learning

Dr. Sharon Campbell-Phillips

 pencil

ISBN 978-93-5458-405-3
© Dr. Sharon Campbell-Phillips 2021
Published in India 2021 by Pencil

A brand of
One Point Six Technologies Pvt. Ltd.
123, Building J2, Shram Seva Premises,
Wadala Truck Terminal, Wadala (E)
Mumbai 400037, Maharashtra, INDIA
E connect@thepencilapp.com
W www.thepencilapp.com

DISCLAIMER: *The opinions expressed in this book are those of the authors and do not purport to reflect the views of the Publisher.*

Author biography

My name is Dr. Sharon Campbell-Phillips. I am from Trinidad and Tobago. I am very enthusiastic about community work and the development of others. I am also very passionate about conducting research and writing as it allows me the opportunity to share my knowledge with others and educate them as well as enhance and develop myself.

I am currently employed with the local government of Trinidad and Tobago where I work at the Division of Community Development. This Division is dedicated to developing communities so that persons' standard of living can be enhanced.

My writing career began when I was approached by a classmate from Bangladesh to collaborate and write professionally. I accepted the challenge and we began writing together. When I received my first publication, I was very excited and was motivated to continue writing, I am also a Doctor of Health Sciences

CONTENTS

Chapter One Education and its Benefits Chapter Two Education and Society Chapter Three The Impact of Effective Education Chapter Four Social Networking and School Chapter Five Blended Learning Chapter Six The Pros and Cons of Online Learning Chapter Seven Boarding Schools Chapter Eight Adaptive Physical Education Chapter Nine The Importance of Grouping Chapter Ten Cross-Cultural Differences in Cognition.....16

Preface

Schooling has grown to be mandatory for all teachers at different degrees of training beneath the six-three-three-four system to undertake the techniques of non-stop assessment in evaluating college students' performance in all school subjects. It turned into also stated using various researchers that the coverage (1981) gives that, "academic evaluation and evaluation may be liberalized by way of basing them in whole or element at the continuous evaluation of the development of the person. It is therefore vital to observe that education, in the many disciplines, is vital to students' improvement. Researchers suggested that continuous assessment during studying is a technique of evaluation that involves a non-stop manner, for figuring out the cost of the method, an motion, a function or tool, that consist of a complies with up. The thing committed its attention to the application of non-stop evaluation method in the assessment of college students' performances in training. Blanketed the numerous factors which can be taught and allow students to express themselves and be assessed. The evaluation of the conventional topics was taught and examined to decide how nicely the trainer might have taught, whether or not the scholars could have found out, what comments are necessary to take delivery of to the scholars and what the instructor can do in another way. Greaves, 1983 argued that the subsequent strategies help more youthful children's linguistic expression, which includes their writing. they're all components of developing what Greaves and the 'writing network' and what I call a network of creators: Encouraging youngsters to work collaboratively for a while; allowing children manipulate over their writing processes, which incorporates giving them time to compose; Use of phrase processor by kids for drafting, modifying and re-drafting; Emphasizing various audiences for writing (along with for each different, for more youthful children, for oneself, for dad and mom, for the local community, in addition to for the teacher); stepping into children's resourceful worlds and Listening carefully to the children's perspectives of and reactions to writing.

This book is designed to analyze and recognize instructors' perceptions regarding the effectiveness of the implementation of continuous teaching that could assist college students to excel. This e-book is of crucial importance because it goals to teach and bring about cognizance. It's also crucial to emerging as privy to the brand new and to be had fine practices in training locally, and globally. The current education environments advocate that there's a need to empower instructors and encourage them to embrace the applications and are searching for to successfully enforce them. Globally, there has been a breakdown inside the place of technology training; therefore there's an extremely good need for curriculum reform in order that the vision and project will be truly stated and that the stakeholders can be truthful when remodeling the curriculum in order that it satisfies the needs of students. There have been hints for schooling packages emphasized troubles, which include up to date medical and technologic know-how, application of modern-day learning concept and teaching techniques". Also, there's a consensus among technology teachers that scholars look at too many regions, without enough intensity in each, therefore, a reform of the curriculum is of great need. Rodger W. Bybee of The National Academy of science also well-known shows that the level of assist for curriculum reform is unparalleled inside the history of Yankee training. Moreover, the curricula in center faculties comprise too many disconnected issues. Further, every topic is given identical priority which discourages the in-intensity study of foundational subjects. It's therefore recommended a revised curriculum that emphasizes a greater practical set of foundational subject matters and ideas are wanted within the observation of science. For this observation, the researcher used a mixture of methods to accumulate data that became then analyzed. Questionnaires, surveys, and commentary have been the channels to accumulate statistics. The motive of the look at is to study if training and curriculum reform can impact the way we research, and how. They analyzed statistics that can be used for similar studies, in addition, to influence curriculum reform in academic systems.

Introduction

Education plays a critical role in our lives and it is a bit blurry when to imagine what type of society we would have without education, and how we will function as individuals. Attending school and acquiring education is very critical to our development and it plays a major role in our life's journey. Education is the foundation of a successful career, financial freedom, the ability to think and reason critically, and to make informed decisions. Without education, we will be limited to perform tasks and we will be ignorant to the things that are happening in and around our surroundings, and according to Martin Luther King, a people without knowledge is like a tree without roots. For education to be of great value, there are many factors that need to be considered, for example, curriculums should be implemented. Curriculums are learning guides that are governed by a school board that is designed to address students' educational needs, facilitate learners while establishing relationships between teachers and students. They state the learning objectives, the grade letter and percentages, and the topics that are to be taught, and the specific order. It also lists the content, materials, resources, and the process for evaluating the set objectives. Education and curriculums are connected and share a relationship in which both of them are enhanced. Education is highly recognized when its foundation is that of an effective curriculum. It is very important as students pay close attention to such especially when comparing and selecting schools in which to attend. Curriculums can enhance education, boost the reputation of schools and attract learners. In Trinidad and Tobago, the education system caters to children from ages five (5) to eighteen (18), which is within the public sector. The education system consists of both primary and secondary schools. However, within the private sector, there are schools that include kindergarten, primary, secondary, colleges, and universities. The education system in Trinidad and Tobago is influenced by politics, the government, and wealthy entrepreneurs. For the public sector, the purposes of education are 1. to develop the country, 2. to develop the citizen's minds and character, and to educate them about what is current about what is currently taking place in their environment as well as globally. The education system within the private sector takes into consideration the working class who are interested in pursuing their education. Unfortunately, despite the many persons educating themselves, jobs are still unavailable and many persons unemployed. Some of the reasons for education in Trinidad and Tobago are similar as well as different to that of other countries but one of their common focuses is developing their country. Education is a process that facilitates learning while providing knowledge and skills which is transferred from persons to persons. Learning is done through different mediums such as research and discussion. Dictionary.com defined education as a process whereby persons transfer knowledge and information.

According to the World Bank's view, as it relates to

education, it is said that education plays a critical role in poverty reduction, enhancing one's standard of living and creating stability. It is both a guided process and an individual's self-educating commitment. Based on one's society and culture, the younger persons are usually trained by those that are older. Due to a person's understanding, knowledge of subjects and topics, and life experiences, he/she is considered well-educated and academically wealthy.

In order for learning to be achieved, there are educational instructions within the system that must be followed, so that persons can understand, assess, critically, and successfully analyze, evaluate, make informed decisions and judgments which is very important to one's development. The education process includes years of attending a school that ranges from preschool to university while incorporating many subjects and even cultures. Also, for learning to be realized, each teacher must teach truthfully and with clarity. Both students and teachers must be clear with the topics discussed otherwise confusion in the mind will be developed and the learning outcome will be a negative one. In some societies, learning is not achieved due to the unavailability of education as a result of a variety of barriers. However, every individual should have an equal opportunity to education without being discriminated against. The way in which a teacher presents students with a subject matter is very critical towards their learning; teachers should be well organized and should interact with each student. They also need to reinforce behaviors by using the various methods that are available. It is expected that teachers will be committed, focused, and willing to work with the students and impart knowledge to them. It is important that both the teachers and the students succeed at the objectives that they had set forth. Sadly, just like the American, many children do not receive the level of education that they deserve. Education should be a priority in society because, without it, the countries will be underdeveloped in all areas, citizens will be unable to achieve and it will increase crime and poverty. Lack of education is a burden on individuals and by extension the society and it will also increase the rate of illiteracy. As a people, we need to understand that we have a responsibility to impart our knowledge to others by educating them so that they can be equipped to make positive contributions to the development of society. Education is both theories as well practical and it is the foundation for all career paths; it also helps in enabling persons to resolve problems and issues that they are faced with. It also helps in forming relationships and helps in building communities while enhancing the stand of living for many persons. Education is a very important factor in our lives and is crucial to the way we live. As a teacher, when I teach, I include the various factors of the environment.

It is important that children learn not just about the physical, but the social elements that influence learning and help in the personal development of each learning. The physical factors of the environment include the structural classroom where students and teachers spend a certain amount of face-to-face contact hours, and students are provided with desks to sit on while the teachers teach and they have interactions. The physical structure is equipped with lighting, labs, technical equipment, and other fixtures that are used for resources and supplements. Factors of the social environment that I use when teaching include the building of relationships between myself and the students. I also teach in regards to culture and its norms which is of great value to the classroom. I also aim to be very polite and approachable to students and encourage communication which helps in motivating them and allows them to seek my assistance when they are faced with situations. My philosophical stance is that students must be developed holistically and not be limited to textbooks. Holistically means that focus will be placed on the physical, emotional, social, and spiritual. My belief has allowed me to have successful learning outcomes among students and it has been endorsed by my superiors. However, from the many global perspectives, I learn the differences and similarities among cultures about their views on the purpose of education. It is somewhat alarming to me to see how and what students across the globe are trained to learn. A classroom environment is very important to the learning outcome and development of children. It should be one that is student-friendly and promotes learning. It is the place where teachers influence the behavior of students so that they can develop, excel and achieve their academic goals. Within the classroom, students learn to form positive relationships; learn the value of teamwork as well as working independently, voice their opinions, understand the benefits of collaboration, and also discover their strengths and weaknesses. The classroom environment serves as a human development center where the focus is on the holistic development of the students, allowing them the opportunity to live their full potential. This is where students spend most of their time with their teachers as they learn the necessary skills which are useful and helps them in achieving their learning objectives. However, within the classroom, there must be established rules and procedures that will enhance learning. Without rules in the classroom, there will be no order and the classroom will be disorganized and learning will be affected greatly.

Rules also help teachers to discipline students and teach them responsibility and self-control, therefore, rules should be reinforced regularly. Based on the rules and procedures that are used in the classroom can either promote and enhance learning or hinder the classroom's objectives, therefore, teachers need to be mindful of their approach when creating and setting rules within the classroom as have a positive or negative effect on the students and their learning outcomes. For rules and procedures to create positive classroom environments and they must be clear, easy to understand, and remember, they must aim to create order within the classroom and they must be in accordance with the school's policy. They must be generally fair to the students while addressing their needs and should be easily enforceable and they should satisfy the students' parents. Teachers also need to clearly explain to the students what is expected of them and the consequences for not adhering to the rules. It should not be expected for students to change their behavior automatically, and because of such, the procedures and strategies that teachers may use within the classroom should empower students to do better. There are simple things that can be done to enforce those rules which include teachers providing each student with a list of the rules to take home so that their parents will be aware of them, and sticking up a list of the rules on the walls of the classroom. Also, teachers can have the students write down the rules in their books and then discuss them with them so that they will understand.

It is believed that when the learning environment is positive, the learning outcomes of students are also positive. According to supporting writers, students learn better when they view the learning environment as positive and supportive. A positive environment is one in which students feel a sense of belonging, trust others, and feel encouraged to tackle challenges, take risks, and ask questions. Such an environment provides relevant content, clear learning goals and feedback, opportunities to build social skills, and strategies to help students succeed. Some types of rules within the classroom should be encouraged and some should be discouraged because of the fact that some make positive contributions and others negative ones. Those that contribute positively should be reinforced as they impact the students' lives and help them to achieve success. On the other hand, those that are negative should be discouraged because they will affect learning negatively and will deprive them of succeeding academically and otherwise.

When rules are created within the classroom, teachers can know if they would have created a positive or negative classroom environment; they will be change positive or negative and can be easily recognized as well as the behavior of the students socially and towards their education. If after implementing rules within the classroom, if the environment is one that is hostile, disorderly, and chaotic, while a positive environment will be one that creates a feeling of safety, welcoming, and appreciation, and one that is very supportive and promotes learning. When the classroom environment is positive, the teacher will notice that the stress levels of students are reduced and their cognitive functioning increased. A negative environment also seems to be one that is associated with threats and negativity, and the students' self-esteem is usually affected. Learning can only take place when students feel comfortable in their environment which allows them to make positive classroom contributions as well as learn from others. A learning environment is one that seeks to address the needs of the learners and encourages interaction for growth among students and teachers. Additionally, teachers need to manage the classrooms in order for it to be positive so that learning can be achieved. They need to provide positive criticisms as opposed to negative ones, and compliment or award students on their achievements; they need to show appreciation so that it can be viewed as a motivation to the students. Teachers also need to discipline students in a professional manner instead of humiliating them and allow them to express themselves and state their opinions and views. However, while students should be allowed to be expressive, they need to be encouraged to maintain respect and positivity at all times. Critically, teachers need to be mindful of how they address situations; when they seek to correct the students' negative behavior, they need to do so professionally and not highlight the individuals who have done wrong. In that way, the message is for everyone and not just a few.

Chapter One Education and its Benefits Chapter Two Education and Society Chapter Three The Impact of Effective Education Chapter Four Social Networking and School Chapter Five Blended Learning Chapter Six The Pros and Cons of Online Learning Chapter Seven Boarding Schools Chapter Eight Adaptive Physical Education Chapter Nine The Importance of Grouping Chapter Ten Cross-Cultural Differences in Cognition

Chapter One

Education and its Benefits

1.

Training is a manner that facilitates studying while offering information and capabilities which is transferred from individuals to humans. Studying is completed thru special mediums which include research and dialogue. Dictionary.com defined education as a procedure wherein persons switch understanding and data. In line with the sector bank's view as it relates to schooling, it's far said that schooling plays a vital role in poverty reduction, enhancing one's widespread of living and creating balance. It's far both a guided manner and a man or woman's self-teaching dedication. Based on one's society and lifestyle, the younger persons are usually educated via those who are older. Because of men and women's knowledge, knowledge of subjects and subjects and lifestyles experiences, he/she is considered properly-knowledgeable and academically rich. So as for studying to be done, there are instructional commands that should be followed, so that human beings can recognize, investigate, seriously and efficaciously examine, evaluate, make informed decisions and judgment which is very crucial to at least one's improvement. The education manner includes years of attending a school that ranges from preschool to college at the same time as incorporating many subjects or even cultures. Additionally, for gaining knowledge to be found out, every trainer needs to teach actually and with readability. Both students and instructors need to be clean with the subjects mentioned in any other case confusion inside the thoughts could be developed and the mastering final results might be a poor one. Instructors might be devoted, targeted, and willing to work with the scholars and impart expertise to them. It's far critical that both the lecturers and the scholars succeed at the goals that they had set forth. One way in which instructors can know the scholars' stage of understanding is by using assessment.

Assessment permit instructors to understand if mastering is taking vicinity inside the classroom. The assessment facilitates to build of teacher/scholar relationships which can be important toward mastering even as promoting a pupil-mastering pleasant schoolroom environment. It's also a method that teaches duty that speaks to the measuring of powerful school room teaching and practices which strengthens relationships with the various instructors and students. Powerful teachings encompass assessment which determines studying results and that a powerful teacher-scholar dating can be the keystone that permits the opposite components to work well. The relationships between teachers and students can be influenced by assessments which serve as a form of encouragement that enhances their educational increase. Moreover, gaining knowledge is a process that entails cognitive and social psychological dimensions, and each process has to be taken into consideration if educational fulfillment is to be maximized. Schooling is one of the driving forces to our development; it's miles as essential as the air we breathe. It's the maximum critical possession someone ought to have.

It's far useful in lots of components of existence specifically, non-public and social, and it's far the handiest possession that can't be taken far away from us. Education is vital as it serves the cause of starting up the windows of opportunities. In this competitive world having terrific schooling is essential because the air we breathe because it's far our weapon to overcome the sector. it's going to help you develop as a character due to the fact the more information you've got the higher expertise you will have in any given hassle on the way to come to your manner. It going to come up with self-pride and could enhance yourself-self-belief. As a man or woman, I know it will help me in a whole lot of components in my lifestyle. It will provide me financial stability due to the fact you may be able to land a good activity and an excessive paying income. You discover ways to spend your cash and could discover ways to invest it accurately. The greater schooling you have, the greater admiration and acknowledgment you will get from people. Know-how is truly vital that is why we need to take it seriously. It's far the robust weapon you may have to triumph over this complicated international. When you have a very good education nobody can fool you and you may no longer tolerate any mistreatment from human beings. It'll give you better perspectives in life if you are well educated. Inside the social aspect of my lifestyle, education will supply me with higher expertise on a way to speak to human beings effectively. You'll understand what's occurring around me. For example voting, you may have sufficient information to carefully pick the candidate that you will vote for. You'll know what to keep in mind in deciding on the proper candidate to serve and shield our USA. You may be capable of apprehending the social issues that our country is going through and could be successful to assist in my very own little way. But, it's miles apparent on this competitive international that maximum of the hit person have the right schooling especially the better position in society they have proved that education will give you the threshold in life.

Education is essential in any society and it is recommended via parents, instructors, or even political leaders. Many people do now not understand why there's a lot of emphases located upon obtaining a terrific education and how precious it's far, this is why a few human beings do no longer put in as an awful lot attempt as they should, whilst others take it without any consideration. It's far important that everyone remember the fact that there are many advantages of schooling which include getting a job, earning an income, becoming aware of situations, becoming informed, and make better existence alternatives. This knowledge will assist you to develop a mindset that is conducive to mastering and will allow you to revel in the authentic advantages of training.

The time period twenty-first Century capabilities refer to knowledge, work habits, abilities and persona traits which are believed by way of the schooling global to be vital in nowadays world and particularly in nowadays offices. Whilst damaged down, the 21st Century talents can be categorized into three categories: lifestyles abilities, literacy abilities, and mastering talents. Getting to know capabilities contain the four C's: vital thinking, creativity, collaboration, and conversation. Literacy skills closely conscious of trustworthy assets and include data literacy, media literacy, and era literacy. Life abilities contain the tangibles of a student's normal existence: flexibility, management, initiative, productivity, and social capabilities. This paper will pick out skills that might be critical for college kids to achieve success as beginners, figuring out how they impact coaching practice, and making connections how they correlate with the worldwide Baccalaureate, or IB, concepts.

Exposing college students to a ramification of experiences that involve collaboration can't be underestimated in these days' classrooms. Within the Social abilities element of the procedures to mastering, there are the factors of respecting others, supporting others, social intelligence, and resolving battle. All of these connect at once to running in corporations or participating. This highlights the importance of making plans for and implementing studying opportunities wherein students are exposed to a diffusion of perspectives, viewpoints, and strategies by working with others. Teachers want to ensure they're offering these possibilities via the year in a selection of settings. Students nowadays are required not best to be literate within the language experience, but also media. As twenty-first Century talent in conjunction with an IB technique to studying, Media Literacy is diagnosed as ingesting and processing, considering online views and growing. Curriculum and instructors need to provide possibilities for students to apply those abilities. Facts literacy is another IB method to getting to know, under research talents, statistics Literacy is diagnosed as formulating and making plans, accumulating and recording, synthesizing and decoding, and evaluating and communicating. With an ever-converting international around us, a key ability for college students to study is flexibility. One Learner Profile characteristic from the IB that resonates with flexibility as a 21st Century ability is that of being open-minded. Constructing resilience permits students to end up bendy as beginners. Teachers must spend time on strategies for adaptation when things do not continually pass the manner that favors the scholars. As a 21st Century talent, important questioning is of the maximum significance for students to end up hit life-lengthy learners. Inside the IB program, crucial wondering is a major piece of the wondering competencies element of the processes to getting to know. It consists of analysis, evaluation, and forming selections. To embed those skills into the day-by-day curriculum is vital. Consequently, instructors have a responsibility to devise for students to learn about and think about questioning. This creates a shift from the traditional manner of focusing on the content to emphasizing incorporating expectations, language, modeling, opportunities, exercises, interactions, and intention putting. Standard, if there was one to be selected because the most important of the 21st Century competencies, it ought to be vital wondering. Out of all the skills stated, that one is utilized in every issue of studying and needs to be integrated into everyday practice. If college students can analyze, compare and shape selections, they are in true stead for being organized after their secondary training for whatever they put their minds to. If instructors are preparing novices via facilitating the

Cultural Forces of wondering, they're placing college students up for success.

Chapter Two

Education and Society

Schooling is a ray of light inside the darkness. It virtually is a wish for an awesome life and it's far a primary right of every human in the world. Schooling could be very important and noticeably valued in nowadays society; it is also important for success in life. Schooling is supposed to offer students the essential competencies that prepare them for the sector of work later in existence. The education gadget additionally serves to teach people the values and morals of society. The government ought to pay extreme interest to school and aid it economically although this is now and then not the case. College students need to be equipped with information and abilities which are needed to take part successfully as a member of society and make a contribution in the direction of the improvement of shared values and not unusual identification; the schooling system serves this purpose. The current decades within the US seems to have contributed to substantial racial, ethnic, and linguistic diversity in public schools, in particular in large city-regions. regardless of the impression of the public college device that racial segregation has been the subject of fifty years in the past; the progress of college integration has fallen far quick of expectations, black and white college students stay segregated throughout public faculties today. An intensive exam of the styles inside the big apple city public schools is applicable here. The theories of Marx, Durkheim, and Weber provide one-of-a-kind insights on the function of public education in society. whilst Marx views the schooling gadget as reproducing inequality, Durkheim feels that the training system is beneficial to all and sundry and it additionally capabilities to socialize young human beings right into a commonplace tradition. Weber, however, believes that a person's magnificence scenario will surely determine their social fame and in view that social reputation is tied to lifestyle, which shapes most of the people's beliefs and convictions the transition from reputation to an association to a positive political celebration is the natural development. This capacity to control one's environment comes again to Weber's perception that class is likewise decided by way of someone's opportunities to change their existing state of affairs. Even though these sociologists have debated the purpose and characteristics of the instructional structures, maximum agree that get admission to academic possibilities has a profound effect on man or woman lifestyles possibilities and attainment. Unique education guidelines and practices such as school preference, curriculum differentiation, college finance, and faculty challenge form the range of instructional opportunities to be had to college students.

Differences through social magnificence, race/ethnicity, and gender exist within the NYC public schooling gadget. The central query is whether or not or now not schools function to sell social mobility, fulfillment, and monetary properly-being or whether or not or not faculties function to breed social inequalities. Although instructional attainment is related to a character's family historical past (socioeconomic fame), the general public education machine is supposed to feature as an equalizer for those who cannot find the money for non-public schooling. In this case, I see the NYC public educational establishments in our society no longer as selling social equality but as promoting social inequalities. For two years, Jonathan Kozol writer of, Savage Inequalities visited the USA's public schools. He interviewed instructors, students, principals, and superintendents, as well as city officials, and newspaper journalists. The e-book exposes the extremes of wealth and poverty in America's public faculty machine and the impact it has on bad kids. He files the inequalities inside the USA's public education system among prosperous and poor districts. one in every one of his fundamental points is that the government does now not spend enough on the education of poor children, whilst spending far greater at the schooling of extra wealthy, white kids. In keeping with Kozol, the issues the colleges are going through are not the fault of the youngsters themselves, but as a substitute for a system that has let them down. Kozol offers thorough research and statistics, his appendix sincerely suggests how much greater is spent on youngsters residing in wealthy districts than on kids living in poor districts. Similar to his statistics, the strongest part of Kozol's e-book is his selection to allow the children to communicate for themselves.

Thus, "New York metropolis's public faculties are subdivided into thirty-two college districts. The district incorporates a big part of the Bronx, however, is an effective, separate district. The sort of district, Riverdale, is the northwest phase of the Bronx. Home too many of the city's state-of-the-art and nicely-educated households, its essential schools have exceedingly low-income students. The opposite phase to the south and east is bad and heavily non-white". Public faculty two hundred and sixty-one in District capability is meant to be nine hundred college students, however, a lovely 1000, three hundred attend. The elegant sizes make up thirty-two kids in all, with the simplest one trainer. Even greater, textual content books are scarce and students should proportion with one another. The college itself is 90% black and Hispanic; the other ten percent is Asian, White, or middle eastern. The college library is small and windowless; there are only about seven hundred books. The school most effective has twenty-six computer systems for its a thousand, 3 hundred attend kids. One instructor comments, "They realize what suburban faculties are like. Then they look around them at their faculty. This became a roller rink, that they don't comment on it however you spot it of their eyes. They understand." in line with a record by the community carrier Society, some of the allocations derive from state legislators where they have political allies. The poorest districts in the metropolis receive about 90 cents in line with pupils from those legislative offers, even as the richest districts get fourteen dollars according to scholars. Even more, an official of the Board of education believes that there is no factor in putting further cash into some terrible districts due to the fact new instructors could not live there. Here we will see that the notion of poor districts being beyond help; or in other words, they're in the end pronouncing that youngsters who stay in those neighborhoods are poor investments. The blackboards are badly cracked, there are gaping holes within the flooring, plaster and ceramic tiles have peeled off or are within the procedure of; "a landscape of hopelessness-burnt out residences, boarded home windows, the vacant lot upon rubbish-strewn vacant lot" surrounds the faculty. Of the scholars in this college, thirty-8 are black, sixty-two percentage Hispanic. There are no white college students within the building. In line with a small child, Alexander who's sixteen, "you may recognize things higher when you cross among the rich. You look around at your college, although it's rude to do this, you are taking a deep breath at the sight of all the one's lovely surroundings. Then you come again domestic and see that there are belongings you do not have. You believe you studied the distinction. Not at first. It takes some time to settle in." then again, there are the one's colleges which might be intended to be enclaves of advanced education, non-public faculties, basically within the public device, says Kozol. At one faculty, the crenelated ceiling, which is white and spotless, and the polished dark-wood paneling assessment with the collapsing structure of the target market at Morris excessive. All the college students are white. The trainer relates that the students are reading Robert Coles, Studs Terkel, and Alice Walker. One student, Jennifer relates that the weight of assisting terrible kids ought to no longer be their hassle, and that taxing the wealthy to help the negative wouldn't make a better instructional revel in for her. Kozol factors out that in the big apple the prejudice is even more excessive considering each youngster within the suburbs receives an education well worth $11,000 a year, while an internal city toddler gets the most effective $5,500. It's far vital to notes that the Board of training complains about unequal spending among towns across the county however shall we the spending be so unequal in groups' facet with the aid of side. This spending sample is an important part of public coverage in any respect levels of government and it cheats minorities and the terrible out in their rightful education and out of the life of success and self-improvement which stems from a very good education.

Training teaches the capacity to study and write. Reading and writing is step one in education. Most information is performed with the aid of writing. Therefore, the shortage of writing talent way missing out on quite a few data. Consequently, training makes people literate. Education is extremely essential for employment. It definitely is a superb possibility to make a respectable dwelling. This is due to the capabilities of a high-paying job that training gives. Uneducated people are in all likelihood at a large downside in terms of jobs. It looks as if many bad human beings enhance their lives with the assist of schooling. Better communique is yet every other position in education. Schooling improves and refines the speech of a person. Moreover, people additionally improve another method of verbal exchange with education. It makes a person a better person of era. Education surely presents the technical capabilities essential for using technology. As a result, without training, it'd likely be tough to master your competencies and talents. Humans become more mature with the assist of training. Sophistication enters the existence of educated people. Particularly, education teaches the cost of the field to individuals. Educated human beings additionally realize the cost of time a whole lot greater. To knowledgeable people, time is identical to money. It permits people to specific their views successfully. Knowledgeable individuals can explain their evaluations clearly; consequently, educated humans are pretty probably to persuade human beings to their factor of view. Pronouncing that education is vital is a real understatement. It's a weapon to enhance one's lifestyle. It might be the maximum important device to trade one's lifestyles. Schooling for a child begins at home. It's a lifelong technique that ends with demise. It definitely determines the exceptional of a man or woman's lifestyles. Education improves one's understanding, talents and develops the persona and mindset. Most noteworthy, training impacts the chances of employment for humans. A highly educated character is probably very possible to get an amazing process. In this essay on the importance of training, we will inform you approximately the fee of schooling in existence and society.

Significance of education in Society

Education allows in spreading understanding in society. This is perhaps the most noteworthy component of schooling. There may be a brief propagation of information in an educated society. Furthermore, there may be a transfer of know-how from one generation to another via education. It enables the development and innovation of the era. Most noteworthy, the extra the schooling, the more era will spread. Essential traits in conflict gadget, remedy, computer systems, take region due to training. The price of education has changed over its route of decades. It was a privilege for a young person to attend faculty and similarly their schooling, but today's society has appeared to make training into more of a satisfaction booster rather than a privilege. There are such a lot of opportunities for a few teens to visit college, but many do not pursue it. Offers, scholarships, housing assistance, online textbooks are a few examples of methods to reduce down the cost of schooling. Even though many teens have the full possibility to attend college, many college students do no longer have a circle of relatives support or feel a feeling of self-confidence to have the ability to complete faculty and further their education. Many excessive school students have dropped out of faculty for numerous reasons; styles of crime among students are escalating amongst faculty dropouts within society. The theoretical version of this has a look at proposes that the social bond is bolstered or weakened idea socialization stories within the circle of relatives, school, peer groups, and the network and that this system influences on the difficulty of dropout status. The lack of possibilities in college, prosocial sports, and interaction with prosocial others increases the vulnerability of the at-hazard baby for dropping out. Even though dropouts showcase extra frequent and extreme crime among students, patterns of deviant behavior range according to the motives for leaving school and the extent of different social and personal troubles. Dropping out of faculty has many effects which include engaging in criminal sports, and crook conviction. Logistic regression showed academic achievement, academic aspirations, and leaning-centered school settings to be associated with a decline in deviant results independent of the outcomes of disadvantaged socioeconomic background, low intelligence, formative years conduct troubles, and having deviant pals at some stage in childhood. Associations among college struggle and later deviancy had been mediated by deviant peer relationships in youth and other college characteristics.

Many research reporting continuity of adolescence conduct troubles and the have an effect on of adolescent affiliations with deviant peers on bad consequences changed into support. Numerous theoretical positions may be appealed to regarding the connection between dropping out of school and criminal activities. The two criminological theories which have received the maximum interest in terms of criminal behavior in kids are strain theory and social control theory. Today, there are a huge variety of juveniles losing out of school for numerous motives. The hassle offers a domino impact. Essentially, as soon as a juvenile drops out of middle and excessive school, the chance of the juvenile dropout turning into deviant may be very high. Whilst students pick to depart the educational organization, they placed themselves at an extreme disadvantage. Society in widespread locations an excessive top rate on schooling. Training and the acquisition thereof assist the direct connection to the activity markets. Therefore, the cause of this research is handiest to stumble on and analyzed the reasons why juveniles drop out of college and explore juvenile dropout acquaintance with the crook justice gadget, because of their deviant behavior. Fisher (2010) keeps juveniles who drop out of college have interaction in gang violence, toddler prostitution, and crime. a number of the extra standard regions consist of unmarried figure homes, peer pressure, and childhood pregnancies. According to the pressure principle, delinquent behavior is an edition to a feeling of dissatisfaction, displeasure, or intention blockage. In traditional strain theory, youth who enjoy educational and social failure in school have two feasible publications of movement. One answer is to stay in college and decrease the pressure produced with the aid of one's terrible college stories using conducting delinquent conduct. Because delinquency presents a feel of status and fulfillment that isn't received in school, involvement in delinquency is anticipated via the principle to result in a discount in stress. The second possible solution is to eliminate oneself from the supply of stress and depart school. As soon as one has left college and no longer feels strained by using college failure, the motivation for delinquent behavior is faded. Consequently, conventional strain theorists might predict an inverse courting between dropping out of college and next delinquency because leaving college could lessen strain and, consequently, the primary motivation for delinquent behavior. This principle focuses on the relationship among demographic factors, together with socioeconomic status, gender and ethnicity, and dropout. Boys are more likely to drop out than girls and dropouts are maximum possibly from a circle of relatives with low socioeconomic popularity. There was rivalry over the have an effect of ethnicity on dropout prices. But, it does have a few impacts. Low socioeconomic status is a substantial predictor of dropout beyond negative academic fulfillment.

In current years or even in today's society, Trinidad and Tobago have been experiencing an increase of social issues within the academic device bearing on to school dropout and crime.

Many individuals trust that the educational device is in part responsible for the number of college dropouts and criminal activities that exist among our youths, and consequently, wishes to put into effect and/or regulate its sports so they may be served as crime prevention measures, and as a result, cast off the number of ability criminals that are inside the colleges. maximum of these students, who've decided to give up on college and their training, started showing their crook behaviors within the college even earlier than they have become dropouts. It is absolutely discovered inside our groups that numerous of our faculty dropouts are carrying out crook sports. Even though college crowning glory charges have continually grown for the duration of most of the past years, dropping out of school persists as a hassle that interferes with academic gadget performance, and the maximum honest and fulfilling path to character instructional dreams for young people. There are numerous motives why students drop out of school; a number of those motives are academic struggles, peer pressure, lack of parental aid, loss of monetary guide, and many others. The reason for a scholar dropping out is often termed because of the antecedent of dropout because it refers back to the pivotal event which ends up in dropout. This occasion, but, is the fruits of a miles longer manner of leaving college that began long earlier than the date that a student simply discontinues attendance.

Dropping out of college is a serious national, kingdom, and nearby trouble. Students who drop out of school have fewer alternatives for employment and are at more hazard of low self-esteem. school dropouts usually become operating low-professional and occasional-paying process-positions with fewer possibilities for development, or maybe accomplishing crook sports as a means of survival or to healthy within a gang/ institution. Crime is a poor externality with great social prices. If training reduces crime, then schooling could have social benefits that are not taken into account by people. The social return to training can also exceed the personal go back. Given the big social prices of crime, even small discounts in crime related to education may be economically vital. There are several reasons to believe that education will affect the next crime. First, training will increase the returns to legitimate work, raising the opportunity costs of illicit behavior. Additionally, punishment for crime commonly includes incarceration.

By way of raising salary charges, schooling makes this 'misplaced time' dearer. Second, schooling may additionally at once affect the economic or psychic rewards from the crime itself. Sooner or later, training may additionally adjust choices in oblique ways, which may additionally affect decisions to interact in crime. As an example, education might also increase one's patience or threat aversion. On the internet, we assume that most of these channels will lead to a terrible courting between education and usual violent and assets crimes.

Students who get to go to university without worrying approximately paying off college, living charges, and so on. Are the scholars who need to discover ways to be humble for the scholars who aren't as fortunate as they are a few students don't have any help from their own family, struggle with the pressure of budget and housing, and but are treated the same as the students who're greater lucky than they may be. Incoming freshmen shouldn't experience like they need to be there; that they have to work to get to that factor. Incoming freshmen want to learn how to be humble to their surrounding friends before they may ever truly need to be in university. Many recent articles were complaining approximately the price of college, and if the value is virtually really worth going. Many dads and mom say they spend most of their profits on paying for faculty for his or her kids, however, there are also many economic options for supporting pay for college. Grants can be presented to what degree is being pursued, what race or ethnicity someone is, low-income families, and the list is going on and on. Scholarships run the identical way; alongside grade point common, writing skills, and hobbies in companies. With a little work, the university can be less expensive, similarly to being a laugh via being a part of the college itself. Some organizations will award grants and scholarships to students which will have possibilities to collect training in their subject of preference.

Education is the know-how of information, abilities, and moral values. It is critical for the boom and improvement of college students. It serves because of the route of the thoughts of a young grownup. A college education is a critical degree as it facilitates college students to recognize and respect the importance of training within society. It's an optional level of a formal device of education that offers vocational gaining knowledge. The university experience teaches the young technology to work with the aid of getting ready psychologically for the actual global. College students learn how to replicate, explore, concentrate, and suppose beyond their obstacles. The general higher schooling supplied in schools includes relevant, theoretical, and summary studies, and applied aspects. Socially, a body of workers that has many human beings with studying skills complements productivity. High productivity improves the output and incomes of the economic system. In some regions, university education has decreased crime prices, improved the significance of civic participation, and stepped forward the social, monetary activities. Schooling presents a high cost to the economic system due to the fact educated people to stay and work in standard. Earnings vary with academic attainment. For instance, those who have attained a university diploma earn extra than people with excessive faculty diplomas. The university revel in improves the pupil revel in because of the meet with humans from distinct parts. It provides extra information about the society and present-day events. Schooling complements a person's popularity and social image with a sturdy education foundation. College schooling has stepped forward social fairness in society. For individuals without a fortunate heritage, training affords the same platform with their opposite numbers. In the long run, training improves human lifestyles with the aid of coaching the more youthful generation on the significance of expertise, competencies, values, and customs. At some stage in the university lifestyle, individuals face one-of-a-kind demanding situations. But, these demanding situations allow the graduates to find out their weaknesses and strengths. Economically, college schooling has contributed a lot compared to the high school level. As an instance, college graduates earn a good revenue hence they may be less reliant on authorities.

Every twelve months the Mauritian authorities devote an increasingly more massive proportion of its finances to the improvement of the education region. The purpose for such a boom in authorities' investment in schooling lies in the perception that schooling has an instantaneous impact on the monetary boom of the USA. In most developing nations, like Mauritius as an instance, training is regarded as a powerful tool for lowering poverty and casting off social and profit inequalities, enhancing financial increase and standards of dwelling, and helping the United States of America to reinforce its autonomy. Many researchers recommend that education also has a few superb oblique results consisting of increasing longevity, enhancing democratization and political balance, and reducing poverty and crimes. Education in many countries is considered as funding in human capital. Human capital can be described because the knowledge, abilities, and competencies of an individual, obtained via training, training, and enjoyment, which assist the latter to be more efficient and as a result enhance his capability profits earning. Ismael has emphasized the reality that, via investing in human beings, we will benefit from a few varieties of benefits in the future. However, Blankneau and Simpson (2004) discover no clear evidence of the link between authorities' spending on training and economic growth. Human capital is one of the most important additives of sustainable financial improvement of a country as illustrated by Lucas (1988) and Romer (1990) in their "new growth" literature. The improved neoclassical growth model advanced using Mankiw, Romer, and Weil and the endogenous growth fashions developed using Lucas (1988) and others have handiest these days harassed at the significance of human capital in growth theories.

Even though human capital incorporates health, experience, abilities, education, and other social elements, in this paper we can listen simplest at the role of education and its results on the financial development of Mauritius. One problem that arises is while coping with the size of human capital. In fact, there's no agreed definition of which proxy ought to be used to symbolize human capital. Commonly, the average quantity of years of education has lengthy been seen as a handy proxy. Some researchers, for example, Mankiw et al. (1992) use secondary enrollment as a proxy for schooling and Barro (1998) uses enrollment in different ranges of education, i.e. primary, secondary and tertiary, and also enrollment using gender as proxies. In our take, a look at us can be the use of the common wide variety of years of various training degrees as proxies for education. Petrakis and Stamatakis (2002) have careworn on the truth that each unique stage of education has a distinctive effect on the boom. As an instance, they find that the effect of number one and secondary education at the economic boom of growing countries is extra widespread than that of tertiary schooling, and for advanced countries, it's miles the reverse state of affairs that takes region. Because it improves human capital, we could say that schooling does have an effect on economic increase predominantly, but surely, the effect of education on economic improvement is quite ambiguous. There were limitless debates over the years through researchers over whether training has a fantastic, negative, or no courting in any respect with the economic boom of a rustic. Barro (1991) unearths that training has a high-quality and giant impact on economic growth. He observes that any rise in enrollment price increases GDP too. De Meulmester and Rochet (1995) offer evidence that this relationship may not continually be genuine. Devarajan et al. (1996) locate that education has a poor impact on the economic boom for a few developing countries. They deduce that growing international locations are not effective at the margin due to the fact those countries do now not fairly allocate their public capital expenditure and this explains the opposing dating between training and financial boom. a few different researchers, along with Hanushek and Woessmann (2007), locate that it's miles in fact the first-rate of education that promotes monetary development and now not the amount of training or schooling attainment. They study that the competencies of the population immediately affect the distribution of income and monetary boom. The motive of this paper is to determine the effect of education on the economic increase of Mauritius.

Education is in no way a finishing procedure and as stated in a famous diction, "education starts from the womb and ends inside the tomb". schooling benefits the society via assisting to boom monetary boom, reducing poverty, reducing crimes, increasing employment and also allows the character to earn higher earnings and therefore improves the latter's residing fashionable. There is irrefutable evidence that connects training to financial boom and training in the shape of human capital boosting productiveness. Training is in truth "productiveness-improving". It's far stated that a person without fundamental literacy and numeracy competencies has many problems in finishing basic duties of everyday lifestyles, which therefore suggests the importance of education. It influences the growth of the economy in various approaches. We here talk about the direct consequences of education. Schooling is stated to be linked to the perception of empowerment. People with a certain level of higher education no longer simplest have a top job with interesting wages however additionally augment the productiveness of the economy. A few studies have shown that GDP per capita rises through one to three percent factors following a one percent factor increase in faculty enrollment quotas. Therefore, schooling is said to increase individuals' wages together with the augmentation of productivity and sooner or later GDP per capita. Mother's training has oblique positive results on the economy. It is stated that a further yr of mom's education will induce the kid to be in better fitness and encourage them to research so one can finally boom their probabilities to be an effective man or woman within the future and affect the financial system positively. Furthermore, knowledgeable people are more likely to be aware of their own family making plans and this may in the end lessen childbirth. This affects families having more or much less 1 to two youngsters, that is, a smaller family where greater time is devoted to the children's training. This interest in return motivates the youngsters to be extra inspired at college and have higher consequences. These children are for that reason recommended to pursue their schooling to better degrees. Moreover, knowledgeable people are more likely to evolve to a new era and new running strategies easier than illiterate people. It's also said that an educated body of workers is greater productive than an uneducated staff, this is, the return of an educated worker is better in comparison to that of an uneducated one. Better returns have a positive impact on the financial boom. Michaelowa (2000) uses the example of a knowledgeable farmer who makes use of "new agricultural techniques" to supply goods. Through training, the farmer will accumulate the information and competencies required to apply those new agricultural techniques and therefore he could be more effective compared to different farmers who're still the usage of traditional strategies.

The alternative farmers in the neighborhoods will tend to do the equal on the way to acquire higher earnings, so this causes both the farmer and the pals to have better returns and in flip increases GDP consistent with capita. There is a dating among training and character income which in turn produce private returns. The Mincerian equation enables us to distinguish between the unique levels of education and distinguish their results in the financial system. He additionally claims that an additional year of education will cause higher personal returns. Ramsey (1928), amongst others, evolved the neoclassical version of economic increase. In his model, Solow (1956) claimed that important factors determined growth, specifically the amount of hard work and the capital stock. The neoclassical model assumes diminishing returns to capital and labor independently, and the enter-output ratio is decided with the aid of exogenous technological elements. This model does not recall the outcomes of things including human capital, health, and so forth at the financial development. In reality, Schulz (1961) proved that labor and capital did no longer explain absolutely the growth in output and Lucas (1988) talked about that funding in human capital is one of the fundamental determinants of monetary improvement. Moreover, that allows you to offset the damaging outcomes of diminishing returns, as a result permitting the economy to grow, the neoclassical version suggests that the USA needs to invest heavily in a generation. In theory, this is one of the reasons why low-income international locations with low ratios of capital to labor are in all likelihood to develop quicker than wealthy countries. But empirical results have proven some inconsistencies with this hypothesis as tested with the aid of Summers and Heston (1988). Also, Lucas (1988) and others evolved the endogenous increase models to overcome the shortcomings of the neoclassical boom models. Inside the endogenous increase model, exogenous technological progress does not affect constant boom. This model introduces human capital as an entering within the form of effective hard work and means that the accumulation of human capital immediately impacts labor productivity. The principle difference between effective labor and bodily labor lies in the truth that the previous is calculated through contemplating labor nice along with academic degree, education, and abilities. Each Lucas (1998) and Romer (1990) have used agents to symbolize the outcomes of the human capital of their fashions respectively. Human capital is the decisive input that generates new merchandise and era in the research & improvement zone and consequently, this implies that international locations with high degrees of human capital shares will develop quickly due to the extra speedy improvement of new merchandise and generation generated through them. Lucas (1988) incorporates human capital in his version and claims that the accumulation of human capital will enhance the productivity of other elements and as a consequence will raise the monetary boom. He additionally affirms that in no way finishing will an increase in human capital will result in by no means-finishing financial boom. In his version, human capital is a measure of talents and skills utilized in manufacturing with the aid of an employee. However, Grossman and Helpman (1994) kingdom that its miles a few shapes of expertise which could finally reason by no means-ending increase, no longer human capital.

Schultz (1999) outlines the significance of human capital through training and fitness in figuring out economic increases. He insists that schooling will increase each human beings' cognizance and their investments in fitness offerings, and additionally, healthy humans have a tendency to be extra efficient and consequently greater efficient. Barro (1991) finds that training and financial boom are highly correlated. He makes use of enrollment charges as a proxy for education and in step with capita GDP as a proxy for monetary increase. information is accrued throughout extra than 100 countries at some stage in the years 1960 to 1990 and Barro unearths that every additional 12 months of enrollment increases in step with capita GDP. Bils and Klenow (2000) additionally come upon comparable outcomes of their research. They locate that variation in education explains about one-third of the variant in economic growth. even though Bils and Klenow (2000) provide proof of the nice courting among training and monetary improvement, additionally they claim that more boom could bring about extra education and now not the alternative, i.e. there may be an opposite causation effect. Barro and Sala-i-Martin (1995) use pass-united states statistics made from ninety countries over the time span 1965-1985. They appoint the AK framework, which displays consistent go back to the capital as it assumes that the opposite elements (exertions and generation) that decide GDP develop proportionately with capital. In other phrases, each capital increase will increase output correspondingly. Their effects suggest a strong high-quality relationship on the lengthy-run among common GDP in line with capita and the extent of tutorial attainment, terms of trade, and lifestyles expectancy. but, a few researchers claim that the kind of regressions performed via Barro and Sala-i-Martin (1995) may be difficult to reverse causation impact as said earlier. For instance, an upward push in GDP may want to increase funding in schooling because the economic system develops. Such types of outcomes will have a splendid effect on our research as we want to study the effect of education on the monetary boom and now not the opposite. Akcabelen (2009) uses the ARDL technique to decide the quick-run and lengthy-run outcomes of various tiers of training on Turkey's financial development. Secondary enrollment and tertiary enrollment are used as extraordinary proxies for education and this allows us to observe the effect of each degree of training at the monetary growth.

Akcabelen concludes that there is an effective correlation between all ranges of training and the lengthy-run economic development of Turkey. Loening (2002) makes use of time-series records from 1951 to 2000 and applies the error-correction methodology to research the effect of education on the economic increase of Guatemala. He observes that output in step with the employee will increase via zero. sixteen percent following a one percent upward push within the common years of schooling. So he concurs at the reality that education does have a superb impact on the overall financial development of us of a. moreover, Afzal et al. (2010) use time-series information from 1970-2009 to analyze the relationship between training, bodily capital, inflation, poverty and monetary boom in Pakistan. According to their findings, training and bodily capital have both a tremendous and tremendous impact on monetary growth inside the short-run in addition to inside the long-run-in addition they find that inflation slows down the financial boom in the lengthy-run and poverty has no impact in any respect on the financial development of Pakistan. other researchers, including Kakar et al. (2011), have used time series data for the time span 1980-2009 and practice the mistake Correction model (ECM) and are available to the conclusion that education influences Pakistan's monetary improvement handiest inside the long run. additionally, the study that the 'great' of education is greater critical than the 'amount' of training in reaching economic boom, so the government should increase its investment in training to enhance the satisfaction of training further. When you consider that Mauritius is part of Africa, it is also appropriate to peer the consequences of researches performed in different African nations. Fonkeng and Ntembe (2009) use enrollment and GDP as proxies for training and economic development and they note that schooling at a higher level, i.e. at the tertiary level, is positively correlated with the financial boom of Cameroon. Musila and Belassi (2004) use government expenditure on training as a proxy for education for the years 1965 to 1999. They practice the cointegration and the ECM strategies and discover that there's a nice correlation between the average worker's expenditure on schooling and the economic increase of

Uganda. Ndiyo (2007) makes use of time-collection statistics from 1970 to 2000 on actual education expenditure, actual capital formation, and GDP, and employs the VAR method. Based totally on the effects obtained after computations, Ndiyo (2007) demonstrates that schooling does no longer have a high-quality effect on the financial improvement of Nigeria. He indicates that this result may be defined by different factors along with exertions marketplace distortions, redundancy, mind drain, industrial disputes and activity discontinuities, and government failure, and many others.

Khorasgani (2008) analyses the impact of higher schooling on Iran's monetary development for the length of 1959 to 2005. The proxies used for human capital are educational attainment and study prices. Khorasgani (2008) makes use of the Cobb-Douglas manufacturing feature collectively with the ARDL method to determine the fast-run and long-run results of better training at the economic boom. The take a look at demonstrates that actual output increases by 0.314 percentage ultimately and 0.198 percentage within the short run following a one percent growth in higher training attainment. For this reason, higher education has a positive and tremendous effect on the economic development of Iran. Many philosophies govern schooling, and they all are very critical to a person's holistic development. Schooling could be very important to everybody regardless of their vicinity. Each the Western and the Non-Western countries value education however they have got specific views, special academic systems which can be ruled by way of their very own policies and ideas. In each culture, education is relatively promoted as a basis of fulfillment and they're both challenged with the lower class and the upper elegance that can on occasion decide the population that gravitates toward training. The cause of the training system across nations and cultures ought to be to instill the belief in men and women that discipline may be very vital and that it surpasses academic problems that can have an effect on their performances and to foster innate curiosity in scholar which will work diligently in my view in addition to within. The diverse philosophies share a few differences as well as similarities within their schooling structures. But, their not unusual goal should be to allow college students to know that they're all equal and has an identical possibility to schooling. The non-western training machine encourages college students to study and does now not show bias and discrimination; it promotes oneness, letting all students recognize that education is for all regardless of their variations. This gadget also holds both mother and father and college students liable for students' academic failure. consequently, it is of extreme importance that they both take into account that due to the fact training is similarly available to every pupil, it's far expected that the enterprise to be triumphant in any respect cost.

Allison stated, "Whilst many were more youthful, I firmly believed that my schooling did not count. This becomes due to the surroundings wherein they lived. Throughout their freshman months, they had no interest to pass any of my classes. They may want to care much less due to the fact they used to be an illegal immigrant and all odds of themselves ever to wait for college had been nowhere to be seen. This all started while they found out that their massive brother became forced to withdraw from his magnificence due to fame in the USA. It broke their coronary heart to peer him spoil into tears as he turned into compelled to let cross of his dream. They did not need that to manifest to me, so they had determined no longer strive in any respect. My sophomore year became an educational repeat of their freshman months. In different words, they did not achieve this properly that year. Their mothers would lecture on and on about how they had to not let everybody or any rule dictate how they took care of their future. They thought how they had allowed down their dad and mom for all their tough work overtime. They went to hell and lower back just to get their family and in which they are now. Their parent's type driven them to want more for themselves .they knew it wasn't truthful for me to give up earlier than even attempting, but once they started to use myself greater in faculty they figured out that faculty became, so clean. They started to understand the capacity and what they used to be capable of. They additionally realized most people inside the equal classes were like me; they didn't even care. The academics knew too, so most of them didn't care if the maximum of classmates exceeded or failed. They made a drastic alternate that helped them with my non-public development and the selections they made in life. After on foot across the stage and receiving a high college diploma, lifestyles progress in a rush. No longer are the carefree days of excessive school simply across the corner. A new truth exists and existence-changing decisions want to be made if they have not already.

For some, college awaits a bit beyond the horizon. For others, the chance of reaching full-time employment can also seem a better choice. With university come the prospects of increased obligation, time management, and for quite a few, eliminating those dreaded university loans. Without steerage, scholar-debt can quickly become a tough lesson in excessive finance. Currently, media outlets have begun to color a bleak image of college students accumulating insurmountable quantities of debt; but, it isn't always the entire image. People who opt out of university-run the chance of costing themselves ability career possibilities and a higher widespread of living. The direction to fulfillment requires difficult selections and calculated dangers. The gold standard way to succeeding in our society is through university schooling. Despite the fees, better schooling presents a valuable asset to long-term achievement and excellent lifestyles. In a capitalistic society, cash, above the entirety else, separates us. From the beginning, each every year step of training grants introduced earning capacity. College students with three hundred and sixty-five days of college earn an eleven percent higher income than those simply graduating from excessive school. A second-year gives another thirteen percentage growth. The 0.33 months of training gains a further fourteen percentage in income. The share of ability earnings boom grows with every year of university attended. There are lower, measurable, quantities of earnings growth for those with a few colleges. However, the large income leap begins with acquiring a degree; every person disregarding the relevance of schooling does now not examine to individuals who achieve a four-year degree. Without education options cut in half, we doom no longer handiest ourselves but additionally our destiny.

I asked myself, "So, what's schooling?" I used to be able to know its which means however turned into still dwindling with the concept of getting training and what can or not it's used for? "Study hard to emerge as a hit individual" these phrases from my dad and mom and another circle of relatives contributors constantly inspired me to move to school. getting to know officially by using going to school intended education to me, but become this enough to recognize the real that means of training? Is satisfying our dreams, making our mother and father, family proud of ourselves using getting the very best degree of education, or by way of having a vivid future is what an educated person meant to be? These questions stored difficult for me; I was on a quest to unravel those mysteries. One aspect that changed into certain to me about the significance of education turned into to have a vibrant future and come to be a successful character. I used to be not sure if gratifying dreams and our dreams lie at the back of the principal importance of training. I kept on asking my instructors and parents but everybody saved me announcing the identical element "get training, go to school, and feature a terrific destiny." What approximately those a hit businessmen who had no any school training; they nonetheless have the excellent fortune and feature a vivid future?

My grandma had no formal training, but she changed into skilled sufficient to know about numerous things. It bothered me difficult, I was mastering something from my Grandpa in an informal way, and the matters I discovered that volunteering activities all were a part of getting casual reports. Education is indeed the key to achievement in life. Now not most effective does it prepare you for life, however, it also is the inspiration of our development, and it shapes who we are and what we may also turn out to be in life. There has to be no confusion on the significance of training; but, how one is taught can be a topic of debate. There are dozens of getting-to-know styles that can be used to cater to a person's manner of studying. How the information is delivered to an infant is simply as essential as the material being taught. If a person is being fed statistics in which they do not comprehend, what is the point? The two fashionable categories which can be utilized in education are Traditionalism and Progressivism. Traditionalism is "described as instructor-focused shipping of preparation to lessons of college students who're the receivers of information." while progressivism is explained to be the mastering fashion which" focuses on the complete infant, in place of at the content material or the teacher. This academic philosophy stresses that students ought to test ideas with the aid of lively experimentation." to provide the best learning in faculties, both Tradalism and Progressivism should be incorporated into education rather than giving one preference over some other. Concerning academic philosophy, I'd say that I'm more a Traditionalist learner; however, I do find that I study with revolutionary training as properly. I locate it less difficult to digest statistics while it's been explained to me.

Training is a vital device which could be very useful in all people's life. It's what differentiates us from other living beings on the planet. It makes the guy the neatest creature on this planet. It empowers people and receives them prepared to stand demanding situations of existence efficiently. With that being stated, training nevertheless remains luxurious and no longer a necessity in ours.

Instructional cognizance wishes to be spread through the US to make training on hand. But, this stays incomplete without first reading the importance of training. Only whilst the people comprehend what significance it holds, can they keep in mind it a need for an excellent existence. We can see the significance of training and how it is a doorway to fulfillment. To advantage information, you want to reveal yourself to a completely new international. Amusing and adventure humans view formal education in a terrible mild. That is education where humans simplest study voluminous books, uninteresting instructors, and difficult checks. Education is truly amusing and adventurous. You study new things, meet new people and pursue new pursuits. It offers you a danger to have interaction with people aside from your friends and own family participants. It additionally presents an escape for folks that suffer from disturbing conditions at domestic. You should undertake a high-quality mindset closer to schooling. This mindset will assist you to spot the laugh in schooling.

Undertake it nowadays. Construct a network you want buddies who care approximately you. Finding excellent friends isn't always easy. It takes time, patience, and perseverance. Experience is typically the great manner of locating good friends. Schooling allows you to advantage this enjoy by using interacting with human beings inside formal and casual settings. You realize people better thru those experiences. This helps you to pick a near institution of precise pals. This group will then come to be your community within society's entangled net of networks. You can call upon this community in instances of trouble. You may discover it tough to construct a network of friends and co-workers without schooling. Because of this, you should pursue training as a lot as you could. In a democratic schooling machine, there's a balance of authority between the nation, the dad and mom, the character, and the educators. At the same time as every organization has their very own declare to electricity over the training of kids, there may be nonetheless the question of who needs to have the maximum. This question regularly comes all the way down to the country or the dad and mom because they're the maximum complicated and influential. The primary goal of democratic education is to equip children with the understanding and ethical person needed to discover fulfillment and contentment in lifestyles and society. Therefore, when training makes a specialty of this aim, the nation must have more electricity than the dad and mom. The state has to have greater authority overtraining due to the fact they'll equip children with the talents wished. Absolutely placed, placing greater authority within the fingers of the country is much more likely to save you bigotry. Gutmann refers to John Rawls' liberal moralist principle, which addresses the significance of instilling a recognition for differences in children. Consistent with Gutmann's evaluation of liberal moralism, the goal of education needs to be "generating in kids the preference and potential to make ethical selections based on principles which might be generalizable among all humans." If the mother and father were loose to educate their biases to the kids, society would end up more polarized and illiberal than it already is. Democratic schooling coincides with Rawls' liberal moralist theory in that both price appreciation for differences. The nation's authority over schooling strives to teach children in a manner that creates an extra tolerant and know-how society, even as additionally preparing them children for fulfillment in that society. A sturdy argument in desire for extra parental authority in schooling is that in step with the statistics of reproduction, teaching their youngsters is part of the determination of individual freedoms. This argument is supported using Charles Fried, who argues "the proper to form one's toddler's values, one's infant's existence plan, and the right to lavish interest on freedom and obligatory.

It is stated that maximum students experience boredom in colleges due to the academics, loneliness, and no cost of the work. However, as we understand, training is an important aspect of people's lifestyles. Education gives people important abilities so that they may get higher careers and maintain financial growth now and within their destiny. Moreover, schooling also allows enhance health care and combat the unfolding of a few commonplace illnesses. Considering that education plays a huge position in human beings' everyday life, human beings want to provide pleasant schooling to their youngsters. The important thing to let youngsters study correctly is to make mastering happier. To try this, college students want to obtain the glide enjoy and their educators; mother and father and instructors also want to help them to have successful results. In his e-book, Ben-Shahar claims that "if he desires to come to be a businessman, then his parents should support him, even though their wish had usually been that he pursues politics. "The identical state of affairs for teachers as well as mother and father, teachers need to also inspire their students to pursue what they want for his or her careers, however, instructors have to no longer tell their students to don't forget their occupations via the value and the benefits. Consequently, college students might be glad after they analyze the knowledge from their colleges. Besides, dad and mom and instructors can also help their children and students by creating a gaining knowledge of condition surroundings. For dad and mom, Ben-Shahar states that "whilst challenged, children, like adults, will find the meaning of their accomplishments and experience the method of attaining their dreams." in this state of affairs, parents should now not guard their youngsters from the tough instances. On the contrary, dad and mom must permit their children to triumph over the demanding situations so they might attain delight after correction. It is a truth that distinctive humans have an exclusive manner of thinking and behaviors; they will see things at distinctive prices. For college kids, it's miles the same circumstance. College students are favored to pick out what they need to do in place of pick out via someone else. When they have a look at schools, students must have the right to pick out what they need to study with a purpose to make their schooling happier. In the article "How high college teachers, mother and father can inspire teenagers to read for amusing." teachers should work with librarians to find books that meet curriculum requirements, however, give teens a diffusion of options to pick out from. Teachers offer books that are proper to satisfy students' ability tiers. Except, exceptional styles of books have interaction with college students. For that reason, they may no longer lose interest without problems. Additionally, he mentions that "a student may not be excited about Shakespeare's 'The Taming of the Shrew,' but he or she may get excited about the 1999 modernization of the story in the film "Ten Things I Hate approximately You." In this example, college students choose the analyzing material that not handiest are well suited to their talent stages but additionally inspire them to study greater because they'll grow to be very knowledgeable about the world they live in.

Why Is Multicultural schooling so important in a state-of-the-art Society?

The world's populace is extensively converting through the years. The census predicts that by around 2020, "more than 1/2 of the kingdom's kids are anticipated to be part of a minority race or ethnic institution," Minorities will in the end be the majority! Because the United States of America is considered the sector's most culturally numerous US, the schools have transitioned to a highly variable population of college students. For this reason, the education gadget has an essential project to adopt; they need to ensure that the early childhood educators are culturally competent; to embrace a culturally various application, and practices wherein the brand new era of students can substantially advantage from.

There's an interconnection between culturally relevant strategies, Anti-Bias Curriculum, diverse family systems, and Multicultural education that constructs cultural competence. Multicultural schooling can be taught to scholars by way of growing culturally relevant methods, an Anti-Bias Curriculum, and diverse family systems. The instructor's priority is to broaden culturally relevant methods, wherein they may have the possibility to learn about the student's own family's heritage, subculture, faith, priorities, and so on. Educators can construct a sturdy relationship with the student, and their families; even as selling figure involvement inside the classroom; so as for the mother and father to witness their children's academic development in a multicultural study room. The scholars will sense welcomed and frequent and be liable to high-quality education and they may work difficult toward fulfillment.

The Anti-bias curriculum is designed to specific diversity within the early childhood lecture room. Educators can teach multicultural training, by imparting multicultural posters around the classroom, as well as books, music, toys, and activities which inspire the children to discover extraordinary cultures. The Anti-bias curriculum no longer only promotes multicultural education, but it also allows the students to discover concrete interactive stories with college students from distinct cultures. The remaining is a diverse family structure; it's far from any other critical factor linked to multicultural training. If educators want to sell multicultural training in their lecture room, they must maintain in mind the distinction among all of the families. Every pupil comes from households who collect distinctive faith, subculture, ideals, and many others, therefore, instructors need to have clean expertise of every circle of relatives needs, so one can promote multicultural schooling. It is imperative to expand a strong, environment for the student; wherein college would be called their second home.

In these days' society, we've got grown up where education has emerged as a critical position in lots of our lives. All and sundry talks approximately the importance of having an education and how being well knowledgeable opens the door for many possibilities. For so long as I can don't forget I've continually been informed via my friends and circle of relatives to take benefit of the schooling I get to now not take it for granted as many desire they could have the possibility to go to school. Each of my parents grew up in Guatemala where they completed a number of their high school education they came to the United States within the early ninety's. They first arrived within America not knowing any English and up to this date they aren't fluent within the language but at the moment can apprehend some of the basics and speak very little. My first language to study become Spanish it becomes and nevertheless is the number one language I take advantage of at domestic to communicate with a lot of my circle of relatives contributors and buddies. At the age of three, I started to examine my second language English no longer with the aid of my parents but my aunt who had attended excessive college here in America and changed into fluent within the language said an educator. I took into account her seeking to teach me to examine, write, and talk this new language. As I became more fluent within the English language I haven't forgotten I cried one time because little three-year-old my idea I might overlook my first language and I wanted to prevent getting to know English however then I used to be defined that many human beings are bilingual in more than one languages no longer simply one. Consistent with Early youth education nowadays with the aid of George S. Morrison, it states that professionalism is built upon individual duty, integrity, and ethical practices that reveal appreciation for all kids and their families. There are four ideas of professionalism which encompass private traits, academic attainment, professional exercise, and public presentation. There is a diffusion of key additives that make contributions to professionalism in a study room and we're going to talk about lots of the one's today. That allows you to practice professionalism, I feel it is vital to speak about and reflect at the country-wide association for the training of young kid's code of ethics and conduct. This touches on more than a few topics from confidentiality, to self-cognizance, as well as a way to publicly represent yourself as a professional. There are numerous key additives to shaping a young child's lifestyle and can be better carried out via professionalism. I like to mirror returned to the "children See kids Do" video, which surely proves kids imitate/learn verbal and nonverbal cues from adults. As a teacher, it's far necessary to be the excellent version of yourself every day, to bypass those actions alongside. This no longer most effective impacts a child's ethics however it additionally generates higher behavior which affects the mother and father's lives in a greater high-quality way outside of the lecture room. This module has taught me many one-of-a-kind strategies whilst running with a misbehaved baby. As an example, I plan to apply self-consciousness in my schoolroom to hold a fantastic tone and do away with poor frame language. I will also use respiration techniques for kids as well as myself to establish a properly rounded schoolroom. Professionalism is such a vital role in shaping our younger toddler's lives and it merits to be stressed more to in flip create a higher studying'.

Gains of bilingual schooling

A totally important key to a person's learning is bilingual schooling programs that emerged during the USA because an influx of immigrants entered the USA because of new immigration regulations, exhibits Brad Brown in his article "The history of Bilingual schooling in the USA." Bilingual training applications involve putting students in surroundings wherein their native language differs from the language spoken at the faculty they attend. Maximum bilingual education programs within the USA. Awareness on coaching students English so the students could have several opportunities and options after they graduate from high school, and be able to easily integrate into nowadays society. In step with M. Lee and Maureen McMahon, disagrees that bilingual training involves putting ESL students in classrooms in which education is given in both English and the scholars' native language (generally Spanish). Pam Bremer, director of Obersee Bilingual school, states that "bilingualism offers kids social, linguistic and cognitive benefits." mastering a second language assists in advancing the scholars' comprehension of "the complexities of languages" and the scholars assume extra creatively (Bremer). Furthermore, whilst students in bilingual training packages are gaining several benefits, students in normal public colleges aren't gaining identical advantages if any in any respect. Coaching students and offering them better knowledge in several one-of-a-kind topics is what faculties attempt to perform and bilingual schooling packages meet those goals. Furthermore, Jeff Bale, a trainer of language and language education at Michigan Kingdom University, claims that students in bilingual schooling packages have the ability to examine other languages at a quicker charge than monolingual college students after they have won fluency in each their local language and English.

With the blessings of gaining several benefits and being capable of learning other languages quicker than students in ordinary faculties, the scholars' performance on standardized assessments in bilingual training packages surpasses the results of college students in ordinary college classrooms, however, simplest after the students in the programs have attained the wanted language skills. Not to mention, studies have tested that bilingual students adapt to exchange simpler, are extra open-minded, and sense extra at ease in environments with humans of many cultures in contrast to monolingual college students (Bremer). However, college students in everyday public college classrooms acquire a few advantages from being round bilingual students.

The difficulty of bilingual education is a very arguable difficulty and plenty of human beings have one-of-a-kind perspectives concerning this subject. "Bilingual education commenced in 1968 as a small, $7.5 million federal program to help Mexican-American students, half of whom could not speak English nicely when they entered first grade". In addition, it started twenty-three years in the past as a historic order for busing students to colleges to reap racial integration. One might consider that the supporters of bilingual schooling are Latino's but in fact, they're black and white specialists who realize the benefits of their kids being bilingual. it's been tested that students who're enrolled in bilingual training have better rankings on standardized exams, consisting of the ACT's and SAT's, than folks who are not enrolled in bilingual training. Bilingual schooling is beneficial for the United States of America and allows college students to examine English as well as retaining their native tongue for destiny success in our worldwide financial system. Bilingual training works in our society and should live intact inside the colleges and have to be funded to allow students who wish to take these classes need to be able to. In think of Rudolph Giuliani's view that bilingual schooling does not work and that it's far too high priced must be a higher notion out and he ought to study the benefits that come from it. Giuliani changed into quoted concerning bilingual training by pronouncing, "It's merciless to them and gives them less of a threat to succeed". That is a weird view that Giuliani is issuing thinking about that it's been confirmed that students who are enrolled in bilingual training perform better on standard eyes assessments. That is an advantage for those students to prevail considering that the higher the test grades the higher the opportunity to get into a good college. in addition you can actually word that knowing more than one language can "utilize the strengths of bilingual kids to prepare all college students to compete in an international economy that increasingly more requires multilingual and multicultural information". Bilingual schooling can be seen as beneficial in lots of faculties and facilitates college students to prepare for a future in the company in the United States. In El Paso at a secondary faculty, bilingual education may be seen as beneficial for both the scholars and the credibility of the faculty.

Bilingual schooling, as educational software, become

initially promoted via educators within the Nineteen Seventies and for the reason that then has been a topic of many debates in the USA. A few argue that bilingual schooling only serves as a detriment to the American subculture. Others argue that bilingual training is useful to individuals who come to live in the USA and want to come to be part of the culture, but lack proficiency inside the English language. Two authors, who've each taken contrary aspects of the talk on bilingual schooling in the United States, are Richard Rodriguez and Ariel Dorfman. Richard Rodriguez believes that bilingual training creates a feeling of separateness between overseas language speakers and American society; therefore, delaying the formation of public identification. In assessment, Ariel Dorfman argues that bilingualism in America will be a bridge to better know-how different cultures. I expect the position of being neither, against, or totally in favor of bilingual schooling. I am in desire of bilingual training because it may be a powerful segue to gaining knowledge of the English language and I trust it's very crucial to stay linked with our own family's language and way of life. however, I additionally understand the bad feeling of separateness from the bigger public that bilingual schooling may have on foreign language speaking households, which hinders my potential to absolutely embody bilingual training. Ariel Dorfman is an Argentinian writer who struggled during his life to discovering stability between the Spanish and English languages. As a result of Dorfman's "bilingual adventure", he argues that bilingual schooling is beneficial to American society. Dorfman believes that bilingualism will serve as a channel to better equip folks to be developed in my opinion.

Advantages of tune education

People with studying disabilities enjoy many highbrow, emotional, physical, and intellectual challenges. Where this happens, the tune can play a crucial function in enhancing the eye, social functioning, self-esteem, and reminiscence of college students with mastering disabilities. The Salamanca Declaration and Framework for action on unique needs schooling is one of the frameworks that urges the global representatives to transport to the concept of inclusive training that tends to profess that nobody will remain unwanted from the instructional institutions due to their caste, creed, and coloration in addition to vulnerabilities. It further states that kids with disabilities or substantial educational needs and capabilities have to have to get admission to ordinary training and child-targeted pedagogy.

As a manner of addressing this, some researchers have promoted the usage of tune and music schooling to beautify the instructional reports of students with getting to know disabilities. One of the principal arguments is that song facilitates students with gaining knowledge of disabilities. Even as researchers recognize that every learning disability (those being, interest deficit/hyperactivity disorder, and autism) may be extraordinary and that this could have an effect on the methods wherein they may be educated, they agree that tune can help improve their confidence and their reviews inside the school gadget. Despite these discussions, there may be little research in Trinidad and Tobago that explores the demanding situations facing unique educators, the specific strategies which can be used to educate people with getting to know disabilities, and the viable effect of song on the learning stories of those children in the schoolroom. Given such, the researcher tends to the cognizance of numerous key thoughts as (i) what are the demanding situations accepted in these areas to teach the novices of getting to know disabilities, (ii) How tune influences the gaining knowledge of those learners, and (iii) how this strategy indicates improving teaching and studying in lecture rooms. hence, these studies tend (i) verify challenges the academics face in coaching college students with studying disabilities, (ii) discover the feasible outcomes of the song as a coaching and learning device in such lecture rooms, and (iii) make tips for enhancing coaching and gaining knowledge of experiences inside schools that cater to the needs of students with mastering disabilities. Obtaining musical know-how gives youngsters abilities and reports that convey through all components of life. But, school boards across the USA have chosen to cut song education due to small budgets, attention on center topics, or meant the loss of hobby. Low-profit colleges, consisting of Haven primary college, placed in Savannah, Georgia, and other similar schools in California, have had to decide to significantly lessen the quantity of time spent in art-associated school rooms or reduce the instructions all collectively. These students are suffering from their loss of song education; at the same time as not simply apparent to many students; teachers, and dad and mom, studies have continuously tested that music education advantages students in numerous ways. Each component of existence revolves around tune; a person's past and present connect to the song, whether it is a liked track or a treasured reminiscence. Therefore, it has to be discovered and shared with others- no longer taken away. Tune gives many benefits inside the lives of children, making cuts unfavorable to their training.

Although it seems as though there are many possibilities for track in faculties these days, struggles hold behind the scenes. Many schools have had to reduce their tune applications in the course of the latest recession. For instance, a district in California that after had 124,000 music students dropped to 64,000 within a few years; this fashion has come to be unfortunately commonplace so that it will save money. but, the redistribution of college students as soon as concerned in arts training into other regions of having a look at has truly proven to be greater steeply-priced, with a mean of $36,000 directed toward the hiring of extra instructors. The rebuilding of those programs may become costing schools greater ultimately. Song schooling is important because it offers many benefits. It facilitates students with their academic fulfillment, attitudes, behaviors, and testing abilities. Many studies were performed to prove these statistics. For example, Dr. Frances Rauscher and Dr. Gordon Shaw carried out a test at the consequences of musical practice on students: The experiment covered four agencies of preschoolers: one group acquired personal piano/keyboard classes; a second institution obtained singing classes; a third institution received personal pc training, and a fourth institution obtained no schooling. The children who obtained piano/keyboard schooling executed 34% better on tests measuring spatial-temporal capacity than the others. These findings suggest that track uniquely complements better mind capabilities required for arithmetic, chess, science, and engineering. It has additionally been verified that once children analyze music early, the mind is enhanced for auditory processing. Magnetic resonance imaging (MRI) research has shown that the fibers within the corpus callosum, which join the left- and right brain hemispheres, are as a good deal as fifteen percentage large in musicians as compared to non-musicians? Clearly, the track affects college students. It is a nice outlet for college kids to express their feelings; it complements the intellectual and social performance and enhances the mind. In the battle, however, many administrators are blind to those superb results, and forget to help song training in faculties. This is nothing new however, song education has been suffering to live alive in faculty curriculums for decades.

Track education is essential as it offers many blessings. It helps college students with their academic success, attitudes, behaviors, and testing abilities. Much research was performed to prove these records. For example, Dr. Frances Rauscher and Dr. Gordon Shaw experimented on the outcomes of musical preparation on students: The test covered four organizations of preschoolers: one institution obtained private piano/keyboard lessons; a second organization obtained singing lessons; a third institution received non-public laptop classes, and a fourth institution obtained no training. The children who acquired piano/keyboard schooling accomplished 34% better on exams measuring spatial-temporal ability than the others. These findings suggest that song uniquely complements higher brain features required for mathematics, chess, technological know-how, and engineering. It has also been confirmed that after children analyze tunes early, the mind is more suitable for auditory processing. Magnetic resonance imaging (MRI) research has proven that the fibers inside the corpus callosum, which connect the left- and right-mind hemispheres, are as a whole lot as fifteen percentage large in musicians as compared to no musicians. Really, the tune affects students. It's a wonderful outlet for students to explicit their emotions; it enhances intellectual and social performance and enhances the mind. Maximum remember the fact that a tune is a beneficial tool for relaxation and entertainment time. Fewer recognize that getting to know a musical device, or maybe taking note of music for lengthy intervals of time, may have a superb impact on one's instructional abilities. Numerous researchers and university professors have regarded this correlation and over and over have produced statistics that confirm this common principle. Studying tune can't handiest improve academic skills, but sharpen motor abilities, memory, and create a nicely-rounded, enriched man or woman. Standardized testing is used across the United States to evaluate college students' development and studying in school. The NAMM (countrywide association of song merchants) basis's Sound of learning software lately experimented to assess the proficiency on standardized checks of college students that have been concerned in a higher degree song software in college. Four thousand, seven hundred and thirty-nine students from center school and standard colleges were blanketed in this examination. The fundamental part of the study showed that scholars enrolled in a top satisfactory music application scored 20% better in math, and 22% better in English classes and checks (track schooling can assist). middle faculty consequences have been much like those of the elementary college students (NAMM takes a look at the famous connection between track schooling & excessive test rating). The president/CEO of the NAMM basis, Joe Lamond, become quoted pronouncing, "college directors, instructors, and dad and mom all agree that track and arts training make contributions to kids reaching their full ability, that's the cause of our educational gadget and something all of us care deeply approximately."

Chapter Three

The Impact of Effective Education

Effective training is the stepping stone to a brilliant and a success destiny. For the reason that the beginning of mankind, there was an ardor for education. People had been searching for high fine education since it's far a fundamental human proper. Consequently, the seventh principle of the United States Declaration of the Rights of the kid which proclaimed by using the overall meeting is that: every baby, with none exception whatsoever, shall be entitled to get hold of training, which shall be free and obligatory, as a minimum in the essential degrees. He will be given an education a good way to promote his well-known tradition and enable him, on a basis of identical opportunity, to expand his competencies, his individual judgment, and his experience of ethical and social obligation, and to emerge as a useful member of society (online). Over the historical years of coaching in schools, it changed into found in studies that Egyptian schools face many challenges that preclude reaching their primary undertaking correctly. A few colleges lack team spirit, others are run randomly. For this reason, school performance and low level of academic attainment among students have to turn out to be a large problem. Moreover, the school climate isn't suitable for getting to know in most schools. Due to the advent of numerous weaknesses and threats in faculties, Egyptian faculty reform has to turn out to be an urgent count number. In Egypt, for instance, every faculty has to respond to diverse and extensive challenges. This might be visible as indicating as a minimum that the principals who lead colleges want to have the personal and professional qualities together with expertise and leadership abilities to meet these challenges. To bring about effectiveness in colleges, teachers and parents should have an energetic function in assisting education gadgets. Lately, there was a hobby in the idea of the 'suitable faculty'. Studies into areas of college effectiveness have advanced hastily and college development is now mentioned more absolutely. Researchers have expressed perspectives approximately how schools are probably made greater powerful. It was discovered that there's a variety of things that result in excessive- appearing faculty. At the same time as the leadership group of workers which includes the college main, heads of the branch, and teachers will probably play the maximum crucial element in improving faculty, numerous factors contribute to excessive-acting faculty. We will take a look at the important thing elements to high school effectiveness and if the achievement is viable in every faculty. It will illustrate the questions of the school climate and creating a suit academic surroundings in colleges, what effective schooling is. It will speak the great and need for continuing expert improvement (CPD) to enhance the school body of workers.

It'll cowl mother and father's involvement, aid, have an impact on and schooling. Plenty of this essay can be approximately how faculties help to deliver first-rate gaining knowledge of and the impact of management and control on the school achievement. Training is a social organization through which a society's kids are taught basic instructional expertise, getting to know capabilities and cultural norms. Every kingdom in the international is prepared with a few forms of training machine, although the one's systems range greatly. According to the World Bank's view, as it relates to schooling, it's said that schooling plays a vital role in poverty discount, enhancing one's well-known living and creating stability. it is each a guided procedure and a character's self-teaching dedication. Based on one's society and subculture, the younger persons are usually skilled by using the older ones. Due to a person's information, the expertise of subjects and topics, and life reviews, he/she is considered properly-educated and academically wealthy. Training performs a vital role in our lives and it's far a piece blurry whilst to assume what type of society we might have without training, and the way we will feature as individuals. Attending college and acquiring schooling may be very vital to our development and it plays a main position in our existence's adventure. Education is the foundation of a hit profession, financial freedom, the capacity to assume and reason severely, and to make knowledgeable decisions. Without training, we will be limited to carry out responsibilities and we can be ignorant to the things that are going on in and around our surroundings, and consistent with Martin Luther King, human beings without expertise are like a tree without roots. For schooling to be of terrific fee, curriculums should be carried out.

However, many children around the world do now not have to get the right of entry to training because of numerous motives which consist of race, gender, and monetary popularity. Those are obstacles that deny humans the possibility to be knowledgeable and carry out at their fullest ability. The variety of instructional studies kids have in my context is incredible; notwithstanding they come from numerous cultures and feature one-of-a-kind backgrounds and distinct experiences; the college is focused on assembly their man or woman wishes. In my context, I can region greater attention on improving success costs inside a framework in which know-how is dealt with in large part as objective, and that is supported using Shisana (2011). I will select classroom issues that commemorate variety and that I teach them to have fun similarities and differences, I'm able to explicit fine interest in diverse cultures, and I can show admiration and empathize with all youngsters. In my study room, the students are advocated to treat each different similarly regardless of their differences. The variety of education studies match with the idea of education having a sociological function and the schooling device sees every student as important. As such, it emphasizes the social factor of college students' improvement. College students from numerous backgrounds learn a standardized curriculum that efficiently transforms diversity into homogeneity.

Classical French sociologist Émile Durkheim become one of the first sociologists to consider the social feature of education. He believed that ethical education was necessary for society to exist because it provided the idea for the social solidarity that held society collectively. The diversity of education in my context additionally specializes in college students' interactions at some point of their college activities and the final results and to peer how tremendous or negative it's far. I agree that interactions between students and instructors and engaging in social activities, assist to shape how we interact and respond to race, gender, subculture, and status which make contributions to our expectations. I anticipate positive behaviors from college students and that I interact with the scholars and speak effectively, letting them recognize what I anticipate from them. I additionally train approximately society's instructional variety, its tradition, values, ethics, conduct, and norms, and that I consider that the socialization feature of schooling helps to encourage people to broaden social control and to lessen deviant behaviors. Dewey argued that the primary motive of education and schooling isn't so much to put together students to live a useful existence but to teach them the way to stay pragmatically and right now in their contemporary environment Dewey (1859). I agree that the reason for school training includes curbing the bridge of social inequality, reinforcing social cohesion, to set up order and keep social roles, and equipping folks with the know-how and capabilities required to achieve lifestyles; because of this, they'll be able to make precise judgments, make informed choices and to use their acquired expertise and talents successfully. Faculties ought to be locations wherein every one of its community tastes the confidence that incorporates achievement in some kinds of other. College to my understanding is the place wherein we train the coronary heart of the scholar so that he can be a very good member of the college and in the long run a good member of society. This shows that preparing top residents depends in large part on all folks that work in colleges and their level of effectiveness. It might seem reasonable to argue that if the faculties are to improve, we want our teachers, principals, dad and mom, and all people who difficulty contributing to achieving that goal.

This could be taken to mean that leadership inner colleges need to be taken to a new stage of making sure that faculty will meet the wishes of every student in terms of learning, attainment, and preferred success. Faculty should demonstrate a few key criteria of what makes college effective inclusive of the college climate, how college students are mastering, discerns involvement, teachers' relationship and the exceptional of teaching and studying. The faculty need to emerge as an area that could be a heaven for kids, a place that facilitates to shape society, an area where every child can achieve success. Subsequently, the excellent college has the perception that every one kid can examine. "Young human beings draw close that the reason of faculty isn't to provide a schooling however to stimulate a thirst for learning, and to present it existence past the college gate". Researchers imply that effective schooling isn't always just a matter of reading an e-book or most effectively a medium to refill minds with information to pass an examination, but its simple objective is the growth of the scholar's character and knowledge. It is the form of schooling that respects the whole toddler and encourages him to be an independent thinker and become a productive member of the network. Plutarch the creek essayist stated "a toddler's thoughts is not a vessel to be filled, but a fireplace to be kindled." consequently, training is a procedure to prepare an accountable and good citizen. This suggests that the college should offer such surroundings that complement students' boom. The school must be a studying network wherein students can correctly extend and increase themselves as people.

Moreover, students need to be answerable for their very own schooling and actively engaged in cooperative studying sports that lead them to recognize the way to attain better effects. This shows that instructors should be ready with competencies and range their techniques of coaching so that they will attain as many college students as feasible within the classroom. Powerful training leads to required and planned trade and contributes to creating a balanced character of college students. The curriculums, therefore, need to be developed in the direction of accomplishing academic goals each cognitive and emotional, and additionally to develop tendencies, competencies, and values. It is tough to achieve these goals without supplying or building a vision of what we are hoping school to be. Operating without vision results in random practice.

The ideas of excellence and vision manual the content and methods of the desired future nation of a college in its challenge as gaining knowledge of the organization, imaging the first-class possible conditions for students to analyze, and for instructors to educate. Taylor and Ryan (2005) see that the imaginative and prescient is the maximum essential component inside the school success and specializes in 'achievement and achievement.' and publications absolutely everyone inside the faculty to accomplish the venture at the right way. School vision: "may be defined as" a photograph of the faculty overall performance that we desire to create. It's determined by using school leaders or faculty principals with the cooperation and participation of the faculty community. In this appreciation, the faculty main shares this imaginative and prescient with the faculty personnel and dad and mom aiming at developing a plan or a selected strategy outlining what the faculty could be like now and within the destiny. The 'college's essential role is to create high-quality weather and suitable circumstances for students, instructors, dad, and mom, and the community to position this vision into practice. Brighouse and Woods (2008) nation that now not best will we want an imaginative and prescient but the school workforce must also be influenced to build their own vision and consider how they could proportion this imaginative and prescient and placed it into practice. For example, teachers should have their personal imaginative and prescient which courses them to improve college students and achieve instructional goals. In other phrases, the task of the school must be made applicable thru imaginative and prescient assertion that describes dreams and strategies. Powerful training is especially interrelated to a vision. Wallace, Jr. (1996) states that the imaginative and prescient is the place to begin for a movement plan to develop and practice a schedule to place the vision into practice. College vision displays the lengthy-term goals for the faculty and identifies predicted results of overall performance. Therefore, faculty vision has to be written in clear language and understood through the humans of the situation in school. Therefore, constructing imaginative and prescient calls for a pacesetter who has the ability to deliver together humans of different views and agendas and facilitate the process of collaboration for the co-introduction of shared imagination and prescient that owned and practiced through anybody involved. In different words, for the shared imagination and prescient to emerge as a reality in faculty, it's miles fundamental to have such form of fundamental who can encourage, plan, facilitate, guide and control.

Leadership and management

Globally, many folks might agree with the proposition that the school leader needs to have the management and management talents and traits to lead the staff, parents, and the community efficiently to position the faculty vision in exercise. It is probably argued that if you want to be a leader, you should be reputable through your team or personnel as a pacesetter. The successful college primary consequently, is a person who fashions for the faculty team the style of behavior she or he expects of them. Due to the fact the pinnacle teacher alone cannot gain achievement, she or he needs to be backed up with a supportive group. Teamwork is the key to achievement. Furthermore, he decides the creating a supportive environment for the export boom of the lecturers and administrators. Regarding this factor, Wallace, Jr.(1996) states that the school predominant's position includes combining and arranging the factors of management to gain the very best wonderful consequences for students. except placing the tone of the whole faculty using modeling the interpersonal regard what is expected of all, school foremost assists schoolroom teachers to peer the relationship among what they're doing and what is planned. For the school head, making plans, organizing, preserving, monitoring, and comparing are key factors to attain excellence and achievement in an internal school. Leadership performs a substantial role in developing educational establishments and society. It's been stated via many researchers that leadership receives things changed.

This shows that if there's no leadership in a society or institution, nothing might be well modified and done in the right ways. Although there are numerous vital arguments approximately the relation between leadership and control, there may be a growing want in all educational establishments, specifically in developing societies for leaders and executives, who are capable of arranging, manage and plan for establishments to improve their overall performance to the ranks of these in greater developed societies. As it is said by way of many researchers educational institutions need a powerful chief who evokes workers and sets instructions for the faculty and permits faculty to deal with change. Effective management can contribute to the improvement of people's capacities with the aid of giving them possibilities to practice and to stretch their limits. Professional operational control can then channel this capacity into appropriate technical abilities. Management is to make certain that people's capabilities do not stagnate but stay aligned to changing organizational wishes. Effective leadership complements humans' adaptive capacities. When the top instructor manages the educational manner of its various components efficiently and effectively, this displays a successful management manner. Therefore, the essential mission of headteachers has something to do with both control and management. Kotter (1990) suggests that "management is set to manipulate complexity management with the aid of contrast, is set copying with trade" Kotter makes a clear mark among the two, control is worried about transactional complexity, while management makes a specialty of trade and transformational. In different phrases, effective leadership worries with generating useful change via planning and constructing an imaginative and prescient while management does care of strolling the company via organizing and provision.

It could be simply visible that each management and control abilities are indispensable demands to attain effectiveness. as an example, faculty heads who can lead however no longer manage, or who can manipulate however offer negative management, chance losing achievement in faculties. Management, therefore, enhances control, it does now not update it. Moreover, Brighouse and Woods (2008) emphasize the want for both leadership and management to reach fulfillment inner our colleges due to the fact control structures aid leadership. It's agreed that successful school management includes a huge range of cultures and practices, so management styles range to match numerous situations. Many kinds of leadership entail a certain social climate. There are many definitions for coaching; however, I consider that teaching is based totally on one's reports. It entails getting to other persons' needs in a way that statistics is transferred to them and it isn't confined to books and rules. Coaching is a completely noble career and it's far crucial to men and women's broaden and how their behavior is formed. Having a tremendous mastering revel in allows students to be encouraged. The behavior of instructors has a wonderful impact and effect on students' learning effects because of the reality that they depend on instructors for steerage and to encourage them to perform. Instructors' behavior closer to college students could have terrible and superb results on students and it can decide their mastering consequences and it could final for a completely long term. Coaching in my view, maybe labeled as effective and rank over different professions and there are numerous questions asked as it pertains to teaching.

Questions about coaching

•   What's the cause of coaching?

I trust that cause of teaching is to educate people through offering know-how unto them and to teach them to do matters which might be set by a machine this is in step with the government. To coach, someone isn't always a count number of having him to commit outcomes to mind. As an alternative, it's miles to train him to participate within the system that makes viable the establishment of knowledge. We train a subject not to provide little living libraries on that problem, but as an alternative to getting college students to assume for themselves, to recollect topics as a historian does, to take part inside the system of expertise-getting; knowing is a system, not a product.

•   What do I trust approximately teaching youngsters?

I consider that coaching children is an extremely good revel in and that it's one of the greatest items that may be presented to them. I additionally consider that coaching child establishes a connection between teachers and students and facilitates shaping relationships. I additionally consider that it helps to form them to gain their character goals. I believe that coaching prepares them for maturity using letting them version the behavior of others to be able to study many competencies they'll need in the future and on an everyday basis.

•   What kind of behavior do I count on from students?

I expect students to be respectable, show nice behaviors,

be encouraging, supportive, and inclined to analyze. I anticipate them to participate in schoolroom sports and are seeking rationalization from me after they don't recognize something. I anticipate them to be responsible and make a motion to pass them forward.

• What do I assume from my students' dad and mom?
As a trainer, I assume my students' mother and father to be supportive, cooperative, and collaborate with me and are searching to recognize approximately what's happening in their children's lives. I assume them to inspire and motivate their children to work hard, to always be respectful, and to be obedient to their teachers. Mother and father are also predicted to be very involved in their kids' lives, provide the important resources that are required for the cause of the children's education, aid the policies and desires which might be set through the school and be right role fashions for their kids

• Do I consider that every toddler can obtain?
I trust that every toddler can attain as soon as given a truthful hazard. What I take into consideration is that each baby is exclusive, has distinct studying patterns and they all examine at their exceptional price. I trust that instructors need first of all to evaluate and recognize students to relate with everyone in everyone one of them. Each infant can attain their dreams but once in a while it calls for more attention, persistence, support, and encouragement but it's far very possible.

Autocratic leadership is a fashion of leadership that takes a tendency of despotism or autocracy. it'd be visible in the dating among both chief and fans and the social surroundings. To my private experience, I've skilled working underneath this style of leadership. The college head was the handiest person who himself determined work policy and additionally decided the form of work that everybody did. Furthermore, he gave many orders or took decisions towards the preference of his group of workers. His best situation becomes to make sure and advantage obedience of college participants. This reduced contact among our college participants. The college group of workers below that style of leadership just performed what the faculty head noticed and found it difficult to see the whole plan. This caused a corrupted college community. Moreover, this created college weather full of aggressiveness and passiveness. We as personnel misplaced self-belief and depended particularly on him. We didn't accept as true with each different and even we hated and didn't believe the headteacher himself. This led some of the school contributors to be hypocritical of this head trainer. Certainly, there are numerous altercations between school participants. In such a climate, you can't work nicely and the 'school's overall performance became negative. Democratic management is any other style which based totally mainly on encouraging individuals to cooperate, percentage reviews. As soon as I worked with such chief who became democratic with the aid of nature. He left the choice of dispensing work to us as school members. He became realistic in his criticism and praise. We were able to pick the work we love to do. We had the danger to specific our opinion. However, the college seemed to be run randomly. The autocratic style is common inside the Egyptian faculties and we leave out the democratic fashion due to the conventional educational gadget which depends in particular on centralization. Situational leadership is the most commonplace and straightforward fashion in which the chief has to use a combination of management patterns relying on the scenario. On managing people this style permits the chief to don't forget the situation he or she faces after which adopt the most right management style. Situational leadership fashion is based on flexibility and cleanness to understand. The qualities of management, particularly headteachers, and the way they deploy their abilities are broadly recounted to be the key elements to high school achievement. Without the proper mixture of them, they have by no means come across an in reality a hit faculty.

However, it is probably argued that something style of management is adopted; it's far essential for the top teacher to have the traits which permit him to steer college in the direction of fulfillment. There's an idea that emanated currently talking approximately the traits of a hit academic leader. Furthermore, Brighouse and Woods (2008) clarify that the faculty head should have energy, enthusiasm, desire, and the capacity to outstanding strength and build capability via having a program for staff development that considers the higher destiny of a person. A hit college head makes positive that the faculty body of workers speaks the identical language and they are members of the orchestra who sing from the same tune-sheet. Successful headteachers have to desirable communicator who connects with a group of workers, dads, and mom and students to invent the future of the scholars. These features need to be practiced within all ranges of headship, from the elegance teacher with college students as much as the chief (ibid). Taylor and Ryan (2005) point out that the national foundation for schooling studies (NFER) have a look which checked out a set of twenty a success headteachers whom they studied shared certain characteristics; they believed in their ability to guide their college to success, targeted on their goals and devoted to bringing out success of their faculty, prepared to take dangers in attempting new methods to encourage gaining knowledge of, were open-minded and allowing new thoughts, were equipped to project policies and do their issue whilst this appears like crucial for youngsters achievement.

Wallace (1996) really defines the school primary and how he affirms the educational leadership function to achieve effective getting to know. Wallace's announcement on the educational leaders visualizes the role and places primary emphasis on powerful scholar learning and the growing of supportive surroundings for the expert boom of instructors and administrators. Eventually faculty major must combine the management and management abilities to create weather for the faculty to flourish. There are a variety of things related to college and contribute to its success or failure to attain its goal. On the top of the listing come leadership and control and the following can be the school climate. Wallace, Jr. (1996) stresses the significance of supplying caring surroundings wherein respect, guide and fairness exist. School climate contributes to understanding the vision of the institution and its message effectively. The great faculty climate calls for establishing or practicing democratic ideas and ethical values. The consolidation of social members of the family in a framework of cooperation, respect, and an experience of safety will really result in high first-class schooling furthermore, growing high-quality relationships between teachers and college students and can undoubtedly affect scholar conduct and contribute towards increasing their educational qualifications. As an instance, academic studies suggest that after students experience that their teachers assist and care approximately them, they have got the higher motivation to be successful. Also,,, fitness researches show that teens who sense connected (sense like they're part of the faculty; that their instructors treat them fairly) are much less probable to engage in negative risk behaviors. Those behaviors intrude with attendance, attention in faculty, and work of completion.

Brighouse, and Woods, (2008) country that high quality gaining knowledge of climate develops and strengthens high-quality relationships among absolutely everyone in the faculty. One of the exceptional definitions of college weather which reflects its significance is the following college climate is the coronary heart and soul of a school. it's far approximately that essence of a school that leads a child, a trainer, an administrator, a body of workers member to like the faculty and to stay up for being there every faculty day. College weather is about that high quality of a school that allows each character to experience non-public really worth, dignity and significance, whilst simultaneously helping create an experience of belonging to something past ourselves. The climate of a college can foster resilience or come to be a danger element inside the lives of those who work and research in a place call faculty". With attention to, the college has to be understood as a social system that consists of complicated interaction among individuals. Every college has weather that influences all personnel, represents behavior, and determines the levels of overall performance. College healthful climate relies closely on the personal characteristics of the lecturers, mainly those who've huge powers and are in a position to steer the choice-making system of the school. The pinnacle instructors and Deputy without a doubt have the greater impact in figuring out the character of the college climate. Brighouse and wooden (2008) factor out that "language could make or damage a school." This reflects the importance of having concord inside the school. Faculty physical environment impacts the behavior and attitudes of each college student and body of workers in the direction of getting to know and toward college itself. For instance, if the faculty is poor in physical appearance which pulls pupils in addition to all body of workers to do their work, this can lead college students and a group of workers to hate the faculty and have an effect on their performance. Alternatively, if the faculty is rich bodily, the college will simply be a place where scholars like to be. It will be a satisfying and beautiful region. I've skilled running in such an environment. I spent two years coaching in a rural school which turned into rich in color and gaiety, said a teacher. The school building turned into new and properly designed. The surrounding location turned into nearly inexperienced in color. The maximum important aspect I trendy is that the community outside and inside school is supportive and the scholars had the motivation to learn. It became an exquisite opportunity to revel in working in such a supportive environment that allowed me to constantly broaden my skills as a trainer. Kerry and Wilding (2004) suggest some dimensions which need to be taken care of in creating a faculty environment. firstly, attention must now not simply take delivery of to school centers, however additionally to plants, whether or not they may be inside or out of doors college, they must be in precise order, tidy, maintained and taken care of. This could inspire pupils to behave properly and have a sense of the area. Secondly, the faculty environment, far from bodily mental factors, must be the form of place where youngsters sense loose to specific their view, ask questions and make mistakes from which they learn. Thirdly, workforce and aid personnel members of the family, there have to be the attitudes of admire and expert agree with amongst them. Fourthly, a team of workers-students relation refers to the great of communication between peers, college students, and personnel because accurate behavior offers a context wherein appropriate relations may be sustained. in the end, home-college relations refer to creating such weather wherein properly members of the family and verbal exchange exist among home and college.

Irrespective of the school layout, kids want a healthful and provoking environment wherein to examine. Faculties must be comfy visually, they need to have first-rate indoor air first-class, and they ought to be secure and comfy. School facilities have a robust impact on coaching and learning. Children are stimulated via light, color, and the surroundings. Children can also react negatively to detrimental situations. As an instance, if the classroom isn't planned to inspire the child to study, there may be no suitable surroundings for a trainer to train or pupil to learn. 'Classrooms' partitions ought to tell about students' achievements, sports, and participation using showing college students' contributions or work. What I like maximum all through my college visits is that the faculty location is selected to be healthy for gaining knowledge of? I mean the inexperienced region outside and inside faculty which provides quietness and adds splendor to the school. Another admirable thing we leave out in most of our schools is the sports activities corridor and swimming pool. Therefore, a successful school should be an area in which capabilities are to be found and practiced. Beard and Corkery (2010) nation aging college buildings that might be in a poor situation cannot meet modern-day teaching or learning strategies. Colleges with new construction and nicely ready witness development in students' achievement and attainment.

Teaching, getting to know, and assessment

The exceptional of learning and teaching is the fundamental position of the faculty. This takes us to say that school is the location wherein kids discover ways to study and write to apprehend the sector around them, to utilize their intelligence and imagination, to stay and work in harmony with others. Consequently, faculties are required to provide high first-class training via keeping effective instructors who trust that 'all kids can examine correctly and they could teach any individual to succeed'. Consequently, the college's responsibility is to draw teachers who can make a contribution to the teaching and studying procedure and consider a way to enhance the same old of success. The college imaginative and prescient which includes the faculty philosophy need to cover those problems of teaching and gaining knowledge. Brighouse and Woods (2008) suggest that each faculty ought to have a policy for teaching and gaining knowledge of which may be built to emphasize; creating and keeping gaining knowledge of the environment, tracking and comparing teaching and gaining knowledge of, the usage of evaluation for studying and the use of learning resources.

To my understanding, students are more and more uninterested in the traditional passive learning manner genuinely because it does no longer fit their mastering fashion. Mastering style is a unique manner wherein every child research and learns. As an example, a few scholars need a quiet room to take a look at, others like to have a look at even as being attentive to tune. This requires the instructor to understand and guide extraordinary styles of interior study rooms. The instructor, who insists on equal habitual for all students, will not be capable of broadening each child's potentials. We live inside the international of modern technology along with a laptop, smartphone cellular, and the net. Consequently, proper faculty ought to pave the manner to more accomplishing an energetic getting to know system via making desirable use of modern era sources. Through generation, instructors could make studying something thrilling and amusing. As an example, the usage of the clever board interior in our classes makes students more likely to engage in the lesson. Contemporary era assets assist teachers to manage to get to know now not gift information. "The use and the control of gaining knowledge of technologies are essential to powerful gaining knowledge of and success". Arguably, desirable college complements creativity and extends lively studying opportunities using listening to personalizing studying, getting to know styles and the usage of generation. A student ought to be responsible for their very own mastering (learn to study). The trainer is only a facilitator or a manager. The kingdom that personalizing getting to know is to assist every student to do higher by tailoring education to his or her desires, pastimes, and aptitudes. This can assist college students to be unbiased and lifelong inexperienced persons. For example, kids study in numerous approaches. Some kids examine maximum from looking, a few opt to listen, and others like to do ("visual, auditory and kinaesthetic". To complex further, every other example is that in schools we've fast inexperienced persons and slow novices. The fast newbies examine quickly whilst the sluggish rookies will study however they want greater time and duties. This leads us to the importance of encouraging teachers to offer different kinds of sports which meet their college students' wishes, and capabilities. It's far genuinely crucial for schools to use accurate evaluation techniques in coaching. The conventional kind of summative assessment and grading strategies is not powerful enough to help scholars to be triumphant. Brighouse and Woods (2008) positioned emphasis on the need for 'evaluation for mastering' in place of 'assessment of learning to allow students to work on their achievement and development. Evaluation for studying is a beneficial method that brings excellence to teaching and getting to know. Through formative evaluation 'evaluation for mastering,' college students realize their goals from the start. They recognize in which they're and where they may be going.

It offers non-stop feedback either it's far written or aural. Now not simplest does it assist students to revise their work but it also teaches students self-mirrored image to tune increase thru having a portfolio. Assessment for mastering brings college students in the procedure of assessment to be accountable and in control in their instructional mastering, achievement, and success. Though, instructors can make a difference inside the child's lifestyles due to the fact they have an extra impact on the scholars. To my know-how, accurate instructors are individuals who pay attention to their students. They may be accessible, available, approachable, enthusiastic, lively, and excited. A good instructor gives students self-belief of their capability to acquire high overall performance. Teachers must be company but fair, show care, make lessons laugh and interesting. This suggests that instructors must think about their practices, discover new techniques to encourage their beginners, make use of various mastering styles, and make coaching thrilling and effective. Moreover, teachers must recall how to form the sort of know-how that scholars get to maximize their achievement. It might be reasonable to argue that every teacher ought to do a self-evaluation to be their personal reflection in their work. It is the trainer's document that tells him how he is doing in his profession. Self-evaluation makes instructors recognize their skills and work on improving those abilities thru continuing professional improvement (CPD). Because of the growing demands for high requirements and requires improving excellent internal colleges, teachers want to update and develop their capabilities via continuing expert improvement. The term 'professional improvement' is used to describe moving instructors ahead in knowledge or abilities and all sorts of experts gaining knowledge undertaken by way of instructors beyond the point of preliminary education. Horsley (1996) defines teacher expert development as "possibilities provided to educators to increase knowledge, skills, and procedures to enhance the effectiveness of their school rooms and agencies." In my notion, persevering with expert improvement (CPD) is one of the key problems inside the development of education and college reform.

Glaringly, it's inadequate to speak about schooling and studying outcomes or bringing about adjustments in practice without citing teachers persevering with expert development. Earley and Bobb (2004), state that a trainer's fulfillment in expert development enhances the results of college students' learning. Moreover, powerful CPD provides something to the school's capability to improve. In different phrases, the core of CPD manner is to improve instructor, teaching, management, and leadership capabilities and qualities. Therefore, the reasons for an assignment such expert improvement are to enhance the process overall performance talents of the whole body of workers and individual teacher and permit them to put together for exchange. Brighouse and Woods (2008) show that imparting opportunities for the workforce to study together will make the overall performance higher and extra regular throughout the faculty. Brighouse and Woods (2008) see that properly organized training and mentoring related to pairs or small businesses of staff operating collectively is crucial for first-class continuous expert development. Craft (2000) points out an extensive variety of techniques of professional mastering encompass movement studies, the usage of distance-getting to know substances and the use of statistics generation along with e-mail discussion group, or self-look at the usage of multi-media sources.

In the years following the No infant Left at the back of Act, plenty of the studies on training have justifiably centered on enhancing fulfillment of the lowest reaching college students. Extra lately, however, there is a developing situation that the most talented students may not be accomplishing their complete potential. At the equal time, tighter budgets are actually forcing cuts in the funding of talented training programs. The cause of this dissertation is to inform education coverage using supplying proof of the impact that talented training has on the scholarly fulfillment of both participants and their traditional friends. Empirical studies at the efficacy of programs for gifted college students will be used to manual coverage selections and make certain proficient college students also are no longer "left at the back of".

I aim to decompose the overall effect of talented schooling packages into each of the person elements so that it will determine what factors are most crucial for the effectiveness of proficient programs. So that you can decide the efficacy of talented schooling programs it is vital to determine each the direct consequences on program contributors, as well as any indirect consequences on nonparticipants. Doing away with the proficient and gifted college students from the magnificence may additionally have several effects on folks that stay in regular education classrooms. Having fewer students within the lecture room may additionally permit students to get extra personal time with the trainer, which would cause a high-quality effect on success. At the same time, the truth that the brightest children are pulled out will put off any high-quality peer consequences resulting from their presence within the ordinary schooling lecture room. Also, to quantify the internet effect of doing away with proficient students from ordinary lecture rooms on the one's students who do not participate in proficient programs. Initial outcomes from bankruptcy 2 show a totally massive, high-quality, and extensive impact for each analyzing and math talented application on scholar success inside the relevant difficulty. when student constant results are protected in the model to control for unmeasured scholar characteristics, the value of the impact of gifted participation on math scores turns into greater affordability and stays tremendous and statistically widespread. But, inside the scholar-constant-effects model, the impact of proficient packages on reading pupil achievement turns into statistically insignificant. outcomes from bankruptcy 3 display that when student, teacher, and college fixed results are employed to govern for the impacts of college students, teachers, and faculty-degree assets, participation in talented programs, in general, does now not seem to have a widespread impact on studying or math score profits. When participation is broken down via software kind and the excellent of instructors and peers concerned inside the gifted programs are taken into consideration, in-college gifted software participation has a fantastic, massive, and quantitatively sizable effect on math rating profits, even as having no vast effect on studying success rating gains. In comparison, participation in pull-out talented programs seems to in reality lower pupil fulfillment gains in math. Estimates from bankruptcy four, which account for a pupil, peer, and teacher time-various characteristics as well as both measured and unmeasured time-invariant student, teacher, and school traits yield mixed results. The percentage of talented individuals has a fantastic and giant impact on math gains till trainer and faculty fixed outcomes are added to the version, and then the effect will become insignificant and the signs and symptoms vary. As for the effect on reading profits, the sign is continually poor, however most effective huge as soon as the teacher and school constant outcomes are included. Other fashions, which account for both innate intelligence and the "pull out" out of these college students from the classroom, display that the marginal effect of putting off the brightest college students from the schoolroom hurts everyday pupil fulfillment. This negative impact remains considerable for the analyzing gains even after trainer and college constant results are blanketed

Chapter Four

.

Social Networking and School

Social networking is a structured product of nodes-which can be normally businesses or people who are tied with the aid of one or greater specific kinds of friendship, values, kinship, imagination and prescient, thoughts, sexual relationships, dislike, financial exchange, alternate, or battle. Nodes within the networks and ties are the relationships among the actors. except for the definition captured by way of Wikipedia.com, social networks also can be similarly tricky as a shape of social constructivism in which it has the ability to foster the interaction thru which expertise and that means is built. Also, social networking has the capability to motivate scholar participation and deepen cultural knowledge. It also emphasizes collaboration and interaction within a mastering community. Ferdinand Tonnies and Emile Durkheim have been noted as founders of social networks in the overdue 1800s. Tonnies believed that social corporations have ties that hyperlink those who percentage ideals and values or individuals who've impersonal, instrumental, and formal social hyperlinks. Even as Durkheimn distinguished among a traditional society as "mechanical unity" which prevails if man or woman differences are minimized, and the contemporary society as "organic solidarity" that develops out of cooperation among people with impartial roles. Within the 1930s, J.L. Moreno began recording and analyzing the social interplay of small organizations. For the duration of this time, W. Lloyd Warner and Elton Mayo additionally have explored interpersonal relations at work. In the 1960s to 1970s, several scholars labored to mix the exclusive traditions and tracks of social networking. Among those, H. White and his Harvard university college students and C. Tilley, who focused on networks in social movements and political sociology, and S Milgram, who advanced the "six degrees of separation" thesis, have further their studies on that. Different research changed into also done using Talcott Parsons and others. Social networks research can introduce humans to one another, remedy organizational issues, and came out with new findings. It calls for the names of each respondent and their contacts to be accrued and used in most analyses. Right handling of the data and the evaluation, including complete control by the investigator can truly eliminate damage to respondents and those they nominate.

On the gain facet, academic researchers constantly benefit, corporations, society, and science may also gain, however, man or woman respondents hardly ever do. Research examination shows that 96% of college students claim to apply the internet for diverse reasons inclusive of chatting, textual content messaging, blogging, and surfing the net. But, all students declare that schooling is the past typical subject matter discussed. Regularly, whilst online, approximately 60% of college students research and discuss university plans, alternatives, and destiny careers. Maximum adults fear while college students use the net it makes them more prompted to the crook. But, new studies claim that teenagers are using the internet to engage with people they recognize as opposed to strangers. From research, 43% of college students declare the use of online networking made their relationships closer due to the fact the internet assisted in making plans and staying in touch with buddies. There has been a small five% that have pals who had been located online and had no head-to-head interplay. In the last five years with the expansion and famous call for facebook.com, numerous research has been appeared about who and why people grow to be individuals on the social networking internet site. Studies suggest that individuals who use Facebook look for human beings they have formerly met offline instead of looking for new human beings. Other studies approximately Facebook indicates that the majority of users have the best connection to their past excessive faculty pals. That is the purpose why social networks are so beneficial due to the fact humans can stay in contact online as they circulate the arena with a past pal.

Social networking sites are an exceptional platform for humans to connect to their cherished ones. It facilitates growing verbal exchange and making connections with human beings all over the world. Although humans trust that social networking websites are dangerous, they may be additionally very beneficial. Social networking websites are anywhere now. In different phrases, they have got taken over nearly every sphere of lifestyles. They come with both, advantages in addition to disadvantages. If we speak approximately the academic area, these websites beautify education by having power on the learners. They can explore diverse topics for their projects. Furthermore, the commercial enterprise discipline blessings plenty from social networking websites. The groups use social networking websites to connect better with their potential customers and enterprise partners. Moreover, human beings looking for jobs use websites to connect better with employers and firms. This gives them an exceptional possibility to searching for higher jobs. Then again, the hazards of social networking websites are also very excessive. They deliver delivery to cybercrimes like cyberbullying, sexual exploitation, cash scams, and more. It's very harmful to children as people lead them to victims of pornography and extra. It additionally offers clean get admission to the pedophiles of children's statistics. Most importantly, social networking websites are very addictive. They drop the productivity degrees of people. Students waste their time using it and get distracted easily from their studies. Furthermore, it makes them inactive and boundaries their physical sports. Social networking websites have created a large presence in nowadays world. Whilst there are many styles of those sites, a few are extra well-known than the others. FB-as an instance, Facebook is the biggest social networking site. It has more than 1 billion users which maintain growing each day. Moreover, it additionally enables you to promote your commercial enterprise or emblem through commercials. Instagram-Secondly, there maybe Instagram. It's owned by Facebook handiest. Further, this app lets you to percentage pics and motion pictures together with your followers. It offers customers loads of filters to enhance their snapshots. Twitter-moreover, Twitter is also a wonderful social networking website. It's far ordinarily utilized by celebrities. This website permits you to publish quick messages known as tweets to proportion your mind. Twitter is an awesome platform to carry your message in limited phrases. LinkedIn-furthermore, we have LinkedIn. That is one of the maximum trendy websites which allow experts to discover and rent personnel. Subsequently, it is to be had in more than twenty languages to offer a user-friendly interface. WhatsApp-although it entered the sport pretty late, this instantaneous messaging app made a place for itself immediately. Facebook obtained this app as well. It allows you to share text messages, pictures, motion pictures, audio, files, and extra. Social networking websites are a bane and a boon. It relies upon on us how we use to. Something in excess is dangerous; likewise, social networking websites are too. Use them for your gain and do now not let them control your life. Social media is a device this is turning into pretty famous in recent times because of its consumer-pleasant functions. Social media structures like Facebook, Instagram, and Twitter, and greater are giving people a danger to connect to every other across distances. In other words, the whole international is at our fingertips all way to social media. Young people are particularly one of the most dominant customers of social media. All this makes you wonder that something so effective and with such a massive attain cannot be all exact. Like how there are always two aspects to a coin, the equal goes for social media. Subsequently, distinctive humans have unique opinions on this debatable subject matter. So, in this essay on Social Media, we can see the benefits and downsides of social media.

Advantages & hazards of Social Media
When we examine the positive issue of social media, we

discover numerous blessings. The most critical being an excellent device for education. All the facts one calls for are only a click away. College students can educate themselves on various subjects through the use of social media. Furthermore, live lectures at the moment are viable because of social media. You could attend a lecture happening in the USA whilst sitting in India. Furthermore, as increasingly more humans are distancing themselves from newspapers, they're relying on social media for news. You're always up to date at the cutting-edge happenings of the world through it. A person will become extra socially aware of the problems of the world. Similarly, it strengthens bonds with your loved ones. Distance isn't always a barrier anymore due to social media. For instance, you can without problems talk together with your buddies and spouse and children in distant places. Most importantly, it also gives a splendid platform for young budding artists to exhibit their expertise without spending a dime. You could get great possibilities for employment via social media too. Any other advantage truly blessings groups who desire to promote their brands. Social media has emerged as a hub for marketing and offers you incredible possibilities for connecting with the patron. Despite having such particular benefits, social media is taken into consideration to be one of the most dangerous factors of society. If using social media isn't monitored, it could lead to grave outcomes. It is harmful because it invades your privacy like never earlier. The oversharing going on social media makes youngsters a target for predators and hackers. It also ends in cyberbullying which influences any man or woman notably. As a result, the sharing on social media in particular using children needs to be monitored always. Subsequent up is the addition of social media that is pretty common among the youngsters. This dependency hampers with the instructional performance of a scholar as they waste their time on social media in place of reading. Social media also creates communal rifts. Faux news is unfolding with the usage of it, which poisons the mind of peace-loving residents. Consequently, absolutely social media has both benefits and drawbacks. However, all of it relies upon the consumer on the cease. Young people ought to specifically create a balance between their instructional performances, bodily activities, and social media. Excess use of something is dangerous and the equal element applies to social media. Therefore, we must attempt to live a fulfilling life with the proper balance.

For almost absolutely everyone online nowadays, social networking is the high-quality manner to maintain contact. Humans no longer most effective keep in touch with their contemporary classmates however antique classmates, contemporary co-employees, own family, people half manner the world over, and lots of others. One exciting region of studies approximately it's far how race and ethnicity are associated with each website. In a new report, it turned into discovered that Facebook, Myspace, and Xanga users may be expected based on their race, ethnicity, and dad and mom academic stage. There are some realistic programs to numerous educational opportunities that are provided via social networking. One among the wide use of blogs to improve scholar studying. Blogs improve the study room surroundings in 5 methods. The primary improvement is determined inside the shape of nurturing a collaborative culture. Next, running a blog adds to student writing time, in other words, journaling. Running a blog may also increase publicity for the content material. Reflective getting to know is also progressed through possibilities from pupil and trainer feedback. Finally, the blogs create one-of-a-kind varieties of participation for college students. Collaboration on a venture is tough for instructors to evaluate because the technique continues to crowning glory. The era has now The rain educators to see the research, view the summaries of the studies, and feature the students peer assessment their class of ates work. The students used a chat container in a single lecture room version. The chatbox perchatboxthe collaboration primarily based on various content gadgets needs to be that discussed by way of students. Blogs permit college ents to work outside the four walls of the lecture room. English instructors finding the use of blogs to enhance the journaling time for students. Pupil journaling otherwise regarded these days as blogging is a completely effective ability for applicable and present writing. Richardson (2003) goes on to talk about the availability for college students to struggle with ideas post magnificence time. This interaction with one another in magazine surroundings to remember numerous processing strategies displayed in diverse individuals. Blogging growth publicity to content and reflective learning is advanced. Ferdig and Trammel (2004) determined that if college students work with the cloth via blogging with different college students enhancement of studying can arise. The dialogs back and forth maintain to enhance various points of view from peer to look. The reflective nature of blogging isn't always observed in the teacher posting a question and all students respond in more than one form. But formetricity comes from the pupil to stupid-to-student via from side to side debating. Running a blog in the long, run creates ext, ordinary sorts of social networking. Now not does the flow of information. This a couple of shapes of parshapesation reverses the float of information from pupil to student and from pupil to teacher. This cyclical nature of know-how motivates the students due to the fact they experience liable for the data and mirrored image. Additionally, there is a finished product left for others to glean from. No longer will the students switch on a fashioned paper to later be thrown away, their blogs can be retrieved for in addition discrimination of expertise. As the students build facts networks the scholars come to be authors for public edification. This provides really worth to college student's time and effort as they collaboratively deliver merchandise to fruition. The reader aspect in their cycle through a completed product is found via the studies device the students have to enterprise and also through peer editing to create thematic tones of their completed work. This reversal of expertise then moves the schoolroom from a passively getting to know environment to healthful lively studying surroundings. The scholar will become capable of interpreting facts and an adept player inside the production of new understanding. Students are stimulated active participants as they see everybody can alternate something. The records the scholars assemble may additionally or might not be linear because of their points of view. This active studying environment establishes possession and well worth as the product concludes.

Social networks trade over the years as relationships are fashioned or abandoned. Particularly large modifications in social networks may affect one's social capital, as whilst someone actions from the geographic area in which their community becomes formed and accordingly loses get right of entry to the one's social sources. Putnam (2000) argues that one of the viable causes of decreased social capital within the U.S. is the increase in households transferring for process reasons. Other studies have explored the position of the net in those transitions. Wellman et al. (2001), for example, find that heavy internet customers depend upon e-mail to maintain long-distance relationships, as opposed to the use of it alternatively for offline interactions with the ones living close by. net technology features prominently in a take a look at of conversation generation use with the aid of this populace through Cummings, Lee, and Kraut (2006), who located that services like email and instant messaging help college students continue to be close to their excessive school buddies when they go away home for college. Nicole B. Ellison, Charles Steinfield, and Cliff Lampe brought degrees focusing especially on the upkeep of current social capital after this foremost life alternate experienced with the aid of university college students, specializing in their potential to leverage and maintain social connections from excessive school. Young adults transferring to college need to create new networks at university. But, they frequently go away pals from excessive school with whom they may have mounted wealthy networks; absolutely forsaking these high faculty networks might mean a lack of social capital. Granovetter (1973, 1982) has advised that susceptible ties offer greater advantage while the susceptible tie isn't always associated with more potent ties, as can be the case for maintained excessive college relationships. to test the position of maintained excessive school relationships as vulnerable, bridging ties, they tailored questions on fashionable bridging relationships, inclusive of the ones in Williams (2006), to be particular to maintained relationships with excessive school friends in place of near buddies.

 They call the idea "maintained social capital". They found out that Facebook (considered one of the social networks) has garnered a completely sturdy percentage of customers on college campuses. Facebook members report spending among ten and thirty minutes on common the usage of Facebook each day and document having among one hundred fifty and two hundred friends indexed on their profile and respondents also file significantly greater Facebook uses regarding people with whom they percentage an offline connection-either a present friend, a classmate, someone living close to them, or a person they met socially. Additionally, they determined out that students view the number one audience for his or her profile to be people with whom they share an offline connection. That is suggested properly using the responses to items about how they use Facebook. Students additionally use Facebook generally to maintain existing offline relationships or to solidify what could otherwise be ephemeral, temporary acquaintanceships. There was a slight tendency for newer students to apply Facebook to meet new humans more than for juniors and seniors to achieve this however across all four years in college, respondents stated more use of Facebook for connecting with current offline contacts.

Returning to our original studies query, we can definitively country that there may be a high-quality dating among sure sorts of social network use and the protection and introduction of social capital in students' lifestyles. Even though we cannot say which precedes the alternative, social networks appear to play a vital function within the technique by using which college students form and keep social capital. The reality is that social networks are a rather recent phenomenon, and senior college students to be much less probably to join. College students used social networks to hold in contact with old buddies and to maintain or accentuate relationships characterized using a few forms of offline connection together with dormitory proximity or a shared magnificence. For lots, social networks provided a manner to hold in contact with excessive college pals and acquaintances. This becomes proven through the truth that the maximum generally protected facts on users' profiles turned into probable to be applicable for current acquaintances attempting to find them. Almost all users felt that their high school buddies had viewed their profile, and through respondents' self-stated kinds of use, this offline to online movement differs from the patterns discovered using early researchers analyzing laptop-mediated verbal exchange and virtual communities.

Due to the shape of the website, which blocks entry to the ones without a school email address after which locations individuals into communities based totally on that electronic mail deal with, social networks serve a geographically certain person based totally. Social networks can assist college students to gather and hold bridging social capital. This is the form of social capital that is closely linked to the perception of "susceptible ties" that seems nicely ideal to social software program packages because it permits customers to hold such ties cost-effectively and without problems. Haythornthwaite (2005) discusses the consequences of media that "create latent tie connectivity among group participants that offers the technical method for activating susceptible ties." Latent ties are the ones social network ties that are "technically feasible but not activated socially". Social networks would possibly make it easier to transform latent ties into weak ties, in that the site offers non-public statistics about others, makes seen one's connections to an extensive variety of people, and permits college students to identify people who might be beneficial in a few abilities (such as the mathematics main in a required calculus elegance), for that reason offering the motivation to prompt a latent tie. these vulnerable ties may additionally offer extra statistics and possibilities, that are expressed as dimensions of bridging social capital that communicate to interplay with a huge variety of humans and the more tolerant attitude this could inspire. Facebook seems well-proper to facilitate those reviews, in that precise profiles spotlight both commonalities and differences amongst participants. Eventually, social networks intensity expected accelerated stages of maintained social capital, which assessed the volume to which members could depend upon high college friends to do small favors. For university college students, a lot of whom have moved away for the first time, the potential to stay in touch with these high faculty acquaintances may illustrate maximum surely the "electricity of vulnerable ties". Those potentially beneficial connections may be precious assets of the latest statistics and sources. Moreover, the capability to live in contact with these networks may additionally offset feelings of "buddy illness," the distress as a result of the loss of old pals.

College students overwhelmingly stated that their social life on campus has been stricken by the internet. The net serves two purposes for college kids. The first is the usage of the internet to live in contact with professors and for operating on group tasks, and secondly to be in sync with a circle of relatives participants, and friends. The strong linkage between social network use and excessive college connections indicates how Social network offerings help keep family members as humans flow from one offline community to another. It can facilitate the identical whilst college students graduate from university, with alumni retaining their college e-mail address and the use of social networks to preserve in touch with the university network. Such connections could have strong payoffs in phrases of jobs, internships, and different opportunities. Colleges may also need to explore ways to encourage this kind of usage. With using the internet and social networks, students at the moment are more in fee in their getting to know extra than ever before. They're developing relationships and taking those to the following level by these online surroundings where they could communicate approximately instructions and educational plans. Giving the students this opportunity is not only motivating however an exciting manner to expose their know-how. The usage of an E-portfolio is almost a demand in any published undergrad program. The capability to compile and feature all preceding work to be had at the press of a mouse is a brilliant way to affect employers at interviews. It's also a great manner for reflection of instructors and college students' approximately their previous accomplishments. Instantaneous messaging is a brief and handy way for college students to communicate. This can be used for socializing outside of faculty but also asking questions. Having the capacity to message any other classmate who's wide awake and work through the trouble facilitates the scholars to complete their work as opposed to giving up. Social networking is a large advantage for college kids outside and inside of the schoolroom. Now not most effective are they in steady touch with peers if wished however they have got the ability to go back to preceding work and replicate upon with others. Online social community websites may also play a function extraordinary from that described in the early literature on virtual communities. online interactions do not always dispose of people from their offline global but may additionally indeed be used to support relationships and preserve human beings in contact, even if life modifications flow them far from every different. In addition to helping pupil populations, this use of technology may want to assist a ramification of populations, consisting of professional researchers, community and community individuals, personnel of groups, or others who gain from maintained ties. Even as the use of the interview has limitless benefits there are of course disadvantages. The conversation is ruined. In more youthful youngsters the abbreviated words and emotions are normally used. But it's been determined that as they mature they fast drop the abbreviated words. Those are the scholars who're adapted and used the generation and the way to work it inside and outside of the schoolroom. The new technology that's usually converting is a hard element to learn with each person no matter schooling and intellectual level. Using technology in the classroom is sort of too much for teachers because they're not able to maintain up with their fast-paced college students. E-Ports while effortlessly handy have issues whilst students aren't honest. Figuring out someone's work nowadays is difficult due to the fact there are such a lot of ways to cheat or clear out facts to skip it off as your very own. The students ought to develop and research so much but those drawbacks severely hinder the manner students perceive the educational device. Students these days, not simplest have problems with college and the one-of-a-kind generation inside their study room however face excessive emotional problems. Cyberbullying is an alternatively new idea but is severely risky. Children who're picked on have both ways to be even in addition humiliated or have a manner to take out their anger others. dad and mom and educators want to work together to save you cyberbullying so our college students can cognizance more of schooling while inside the study room and no longer on terrible social reports.

Chapter Five

Blended Learning

How does blended mastering assist in modern-day schooling devices? How does mixed getting to know fit into the nowadays higher education system and what are the views and perceptions of people toward the mixing of combined gaining knowledge of into better education? Mixed getting to know has had and is having a tremendous impact on these days' instructional system. Many individuals and higher institutions have observed the effectiveness of blended learning and spot it as the first-rate manner to train people. greater powerful than Face-to-Face was written through Katie Ash for schooling Week digital directions, she said that a record become launched on June 26, 2009, by way of the US of the United States' branch of schooling. She claimed the document examined several research,46 to be particular, comparing the conventional face-to-face form of learning with online gaining knowledge of and concluded that blended studying changed into certainly more effective than the traditional head-to-head way of learning. Many persons sense that even though mixed studying has many advantages, there is not sufficient evidence to conclude that blended getting to know is better than conventional face-to-face studying. It's far obvious that mixed studying holds remarkable promise for educators. pleasant and powerful training will now not be constrained to the walls of a classroom at the same time as mixing may be an enormously powerful and green way of training, it's miles vital to understand that a success mastering revel in requires excessive nice in all elements of the academic device study room interaction. blended getting to know is a combination of the physical and digital gear, which combine face-to-face pedagogical methods with an aggregate of magnificence education, online work, and peer collaboration all intertwined with choices, creativity, and differentiated preparation that keeps pupils engaged as they study. As a part of the mastering manner, some classrooms offer innovative environments which are flexible, which permit the scholars to work at their own tempo and on their very own time before the subsequent elegance length. via supplying dynamic and enduring practices, instructors can examine their students work and deliver constructive criticism; therefore, permitting their college students to have a significant mastering revel in. faculty hallways and lecture room today are more dynamic than they have got ever been before, and the capabilities essential for fulfillment are measured in teachers. A teacher with strong study room control skills has the ability to set up nice combined mastering surroundings, regardless of what type of era is being used. The capacity for that form of differentiation is right here, so it's miles as much as the trainer to find hard gaining knowledge of possibilities for each learner to feel valued and linked to their community. Combined learning is a time period that has been utilized for decades with the aid of educators and companies, no matter the truth that it most effectively received predominant attention in recent years.

Mixed studying basically manner using more than one studying technique to educate college students. Inside the beyond, blended gaining knowledge of has been regarded as a mixture of traditional face-to-face gaining knowledge of and any ordinary era. This may consist of everything from calculators to private computers to the net. However, combined studying has advanced notably during the last couple of years. The number of educational institutions and businesses making use of combined gaining knowledge is a testimony to the fact that it's miles certainly an effective way of passing knowledge thru. Combined studying entails the integration or blending of mastering packages in numerous formats to achieve a common intention. Blended getting to know programs usually consist of a mixture of school rooms and online programs. Blended getting to know may also be defined as the fusion of traditional face-to-face and online gaining knowledge of schemes to maximize the effectiveness of mastering. In mixed getting to know, the schooling program or direction is broken into exceptional sections and the most suitable sections are selected. The main intention is to take gain of the first-rate functions of every technique. PC-based schooling and CD-ROMs are examples of media that would be utilized in a mixed route.

Blended learning forces us to do not forget the traits of virtual generation, in standard, and data verbal exchange technology (ICTs), extra special. Floridi (2014) suggests a solution proffered with the aid of Alan Turing: that digital ICTs can technique facts on their own, in some experience simply as humans and other organic life. ICTs can also speak statistics to each different, without human intervention, but as linked strategies designed through human beings. We have advanced to the point where people aren't always "within the loop" of technology, however, must be "at the loop" designing and adapting the system. We understand our world increasingly more in informational terms, and no longer more often than not as bodily entities. More and more, the instructional global is ruled by facts, and our economies relax by and large on that asset. So our international is likewise combined, and it's combined so much that we rarely see the personal components of the blend anymore. Floridi (2014) argues that the world has to turn out to be an "infosphere" (like biosphere) where we stay as "informs." what is real for us is moving from the physical and unchangeable to the one's things with which we can interact. Florida also facilitates us to become aware of the next combination in education, regarding ICTs or specialized synthetic intelligence. learning analytics, adaptive mastering, calibrated peer overview, and automated essay scoring is advanced procedures that, provided they may be correct interfaces, can work properly with the instructor— allowing her or him to pay attention to human attributes such as being worrying, innovative, and tasty in hassle-solving. This could, of course, as with all technical advancements, be used to save sources and increase the position of the trainer. For example, if synthetic intelligence may be used to work along with instructors, allowing them greater time for non-public remarks and mentoring with students, then, we will have made a transformational leap forward. The Edinburg college manifesto for teaching online says bravely, "Automation needs now not impoverish education – we welcome our robot colleagues". If used wisely, they will train us extra approximately ourselves, and approximately what is definitely human in training. These emerging blends may also affect curricular and coverage questions, which include the what? And what for? The brand new regular for education will be in perpetual flux. Floridi's (2014) philosophy offers us gear to apprehend and be in control and not simply sit by using and watch what takes place. In many respects, he has addressed the brand new regular for mixed gaining knowledge of.

Generation plays an essential position in gaining knowledge of in today's international, it's miles everywhere. Children are exposed to the era essentially at the beginning. It's far commonplace to look at toddlers looking T.V or pc monitors and infants playing with their parent's mobile telephones or tablets. Instructors from preschool through college have started to contain technology into every day getting to know agenda and they're seeing wonderful effects. Faculties are going as away as the usage of pc based teaching programs a quarter of the college day to enhance students studying. That is not the only way era has assisted getting to know. There are many packages that teachers use to facilitate kids' mastering. Computer systems can assist teachers to make studying fun. Many laptop programs educate instructions inside the form of video games which kids revel in and inspire other kids to need to learn. There are even computer packages like Rosetta Stone that could teach everybody, child or grownup to talk an entirely new language! A generation has honestly skyrocketed human beings' cap entirely to gain knowledge generations are following a fast-accelerating trend referred to as mixed getting to know and that is wherein kids will spend a portion of their day conducting era. Generation isn't only in fundamental faculties, iPads and capsules are even included in pre-school getting to know the curriculum.

Children as young as three are playing interactive games on tablets and iPads. At a totally younger age, children are being exposed to interactive gaining knowledge of and appear to be learning better due to it. Instructors have software that can exhibit what region the kid needs enhancing on whether it's miles vocabulary or essential questioning and provide the child with gaining knowledge of games or quizzes that are aimed to enhance those fields. Gaining knowledge is a fantastically permanent trade in behavior because of enjoyment consistent with Ormrod, 2004 besides that, the definition of 21st-century learning is all approximately collaborate with others and connect via era. Discussing the implementation of generation in gaining knowledge of it's noted the coaching, mastering, and questioning gear that can alternate the way of the cognitive system. A generation has a high-quality capability to enhance education if appropriately carried out and the expectations approximately the function computer technology could play within the mastering manner. instructional technology includes now not handiest the internet, which provides get admission to university websites immediately tied to guides as well as to assets around the world, but also innovations in recording, taking part, and responding technologies that provide more desirable environments for scholarly interplay and intellectual. these technologies are valuable when they serve the larger academic goals of the college to create active newbies who not handiest master the content material of their selected fields, however additionally increase strategies and modes of important thought that activity will permit them to be informed and smart residents and individuals to their professions. Most of the students are immersed in facts generation in their daily lives. They count on that their instructional lives could be in addition wealthy in the era, and that they will leave UiTM as era-savvy graduates. Each school and students are given up customers of educational technology, and from it, they gain large advanced entry to path substances and each other. The educational generation holds the promise of creating greater interactive training, enticing college students greater deeply and more actively inside the route content material. The lack of access to academic technologies and innovations (sometimes termed the virtual divide) remains an undertaking with novel academic technologies. one of the guarantees of online technology is they can increase get entry to nontraditional and underserved college students by bringing several instructional resources and studies to those who may have constrained get entry to on-campus-most effective better education. A 2010 U.S. record suggests that students with low socioeconomic reputations are much less probable to reap better degrees of postsecondary schooling. But, the growing availability of distance education has supplied instructional opportunities to millions. Additionally, an emphasis on open educational sources (OER) in latest years has resulted in giant price discounts without diminishing student overall performance outcomes. Lamentably, the advantages of getting the right of entry may not be experienced lightly throughout demographic businesses. 2015 have a look found that Hispanic and Black STEM majors were appreciably much less probably to take online courses even when controlling for academic instruction, socioeconomic fame (SES), citizenship, and English as a second language (ESL) reputation.

Additionally, questions have been raised approximately whether the additional get entry to afford by using online technologies has truly led to advanced consequences for underserved populations. A distance education document in California located that everyone ethnic minorities (besides Asian/Pacific Islanders) completed distance training guides at a decrease charge than the ethnic majority. Shea and Bidjerano (2014, 2016) discovered that African American network university college students who took distance training publications completed tiers at extensively lower quotes than people who did now not take distance schooling guides. Then again, a take a look at fulfillment factors in k-12 online learning determined that for ethnic minorities, the most effective one out of fifteen guides had huge gaps in scholar take a look at rankings. greater studies wish to be performed, analyzing access and achievement quotes for unique populations, on the subject of gaining knowledge of distinctive modalities, inclusive of absolutely online and blended gaining knowledge of environments. During the last decade, there had been at least five meta-analyses that have addressed the impact of mixed mastering environments and their courting to mastering effectiveness. Every one of those studies has discovered small to slight effective impact sizes in favor of combined gaining knowledge of when in comparison to completely online or conventional face-to-face environments. However, there are numerous concerns inherent in these studies that impact our information on the generalizability of consequences. Dziuban and colleagues analyzed the meta-analyses conducted by way of approach and her colleagues concluding that their techniques have been remarkable as evidenced via an exhaustive look at inclusion criteria and the use of scale-free effect length indices. The conclusion, in each paper, turned into that there was a modest difference in more than one final results measure for guides featuring online modalities—especially, combined courses. However, with blended learning especially, there are some concerns with those styles of research. First, the effect sizes are based totally on the linear hypothesis checking out model with the underlying assumption that the remedy and the error terms are uncorrelated, indicating that there is not anything else occurring in the mixing that could confound the effects. Even though the mixed gaining knowledge of articles was cautiously vetted, the belief of independence is tenuous at nice so that these meta-analysis studies ought to be interpreted with excessive caution. There is a further issue with mixed studying as well. Many people consider that blends are not equivalent because of how they are configured.

For instance, a careful analysis of the sources used inside the approach, et al. papers will perceive, at minimum, the following mixing strategies: laboratory exams, online preparation, e-mail, class net sites, pc laboratories, mapping and scaffolding tools, computer clusters, interactive shows and email, handwriting seize, evidence-primarily based exercise, digital portfolios, getting to know management structures, and virtual apparatuses. These aren't equal approaches in which to configure publications, and such nonequivalence constitutes the confounding we describe. We argue right here that, in reality, mixed mastering is a well-known construct in the shape of a boundary object instead of a treatment effect within the statistical experience. That is a concept or idea which could help a community of practice, however, is weakly described as fostering war of words within the well-known group. Conversely, it's stronger in person constituencies. The creation of the era into the classroom is a movement that every district will or already has carried out. Getting the technology into the schoolroom is handiest the first step. Determining how the era can be used inside the study room to assist enhance scholar fulfillment is but some other trouble. Few school districts aid instructors passed the point of having technology in the schoolroom. There's commonly little to no steering given to trainers by way of administers on the way to merge technology into the study room. Due to this, many teachers will most effectively implement technology up to their comfort level. The one's teachers who experience secure integrating era into the classroom will do so, and people that do not will integrate a minimum amount. Even those teachers who do control to combine a top-notch deal of technology into their school rooms nevertheless do no longer use it to its greatest gain. The one's teachers that now integrate the era are the use of strategies which are ten years in the back of the present-day generation. Although a high-quality deal of studies has been finished on the use of era within the classroom over this time period, generation is changing only a swiftly. The web (internet 1.0) that changed into studied for the past ten years and the present day net (internet 2.0) are extraordinarily one-of-a-kind. A maximum of state-of-the-art instructors uses the web 1.0 era of their classrooms. In this case, they use the internet as every other aid for college students. They keep it to an equal degree as a textual content book or even transparency. Students who're typically shy, reserved, and uncertain of themselves can now come to be engaged inside the content material furnished in the course of elegance. Also, extending the class outside of the ordinary forty-five minutes in a manner that permits students to speak with one another approximately content material makes them more engaged. Dialogue boards allow for the extra idea out solutions to questions and extra in-intensity considering the content. The destiny of generation inside the school-room ought to be these days. Many teachers and colleges lack the expertise to put in force the internet 2.0 thoughts that scholars already use today. Research should be completed to determine the nice methods to educate teachers on a way to combine this technology into the schoolroom. The future classroom ought to characteristic internet 2.0 ideas that assist encourage twenty-first-century talents including collaboration, dialogue, network, and peer evaluation through publishing.

Twenty-first-century learning is formidable, bendy, innovative, tough, and complex; it takes under consideration the hastily changing international packed with new issues and new possibilities. Students expand important questioning and interpersonal communique abilities so one can be successful within the twenty-first century. By imposing an era to create an environment that meets the needs of this generation, studying now not must be a 'one-length-suits-all' device; the possibilities possessed with the aid of era ought to be used to reconfigure 21st century studying. coaching and mastering within the twenty-first century includes greater than the use and impact of virtual technologies; it comprises of more than one idea and practices coming collectively which will re-package deal gaining knowledge of and teaching so one can, in turn, higher mirror the twenty-first-century world. 21st-century studying is aware that during a global statistics society where new professions are continuously emerging, the priority has been shifted to growing appropriate skills and aptitudes our college students want as a way to be lifelong novices. This protected the dilemmas brought on between modernism and postmodernism, and structuralists and poststructuralists. when searching at 'traditional education' of the nineteenth century in comparison to new practices of the 21st century, big changes are being made to equip college students for the world wherein they live (Australian Curriculum and evaluation Reporting Authority [ACARA]. generation in the twenty-first century goes to adapt regardless if one is ready for the modifications aren't. better academic establishments are folks that cannot come up with the money to be left at the back while technology is changing the sector. Technological advances will quickly include modifying didactic teaching that focuses on scholar calls as well as converting the study room dynamic right into a more hybrid fashion of getting to know. Usual those modifications will have an effective impact on higher schooling. Colleges will want to maintain a bendy but distinct style of coaching to place the hobbies of the scholars first. This scholar-centered priority will subsequently promote innovation and creativity. There are several ways education will exchange because of technology. Concerning a greater pupil-centered fashion of coaching, professors can adapt to e-advising. E-advising is a manner for college kids to live have interaction in their research as well as get the guidance they need from their marketing consultant. With new technology at hand, teachers can use cutting-edge video internet chats to communicate first-rate lesson plans for every student. Not simplest will this method decorate customized learning but may even assist the educators to research more various coaching methods. The communication among the teachers and guardians will guarantee to hit school months for each pupil. In today's society, higher schooling manner greater technology. but, technology may also entail monetary burdens for the college board that in the end limits the scholar's get right of entry to these useful packages. Therefore, lengthy-time period trends that affect training are the boom dominance of the era in addition to growing needs for accountability of using public price range. These two traits can be looked at facet through side due to the fact without one; the other won't be as

Famous psychologist Albert Bansura discusses the power of self-efficacy and the way a pupil's self-photo determines how they feel about themselves. He defines self-efficacy "as someone's belief of their potential to succeed in particular conditions. Relying on the cross-evaluation of these three parameters, the course clothier will opt for one of the three alternatives. In his direction scenario, he/she will then must determine which parts are online, which elements are offline? A basic example of that is a path of English as a second language where the teacher concludes that all audio-primarily based activities (listening comprehension, oral expression) will take area within the lecture room where all textual content-based totally sports will take area online (reading comprehension, essays writing). Mixed learning increases the alternatives for greater exceptional and amount of human interplay in gaining knowledge of surroundings. Combined learning allows newcomers "to be both collectively and aside. A network of beginners can interact whenever and everywhere due to the blessings that laptop-mediated educational gear provides. mixed mastering offers a 'top' blend of technologies and interactions, resulting in a socially supported, constructive, learning enjoy; this is particularly large given the profound effect that it may have on distance getting to know. In a great global, an ideal concord can be created between head to head and online learning. Blended mastering strives to try this. In this state of affairs, the benefits of each procedure would be applied, without incurring the poor facet consequences of an unbalanced approach. The assignment, although, is that it's far difficult to come up with a great prescription for a way to relate to all and sundry effectively. Each architecture training has been combined gaining knowledge of environments, considered one of which mixed lecture room and online gaining knowledge of. The conjecture became that blended studying more suitable studio courses with the aid of permitting all direction material to be viewed by all and through having evaluations accessible to all students. although the supposition was that the scholars could be capable of garner expertise from comments made to others in their class and that the digital collaboration could permit for extra flexibility in reviewing, submitting, and refining facts, now not all college students have been capable of figure and follow comments and pointers about their work no longer made directly to them. Teachers also confronted improved workloads and there was faded scholar-teacher interplay, as elegance sizes grew larger because of the web format. Still, it becomes believed to substantially enhance the conventional face-to-face studio direction.

The final structure observes checked out scholar delight whilst comparing PC completed paintings with hand renderings. In that example, even though the scholars said they might use the pc to keep up with modern-day market trends, they desired the appearance and emotional enchantment of the hand-produced renderings. Literature summary the authors inside the studies cited some of the ability difficulties similarly to positive effects when it came to online lessons. The most not unusual online class was artwork history and the majority. There are criticisms regularly heard from parents after they pay attention to the time period of technology-based training. It's also a notable misconception about this model of gaining knowledge. online training is on the rise as noted using the authors of Disrupting elegance after they project that 50% of all excessive school publications might be online by way of 2019, and 80% by way of 2024 (Christensen ninety-eight). It cannot be neglected. A few parents and educators dislike this flow far away from the conventional study room and sense the need to choose one mastering model over the alternative. They fail to recognize that there's every other preference – the nice choice. A growing trend in education nowadays is a blended mastering version that integrates a technologically-based totally technique with traditional classroom instruction. With the benefits of individualized instruction and college readiness, blended studying is the most efficient and powerful way for students to research. Over the last forty years, generation has been incorporated efficaciously into many fields. Simply one instance of that is within the medical discipline wherein the innovation of Magnetic Resonance Imaging (MRI) permits medical doctors to look inner a body without doing the invasive exploratory surgical treatment. This is simply one instance of loads. But, in line with Carol Tomlinson in her eBook The Differentiated schoolroom, "while the rest of the world have stepped forward over the past century, the practice of training has remained static".

Blended mastering is one of the fastest-growing actions in schooling. Via combined studying the potential to customize guidance is made to be had while the high-quality social components of face-to-face getting to know are not completely misplaced. But, most of the studies on mixed studying are based on models applied at higher schooling institutions, or even these statistics are constrained or mixed. The outcry from researchers is for extra statistics at the effectiveness of mixed mastering, first-class practices in the implementation of the mixed model, the right blend of online vs. face-to-face training, the high-quality tools to utilize when the usage of a combined model, how to correctly put together teachers for the web academic detail of mixed learning, and how to scale blended gaining knowledge of up to the institutional stage, especially in structures out of doors of better training. Shifting to a blended getting to know the model is not an easy manner and needs to be carried out well to make certain effectiveness and sustainability. At this factor, it's essential to gather study data as it is very restrained on the technique of efficiently remodeling a public high school from the traditional model. Successful online gaining knowledge in a blended classroom requires an era with Inclusion training. In today's excessive colleges, it has grown to be increasingly greater difficult to satisfy the numerous needs of college students with social-emotional disabilities. These college students face a myriad of demanding situations inclusive of college avoidance and college phobia. Colleges ought to be creative and increase programs to aid each scholar's emotional fitness whilst presenting a rigorous program to meet the student's instructional wishes. One version to address the desires of college students who're college avoidant or have faculty phobia is an off-campus vicinity which is staffed by way of special needs instructors with expertise in mental health and counseling. By using staffing such applications with teachers designed to satisfy the scholars' emotional health, instructional rigor may be sacrificed. Packages that lack content-certified instructors to deal with all college students' instructional needs are turning to online learning platforms. Virtual excessive colleges and online learning guides create a solution to teaching high college students who may not be able to be knowledgeable in a conventional study room putting. Faculties are developing mixed studying environments wherein educators trained in mental health can guide students' intellectual fitness at the same time as accessing content-rich surroundings with online publications.

The significance of abilities Integration in trainer training

Teacher schooling institutions play a completely critical role to produce exceptionally erudite and skillful teachers. From in the modern generation, prospective teachers need to be able to grow such information and abilities. trainer schooling includes the regulations, methods, and provisions designed to combine instructors with the expertise, attitudes, behaviors, and abilities they require to carry out their tasks successfully within the institution, schoolroom, and community. The curriculum of the instructor education must be achieved of presenting a few information, communication talent, networking and soft capabilities .soft talents that enhance a person's interactions, task performance, and career projection. A first-class teacher comes from an excellent training manner. A carefully designed and well-planned education system is important to developing instructor education. This is an interesting and tough time for teacher educators. The character of coaching is changing. So that you can transform yourself into exemplary educator coaching establishments, many programs have become more entrepreneurial, spotting new opportunities and making adjustments required to respond to the needs of 21st-century beginners. This is to explore the desires and software of talents that have been included in the teaching profession. Now this time establishments become extra technological enrichment, educators want primary technological skills for ICT base presentations, prepare documents, and taking attendance electronically.

Cutting-edge university college students lead mixed lives. In truth, if we loosely define the time period combined to mean "partially digital, in part tangible," then we can adequately say all our lives have steadily grown to be increasingly more blended. We get entry to our information online, we pay bills online, and we communicate through email and social networks. People with net access go first to the internet for data. We get entry to the world thru smartphones; why now not access training in that manner too? At its handiest, blended mastering courses are the ones in which a substantial amount of seat time, that is, time spent within the classroom is changed with online sports that contain college students in assembly route goals. Educause, a nonprofit enterprise whose assignment is to sell the wise use of facts technology in better schooling, classifies guides primarily based on the quantity of time spent in each modality. According to its category scheme, blended courses have between thirty percent and seventy-nine percentage of activities online, face-to-face courses can encompass up to 29% of online sports, and absolutely online guides can include up to 20% of face-to-face activities. Garrison and Vaughan (2008) outline combined getting to know as \"the thoughtful fusion of face-to-face and online mastering reports . . . such that the strengths of each are mixed into a unique getting to know revel in. combined studying is an essential remodel that transforms the structure of, and technique to, teaching and studying". The precise characteristic of blended gaining knowledge of is that a large portion of the sports occur in two regions: in-person and online. Numerous different pedagogies - lecture, hassle-primarily based getting to know, just-in-Time teaching, cooperative mastering, and others - can then be superimposed at the blended framework. The assignment of mixed mastering is to link, or combination, what happens in each medium so that face-to-face and online sports toughen every other to create an unmarried, unified, route.

A large body of literature, frequently labeled as the no

great distinction literature, is frequently referred to in guide of the rivalry that there may be no discernible benefit within the learning outcomes of students taught online compared to students taught in a face-to-face environment. In fact, careful meta-analyses of this literature display a vital difference: online learning, and specially combined mastering, can bring about extensively better scholar learning as compared to learning within the traditional classroom. A meta-analysis carried out using the U.S. Department of Education (2009) winnowed down over 1,000 empirical studies to fifty-one that used a rigorous research layout to degree student learning results in each environment and furnished sufficient information to permit calculation of an impact size. The locating became that scholars in absolutely online and blended courses tend to carry out higher than students in face-to-face guides, with students in blended publications appearing significantly better. Any other finding of the have a look at ways that the extra time students spent on the project, the greater the differential in scholar performance. These findings are attributable in part to lively studying strategies, which encompass possibilities for mirrored image and interaction with friends, and an element to the enriched content that characterizes well-designed online and combined publications.

But, a substantial caveat is so as: The studies in this meta-evaluation do no longer demonstrate that online gaining knowledge is superior regardless of how it is implemented. The mixture of elements inside the treatment situations produced the discovered advantages. Among the studies showing an advantage for online studying, the web and school room situations differed in phrases of time spent, curriculum, and pedagogy. The success guides covered additional gaining knowledge of time. On-line and combined gaining knowledge of, lacking the time constraints imposed by face-to-face guides, are a lot more conducive to the growth of mastering time. The successful courses also blanketed extra interactive substances (studying items) and additional possibilities for collaboration. In any other meta-evaluation of the literature, Zhao, Lei, Yan, Lai, and Tan (2005) diagnosed 3 forms of interactions-teacher and students, college students and their friends, and college students, and content material as essential factors in determining the efficacy of a route's design. They similarly said that publications with synchronous and asynchronous additives-for example, mixed courses-document greater fine outcomes than courses that are entirely synchronous or entirely asynchronous.

While the design of the various research is teased apart, it is feasible to institution subsets that identify particular variables. Three components of online getting to know to stand out as contributing to extra powerful learning: discourse, through dialogue forums, blogs, or different media; reflection, either public or private; and writing to examine techniques. To summarize blended getting to know guides hire active mastering strategies through the usage of a variety of pedagogical strategies. The asynchronous nature of the mixed composition of the courses has the salutary effect of expanding the time students spend on the course fabric. Discussions carried out online encourage reflection and typically reach a hundred% participation. As a result, the face-to-face time can be used more correctly, with students extending the fabric beyond what is probably carried out in a conventional face-to-face path. The students in a combined direction make extra and richer connections between what they're learning and what they already realize, growing a strong scaffold to organize the records. The subsequent sections include a more special observe a number of the traits of a hit mixed learning publications.

The contemporary generation is characterized by way of rapid modifications on account of scientific and technological advances, such as the statistics era. Keeping up with those adjustments is necessary for the schooling machine to address issues that may arise from them, including the massive extent of statistics and increase in the number of newbies, coupled with teacher shortages. Those changes in technological know-how and generation ushered in lots of new teaching and mastering methods, consisting of e-learning and combined gaining knowledge of (BL) in particular in research and self-improvement regions, and a revolution in statistics technology, which has certainly turned the sector into a worldwide village. The former caused a more need for inexperienced persons to have interaction in multivendor environments, and the latter, for people to proportion reports with others. E-studying is described as learning that is furnished electronically thru the net, an internal network (intranet, or multimedia, consisting of CDs or DVDs). it is taken into consideration some of the most contemporary gaining knowledge of methods and has been associated with many benefits. Amongst those benefits is its ability to remedy the problem of expertise explosion and developing call for training; cope with the trouble of overcrowded lecture halls, if used as a way for distance getting to know; and provide possibilities for the attractiveness of diversity in education. For example, e-studying lets employees study, knowledgeable, and rehabilitated without leaving their corporations while additionally teaching their housewives, consequently contributing to increasing the literacy charge. e-gaining knowledge allows task interviews to be carried out and stay debates to be available online and offers quickly updated records, simulation and animation applications, interactive physical activities, and sensible applications, which are constant with a learner's desires, and observe his/her pace even as decreasing education expenses (accommodation, tour, and books). Moreover, it improves the retention of and get right of entry to information in a well-timed manner and unifies content material and information for all customers.

Ultimately, it improves collaboration and interactivity among students and decreases their emotions of embarrassment in front of fellow workers while making mistakes. But, e-mastering could have poor factors consisting of technology dependence, lack of motivation, and lack of human touch. Eventually, e-learning exams are constrained to questions that can be normally objective in nature no longer to say the difficulty of the degree of protection with regards to online gaining knowledge of applications. Meanwhile, BL is a contemporary academic strategy that has changed e-mastering gradually in maximum educational establishments. In line with Salama, BL is a logical and scientifically applicable alternative to e-studying, has higher yields, is much less costly, and includes greater state-of-the-art types of gaining knowledge. Similarly, Garrison and Kanuka argued that BL is a time period that explains the diverse attempts made by instructors to include the element of generation into the traditional schoolroom placing, because of the performance this association brings. BL goals at interactive getting to know, resulting inside the blending or blending of a trainer's position in a conventional schoolroom with that in the digital one. The technology carried out in BL is frequently meant to generate the most effective performances via students. in step with Graham, BL systems are meant to promote learning by facilitating the mixing of visible cues and academic standards. Using virtual environments acts to seize the eye of the audience concerned even as augmenting interactions between difficult parties. BL combines forms of direct and oblique online learning and generally entails the net and intranet, even as oblique studying takes place simultaneously inside conventional training. Valiathan advised that different additives implemented in BL are, amongst others, email, simulations, internet-primarily based tests, and FAQ. Three primary fashions, namely, talent-pushed, attitude-driven, and competency-driven models, can be carried out in BL. All fashions entail the assessment of the topics to be included. They also contain the assertion of the initiatives a good way to be engaged inside the delivery of studying concepts all through elegance sessions. An example of this type of mixing could be an education software that gives observe substances and research resources at once on the net, whereas teacher and school room education classes offer intermediate fundamental schooling.

BL additionally pursuits the usage of the contemporary era in teaching without leaving behind the standard educational situation and classroom attendance. It focuses on direct interplay in the classroom through using present-day verbal exchange mechanisms, including computer systems, networks, and net portals. within the evaluation of the influence of BL on interactions between college students and teachers, so and Brush set up that the social presence provided within the environment encourages questions and consequently affords a medium via which clarifications may be made in a timely and green manner. Such mastering can be described as a manner to arrange facts, attitudes, and academic experiences that are furnished for the inexperienced persons through multimedia supplied by cutting-edge or records technologies. This type of gaining knowledge is characterized with the aid of its capacity to lessen the time, attempt, and cost, thru the delivery of information to beginners as quick as feasible and in a manner that enables control and control of the academic procedure, the size, and assessment of newcomers' overall performance, and the development of the overall degree of educational attainment at the same time as presenting an appealing learning surrounding. combined getting to know is defined as gaining knowledge of using distinctive methods related together to teach a specific substance. Those strategies might also consist of a combination of direct lecturing in the auditorium, online communication, and self-learning. Julie believes that combined studying is a newly used term, but it became general before; it blends various academic styles of laptops and provides e-learning thru the internet; it includes email carriers, in addition to traditional education wherein the teacher has the most important position. BL, however, has some negative aspects along with inadequate technical accessibility which may additionally result in losing resources. Technical issues including poor net connectivity and excessive maintenance value are yet any other difficulty. BL can also be challenging for teachers because it demands time for each guidance and assessment. In the end, plagiarism and credibility can also pose the foremost problems mainly for younger. BL has many blessings, such as the subsequent: making computers and neighborhood and international networks of facts to be had for rookies; growing teachers' roles as leaders and mentors to their students in phrases of their information in computer systems and networks of local and worldwide facts, further to being producers instead of importers of understanding; enabling getting to know companies to use multimedia, email, digital libraries, and all internet data collaborative software program; having the potential to mix unique opportunities for exclusive schools and universities inefficient ways, and overcoming the hassle of lasting alternate in the content material of instructional substances. The problem addressed on this look stems from the need to diversify the coaching techniques used inside the discipline of mastering and education, mainly within the English language, in which the results of success checks imply a low stage of instructional success in the English language for college students in English guides in Jordanian universities is widespread and on the German Jordanian college (GJU) in Madaba town mainly. This is reflected in students' low-level conversation capabilities in English, which led instructors to locate various teaching strategies to improve college students' studying.

The instructional system at present is in a transition

degree. to meet the demanding situations of expansion and for catering individuals need it is trying to adopt new technologies and exploring new paths to attain the aim of nice educational possibilities for all, at the equal time due to different factors like poor budgets, loss of centers, advantages of face to face interaction, it isn't completely equipped to depart the traditional modes of know-how transfer. Even the scholars are in a nation of dual thoughts. When a set of teacher trainees were inquired approximately the mode of teaching they will pick from the way of life classroom coaching and ICT supported teaching the students were nearly flippantly divided between both the selections. The traditional model of teaching regardless of its shortcomings offers a far needed human contact to the teaching mastering process. The personality and behavior of the academics at once affect the blooming persona of the students. Best face-to-face interaction meets the affective targets along with cognitive and psychomotor. The face-to-face conventional technique helps in developing a strong value system. Social capabilities like cooperation, sharing, expression, and respecting different views are extra without problems advanced in the traditional model of coaching. college students analyze now not only from books, or from instructors coaching interior lecture room but additionally from the co-college students, thru their peer institution interaction, they research many competencies in the playground and their small social interactions in canteens, front room, etc. All this is essential for a proper character improvement notwithstanding traditional technique has its very own benefits however it is not loose from deficiencies. It has the following shortcomings: it's failing to fulfill the personal wishes of all the college students inside the class essentially due to an improper pupil instructor ratio. It is not adapting itself to meet the undertaking of teaching bodily demanding situations to college students. Teachers are not trained for an included classrooms. It isn't always a match to meet the challenges put forward by way of the abnormal students as attendance is ought to and the evaluation machine depends on the annual exam. If college students fail to take the exam his entire year is a waste, due to tension the irregular students are in a way excluded from the mainstream of college gadgets. In addition absence of professional counselors and a shortage of proper mindset of academics and a dearth of observe-up sports in the schools the kids who stop the faculty for any purpose do no longer get the hazard of getting into inside the formal educational system once more. School isn't capable of attaining every child and so education for all is still a far-sighted purpose.

Kids from deprived businesses, from the areas that are geographically isolated and medically undeserving college students, are not able to advantage benefit from this formal conventional mode of coaching. At the same time, students need to suffer due to the dearth of teachers, their studying has many ambiguities due to inefficient instructors. Direction is not frequently revised, books are not updated and teachers are not interested in upgrading their a hundred thirty combined gaining knowledge of A revolutionary technique knowledge and expert abilities, the result is that our college students are not properly prepared to satisfy the needs of the contemporary marketplace and professions. To make their expertise correlate with the present technological advancement and globalization, to minimize the teaching errors, to improve the best, to increase college students' publicity ICT supported coaching getting to know the process is a great choice. ICT-supported teaching affords a new size to the teaching-learning method, introduces students to the extensive pool of know-how, and opens before them innumerable opportunities to examine, unlearn and relearn, All kinds of learners whether in- provider, bodily challenged all may be benefitted through this mode of coaching. It enables accomplishing to all students. In the words of Swami Vivekanand "if human beings cannot attain faculty faculties have to reach them", ICT-supported studying is precisely doing the identical. evaluation of each the traditional mode of teaching studying manner and ICT supported coaching mastering manner display that both have few merits and demerits, both are catering unique desires, demands, and expectancies from the educational machine, so the answer is to offer and layout any such gadget that is based totally on an incorporated approach, a gadget that consists of the primary capabilities of both conventional method of coaching and ICT supported coaching. The call for of nowadays is a technique that blends the advantages of each the modes for the student's mastering i.e. mixed getting to know.

Major characteristics of blended studying

The principle features of combined gaining knowledge of are-

College students have the option of the two modes- students in combined gaining knowledge of can choose either the traditional model of school room coaching where they could get personal interaction with the teacher and their classmates or they can choose ICT supported teaching gaining knowledge of. This largely relies upon the nature of content material and goals being targeted. Someday course dressmakers or teachers themselves determine the mode appropriate for the topic being treated. teachers are nicely versed with each mode; it is an essential function of the combined mastering that instructors are very dynamic, techno-savvy, and fully educated to work correctly in both the shape and conventional lecture room format and ICT supported layout. they may be properly geared up in using traditional techniques and different cutting-edge technologies college students get head-to-head interaction as well they interact in a digital area- college students get sufficient of time to have interaction with different college students pursuing equal direction. They can have interaction with their interior university campus and also in the digital area. consequently, their group ends up very big and has a lot of variety so the scholar's understanding turns wide and they also expand a sense of expertise, love, and harmony with college students of other cultures and international locations. Students get full enjoy in the use of new era- the present century is the century of ICT. Nowadays the illiterate isn't only the one who cannot study and write but a person who isn't well versed with modern-day technology is likewise illiterate. These days all professions demand expertise in ICT so blended getting to know help to make scholar's ICT experience wealthy. College students worried in combined studying gain functionality to take advantage of to be had technologies to the fullest in their benefit. College students get schooling in exceptional lifestyles abilities- lifestyles talents are the one's talents which are had to lead a glad peaceful and successful life. The predominant life capabilities are empathy, choice-making functionality, love, patience, verbal exchange, self-management, vital questioning. The blended getting to know enables the students to practice those talents. College students get acquainted with few talents like love, empathy, staying power in the lecture room thru their teachers, classmates, and a few like self-management, choice-making, critical thinking, communique via the net reports. All-round development of character is centered. In combined mastering, the scholars get the full opportunity for all-around improvement of the character. All the components of personality particularly- cognitive, bodily, and emotional are developed via blended studying that's difficult to reap in conventional mode or ICT method if observed in isolation. way of life study room coaching is beneficial in memory level and know-how degree of coaching and so help in cognitive domain improvement and at the same time teacher's behavior, playground experience and social group with classmates increase affective and physical domain at an equal time online studies assist in the reflective degree of gaining knowledge of so increase better colleges of min and social networking sites and other social interactions even though internet help in proper kind of cost development. Physical improvement is possible within the faculty campus- the web gaining knowledge of and ICT supports coaching gaining knowledge of manner is regularly centered with the blame that it ignores physical development of the scholars.

The mixed studying overcomes this challenge. As it blanketed school experience additionally so the student gets time for gambling, physical work, yoga on the college campus. college students get wide exposure and new perspectives of the route content-due to the style of revel in college students get huge publicity and their content knowledge is enriched, they get to see diverse new dimensions of the content material benefit realistic beneficial knowledge. It has a human touch- because of the bodily prescience of the instructor thru the traditional approach students get that human touch which may be very vital for a balanced scholar's emotional quotient and really necessarily as much as the secondary level. It offers a multicultural and multi-size technique to coaching gaining knowledge of the procedure-mixed learning approach offers pupil the possibility to communicate and share their views and feeling with the students everywhere in the world for that reason it makes teaching studying process multicultural and form of enjoying deliver with it the interdisciplinary and multidimensional aspect additionally. Makes coaching getting to know manner infant targeted blended studying is designed to provide the most advantage to students and for this reason attain the intention of toddler centered training. Numerous position of instructor- instructor in combined getting to know is gambling exceptional role, the traditional position of an instructor in the study room, she acts as a motivator, as an aid individual, as an organizer, as a developer, while she develops content material to be furnished through ICT, as a manual at the side. Consequently, the teacher gets freedom from the monotonous traditional roles and she or he can attempt her fingers in numerous areas which might be accurate for her professional boom also, the pupil constructs expertise in place of just ingesting it. Blended studying also includes constructivism.

Imposing blended teaching isn't a smooth undertaking. It requires sure essential arrangements in all of the factors of coaching mastering method- teacher, scholar, content designing, and infrastructure. The following are the primary requirements for enforcing a successful mixed gaining knowledge. 1. Nicely trained teachers- even though toddler targeted but instructors are a vital pole of mixed learning. Teachers should be properly familiar with the concept of blended studying and fully educated and skilled to mixture both types of techniques- culture and technological. They have to be taught to broaden content material in digital shape so that it can be available to college students online. They ought to be well versed with net surfing and internet terminology need to be aware of all the websites that can be beneficial for the students even as getting to know online. The trainer ought to realize how to make use of blogs, youtube facility, software like Skype, goggle speak and others for video conferencing and social networking websites for instructional functions. 2. Instructors with a scientific mindset- it is very critical that teachers have a medical attitude. They need to have precise remarkability, they must be positive need to have hassle-solving abilities. A clinical mindset will assist the lecturer to deal definitely with failures she will get at the same time as running on this modern concept and will help to analyze the situations objectively.

This proper form of clinical mood will routinely filter out from instructors to college students 3. Instructors with a wider outlook and advantageous approach in the direction of trade – as it needs to for the success of any progressive concept or technique blended getting to know procedure additionally want teachers which have a wider outlook and should be flexible, they need to be equipped to accept the adjustments and very innovative and dynamic. 4. Complete facilities like well-supplied computer lab, net connection, provision for video chatting- it's the compulsory issue of combined learning. blended gaining knowledge of in large part depend upon infrastructure, school have to not handiest have excellent school rooms however must also have a well-supplied compute laboratories with a sufficient number of computers to cater to all the college students of one class and the net facility, a Wi-Fi campus if feasible. 5. Students have to get admission to net at their personal computer systems- further to high school having completely ICT friendly campus college students should have basic hardware help to study on-line and offline at their residence also. This calls for an advantageous mindset and appropriate investment schemes from the government. 6. Flexibility inside the machine- The device needs to be bendy, flexible time desk, examinations gadget all this is very critical for imposing blended getting to know. 7. absolutely aware and agreed on mother and father- the dad and mom must be made well aware about this progressive approach to teaching so that they're equipped for it and help their wards for the blended getting to know and can receive that this deviation from conventional teaching is beneficial for his or her children. 8. Formative assessment and non-stop internal evaluation- the school authorities and higher educational bodies have to be ready to completely put in force continuous inner evaluation(CAI) and different tools of formative assessment as summative assessment isn't supported within the mixed studying. The supply has to be made for the online exam for making the system extra bendy. These are few essentials and fundamental requirements without which the mixed getting to know cannot be completed successfully.

Chapter Six

The Pros and Cons of Online Learning

Education is the key to success and within the global today, mastering can take area in a conventional schoolroom setting, in addition to online. Even though those are each method of instructing freshmen, some variations benefit the particular learner. A conventional study room setting is wherein studying takes vicinity and the trainer presents face-to-face academic gaining knowledge of to students. Students also are capable of speak head to head with the trainer as well as other students in the study room. Then again, online studying is where guides are taken online, but the instructor and college students have interaction or talk online. This may take area in a video chat room, virtual learning magnificence, emails, digital telecommunications, and so on. If a student misses a class inside the conventional study room, she or he will be capable of asking the trainer or another scholar face to face for notes or assignments that were overlooked. College students are also able to ask the trainer for added assistance while she or he does no longer understand a lesson. However, the scholars will nonetheless have a good way to keep up with new notes and assignments, whereas in the internet getting to know the environment, the scholar can complete assignments at home on their personal time, however, may have a due date. If the student does now not recognize something, he or she can prevent and go over it later or electronic mail the instructor to reply to questions. A traditional classroom setting is a higher choice for college kids with more freedom of their schedules.

Some numerous instructional philosophies and theories govern the manner we train and the way we view training. Out of the numerous philosophies, many thoughts and thoughts were birthed, and these are primarily based on the way of life and different factors that affect educational systems, but which is an appropriate philosophy? I consider that each one philosophy was designed to sell studying and to educate us approximately existence itself, despite their strengths and their weaknesses and their wonderful and poor perspectives. As educators, we have a massive duty to compare every philosophy towards our very own private patterns and our own philosophy so that or coaching may be powerful. When sifting thru these philosophies, we need to pay close interest to the professionals and cons of each so that we can select diverse alternatives and include them in our very own precise fashion. Also, we want to grow to be familiar with even the philosophies that don't practice to us and our subculture to be able to be smooth for us to pick out what we desire to be part of our educational adventure. Our chosen philosophy needs to teach youngsters to understand the fundamental educational standards of analyzing and writing. The manner wherein college students behave is commonly related to these philosophies be it fantastic or terrible. Consistent with the behavioral idea, development as a continuous manner in which kids play an exceedingly passive function and the only things which might be actual are the matters we can see and have a look at, Jean Piaget (1896–1980), therefore, it's far critical that we apply the right philosophy to our teachings. Actually, we can't see human beings' thoughts, but we can take a look at their reaction and their behavior to state of affairs and statistics.

One's behavior has many outcomes and influences one' getting to know and much can be discovered approximately a baby through their conduct. Additionally, consequently the reason it's recommended and recommended by the behaviorist's idea which has advanced many exquisite means of discipline and lecture room management. Kauchak and Eggen defined educational philosophies as a set of ideas and beliefs that courses instructors' moves and gives a framework for considering educational issues. Philosophies are used each day in the lecture rooms and it impacts the relationships among teachers and students both definitely and negatively. Some additives of the numerous philosophies spoke without delay to me and that I believe sure ideas that I had a different view about before that may exchange the academic outlook through the years. However, the philosophy that surprised me rather is the Islam philosophy. No matter it specializes in the standards and the principles which might be involved with training, it criticizes its construction whilst investigating new ideas to upload fee to the philosophy. The Islamic philosophy ambitions to acquire the best, however curiously, their ideas derive from their Holy Quran and no longer always the society. Curiously, the Islamic philosophy seeks to create balance and expand individuals holistically. What's contradicting is that at the same time as the philosophy seeks to develop individuals holistically and that their concepts and ideas are based on their Holy eBook, a lot of them do not help impartial questioning. As an example, Halstead argues that Islamic philosophy and training are not selling crucial wondering. He additionally delivered that Independence of idea and personal autonomy do no longer input into the Muslim thinking about schooling, that is more concerned with the revolutionary initiation of scholars into the obtained truths of the religion. Classroom seating association for college kids is common of the first-rate fee, and it has wonderful outcomes on students and their learning. It's far important for instructors to configure their lecture rooms to their likeness, their unique style, and in a manner as a way to serve each of them and the students well. While a lecture room design is by the instructor's style of teaching, he/she promises shows and instructors with authority, strength, and confidence and it also includes finished with excessive readability and as a result, the scholars gain greatly.

When configuring lecture rooms, numerous factors should be considered which encompass: study room length and form, the level of distraction and its direction, the size and in some cases, the age of the students, and the trainer's teaching style and his/her study room targets. earlier than you readjust a classroom, as an instructor, you need to consider the amount of area this is available even as retaining in mind the vicinity of furnishings and try to avoid everybody getting hurt. Teachers also need to understand the classrooms' distractions and try to decrease them as a lot as viable because distractions limit college students' studying. Distractions can be little things that get the eye of students and preventing them from paying attention to what's being taught. The dimensions of a category need to be carefully taken into consideration and the ages of the scholars. in lots of situations, you find the more youthful college students are those who are greater effortlessly distracted, so they want to be placed in regions that they can have regular eye touch with the lecturers. However, for teaching to be effective, a classroom doesn't have to be configured, the academics simply should discover innovative approaches to education. The teaching style and lecture room objectives are the simplest to me in terms of teaching. primarily based on what instructors are hoping to achieve in the school rooms will inspire them to do their first-rate, giving every scholar an outstanding possibility to be triumphant. As an instructor, the diverse classroom seating arrangements of your preference for the scholars may have tremendous and poor feedback and many impacts on the dynamics of the whole study room. Three study room patterns are Clusters, U-shape, and conventional rows. Clusters usually facilitate institutional work and allow less difficult navigation inside the classroom, however, the bad thing about such a setting is the reality that not all of the college students will be capable of face the trainer which could cause some students to be distracted and distract others. The U-form association decreases many study room challenges and it permits the trainer to easily flow through the classroom and captivate the attention of the scholars. But, with such placing, the dynamics of companies and organization work may be declined to a terrific quantity especially if the magnificence has a big range of college students.

Conventional Row configuration is called the most commonplace study room association. This kind of placing works well with many elegant systems which can be according to a trainer/pupil-based curriculum. With this putting, students are more liable to getting to know, more prepared and attention and it can work with any school room length. However, this putting too has its poor side; when this layout is used, maximum of the students that take part in schoolroom sports are those who might be seated at the front and the center, at the same time as those seated at the lower back turn away.

In keeping with the educational communique idea, the physical setup of chairs, tables, and presentation in a schoolroom can drastically have an impact on learning, and the seating arrangements can affect how the teacher communicates with college students and how the students have interaction with one another, impacting engagement, motivation, and awareness. Harvey and Kenyon in a current study additionally propose that scholars tend to select greater bendy seating preparations. I for my part decide on the conventional rows due to the reality that it accommodates the exceptional class sizes. I trust that installed regulations, studying could be performed notwithstanding the few challenges faced. The theories that govern training, and all are very crucial to the study room in addition to outside of the schoolroom. All of them help in the development of students holistically. My selected instructional idea is humanism, (instructional philosophies of self-evaluation). This theory will pay close interest to college students as people and their self-actualization. This concept also cognizance of how human beings examine, and two (2) crucial and contributing elements are eventualities and observational getting to know which permit students to version the behaviors of others. Humanism additionally believes in people's freedom, dignity, capability, and independence. it's far a central assumption of humanism, in line with Huitt (2001), and it believes that as people, we're responsible to assist others to develop so that they can live their full potential. This method helps men and women to recognize their rights as humans and promotes equality. According to the educational philosophies, humanist educators tend to choose to study from human's capability to grow and turn into their final self. Billings and Halstead (2009) emphasized that "The primary issue with humanism as an academic theory is the autonomy and dignity of people", and Maslow (1954) supported this by saying that humanist educators also assist the pupil in turning into "self-actualized. The philosophy speaks to me and my ideals due to the fact my notion is that as individuals, we want so we can suppose and make decisions on our own and no longer be dependable on others. However, I do trust in the steerage of others however one has to now not be afraid to think independently. also, much like the humanist attitude, I believe that we have to at all times try to see the nice in humans notwithstanding our differences, and we have to endeavor to encourage and support every different in whatever way we will in each issue of life. I agree with equality and that each one of us stocks a few fundamental things and wishes. Additionally, I accept as true that for us to excel in life, it's miles important to suppose independently as well as collectively. That is very essential due to the fact there may be situations that we all will need to face at some point to require our capabilities to carry out character responsibilities as well as group work.

Humanism encourages me to consciousness on college students' development of their self-idea and to recognize how they experience themselves as individuals and if you want to identify their strengths and their weaknesses. This philosophy is set self-recognition and profitable one's behavior, it encourages one to attempt toward growth and to be devoted to their duties. As a humanist teacher, my attempt is channeled into growing students' self-esteem which's critical to their improvement. Humanism also encourages students to set dreams and work hard in the direction of achieving them. It additionally encourages college students' participation inside the classroom day by day. The humanist philosophy, just like mine, discourages students to make receiving rewards to be the reason for his or her work, however as an alternative, they to intention to achieve success because they need to obtain their dreams and dreams. Because of the reality that schooling prepares college students for lifestyles and their destiny, I agree that the humanist approach is the maximum appropriate one. I also consider that the humanistic philosophy permits instructors to create a holistic technique with a purpose to facilitate getting to know using displaying interest in the college students and their training. It also allows students to be accountable and make choices to benefit them at the gift and inside the future. Humanistic teachers design their instructions to house the needs of the scholars, rather than being harsh and rigid. Training and surroundings that are scholar-centered, promotes gaining knowledge of and teachers enable as opposed to strict coaching. This allows the students to be creative and percentage their information with others.

When you are planning to enroll in similar studies, distance learning is one of the nice options you can remember. Nowadays, there are a variety of faculties and institutions that provide distance getting to know guides. Tendencies in generation remain to make it less difficult for the contemporary and destiny students to gain their dreams through distance getting to know programs. Distance mastering is designed to provide opportunities to novices who're not able to pursue the on-site study. Online training, written correspondence guides, and other remote lecture room methods come under the category of distance learning. Distance learning offers college students the pliancy to complete their course from the convenient domestic and different faraway sites; they best need a laptop, a cell, or a pill with internet connectivity. These days, many online publications permit students to watch lectures online and end their assignments and initiatives on their very own time. This could be greater favorable for an operating expert who cannot depart their job to pursue full-time schooling. Every other benefit of distance studying is that it permits students to get the identical getting to know in either format. On the side of this, nowadays online education gives the right to use too many services as on-campus students like professional services, library services, instructional and monetary advising, and tutoring. Distance getting to know no longer only has the benefits however also it has a few disadvantages like lacking the face-to-face verbal exchange that comes with learning on—campus. College students who pursue online observation additionally need to pay extra attention and commitment to their research so that they do now not fall at the back of. Distance mastering can be effective for a few college students and not for others. It isn't always for all people. There are a few professionals and cons of distance mastering which assist you to determine whether or not it makes sense for you or no longer:

• Flexibility

One of the finest blessings of distance getting to know is that it does no longer want you to be present physically inside the classroom; you're unrestricted to set your personal time frame. It presents you the suppleness to finish your direction at each time from anywhere, and your very own pace.

• Getting to know with incomes

Many college students who're working full-time or component-time and do now not have enough time to finish on-campus programs looking to pass further in their careers with the aid of completing graduate or postgraduate levels. In this situation, distance getting to know may be a great alternative for you to complete your observation in an equal time.

• Global get admission to

Distance mastering enables you to complete a course or degree from everywhere around the arena. You may choose any college or university that offers the route you need, regardless of wherein it is positioned around the arena. Or even in case you ever relocate, you do now not need to worry approximately shifting to some other school or university.

• Technological friendly

Online education applications train us to apply erudite generation to bring education. By way of acquiring have a look at substances, submitting projects and assignments online, and take part in online forums to work together with classmates and professors. Distance mastering makes college students extra technical pleasant than their study room counterparts.

- Finances pleasant

There won't be a very plenty difference in costs while you compare traditional and online publications but online mastering definitely extra reasonably priced in assessment to traditional gaining knowledge of. With distance studying, you shop on various expenses like fuel, books, childcare, and many others. Distance studying programs are self-paced, they could provide you the chance to finish your observation in much less time and it cost decrease academic fees.

- No Interrupting task or profession

In distance learning, there's no want to cease your cutting-edge job because those publications are to be had online or even take a go away of absence. So, it doesn't interrupt your modern job. The virtual mastering global turned into added to interest inside the year of 1999.

The era has advanced distinctly considering that then, and it is most effective getting greater complex with time. As generation has immersed itself into almost every part of lifestyles in today's society, it has maximum simply been absorbed into the education international. Whilst one mix era and education, online getting to know are brought to lifestyles. Many accept as true that going to high school online is an appropriate invention because online classrooms can bring education to everyone, in any place conceivable. A few also argue that online training may be less costly than taking training in the traditional study room. even though a massive range of yank college students accept as true that online getting to know is a valuable training device, numerous research studies have proven pretty the alternative. Online college students have decrease communication talents, can cheat easier, and have extensively unique grade factor averages. Lots of college students throughout the US have taken to going to high school online, wondering that they're receiving the identical exceptional of education as a pupil in a conventional schoolroom.

What they do not know is that they are now not getting the sort of educational experience that they deserve. This research paper will cope with just a few of the numerous troubles with online studying and could display the sturdy blessings of going to high school in a conventional classroom. Online schooling is developing in popularity as more schools and universities offer alternative enrollment applications. Whilst there may be blessings and drawbacks of online getting to know. The advantages outweigh the dangers, specifically for people who may also face boundaries in pursuing university schooling. Online education may be an opportunity means to classroom instruction. Online practice allows students to have a flexible timetable while taking college publications. Furthermore, the flexibility and convenience of online schooling options permit students to work route assignments from any area. Taking online guides can lower expenses for college kids by way of disposing of commutes to campus, campus charges, and room and board prices. As we pass ahead, online schooling is gaining more recognition yearly, greater individuals are looking toward the course of online training to earn their diploma. In the fall of 2002, students enrolled in distance schooling become approximately 1.6 million. Five months later, that populace grew to about three. Five million and in 2012 about 7.1 million students enrolled in online learning from just American universities. With the rise of online schooling, there may be an effort to shut the space between online education and conventional schooling. online gaining knowledge has emerged as a critical avenue for people to advantage knowledge and for professors to provide the student with studying revel. delivering training in this layout has its flaws and benefits, with the advent of technology the issues are getting much less complex, and as time proceeds the distance between traditional gaining knowledge of and online mastering is lessening. Establishments and teachers are operating on lessening the distance between online and traditional mastering by consisting of factors that might be present in a traditional academic placing. These days' trend in online schooling consists of the usage of video conferencing in online schoolrooms to emulate the face-to-face feeling in a lecture room putting. As said by using Mader and Ming "majority of guidance [in an online schooling] takes place even as the pupil and trainer are separated". Introducing the usage of video convention offers each scholar and teacher the opportunity to connect everywhere in the international.

Education is turning into one of the maximum critical matters in a person's existence. These days, many individuals are seeking to pass the extra mile and in addition their schooling. That is because several employers require a degree and a big amount of enjoy which will turn out to be eligible for sure occupations. The subsequent question to keep in mind is a way to pass about this. Younger adults with minimal duties truthfully have a broader variety of alternatives. As for working adults who have youngsters and obligations that hold them back, attending lessons more than one times per week can also seem hard and out of the query. Fortunately, the development of generation has had a prime effect on training. The implementation of education became best in a traditional setting earlier than this advancement of the era. Presently, this has altered. With the outburst of the technology industry within the past fifteen years, online training has helped people from all walks of lifestyles retain and in addition their education. This in the end leaves us with a subject at the nice of the schooling provided. There are numerous matters to take into account whilst deciding on which path one needs to pursue. Before committing to any specific diploma program, one ought to weigh and examine their alternatives primarily based on what is essential to them. Despite sharing many apparent similarities, the distinction among each

Our lives are dominated using generation; we rely on cloud computing to synch statistics amongst all of our electronic devices; we can text, email, and tweet nearly simultaneously from our clever telephones; we have to get admission to statistics 24/7 via the internet. It's no surprise then that the technology that lets us do all these things is likewise increasingly being implemented to mastering. Increasingly groups are turning to e-studying to offer training and expert improvement possibilities to their employees, way to its accessibility and adaptableness. As companies start to draw close to the importance of adopting expert improvement strategies for their personnel, they start to look for appropriate answers and pleasant practices. E-gaining knowledge is quickly coming to the vanguard of those solutions. A generation has been verified to be a wonderful enabler for getting to know with the aid of granting wider access and facilitating persevering with training for the duration of an enterprise. It provides an infrastructure via which organizations can increase interactive and attractive platforms to deliver ability-constructing, education information. However, like most new generations, e-mastering nonetheless has its drawbacks. Wider get admission to can also mean much less manipulation and ability technology troubles. Right here are a number of the pros and cons of adopting e-gaining knowledge of your organization's education and development wishes.

Benefits and drawbacks of online mastering

As a result, there are strongly discovered benefits and disadvantages of distance studying vs. face-to-face coaching. One downside is a lack of interplay with a professor at some stage in practice. Every Another downside is conventional enrollment offers more diploma alternatives, counselor advisement, and student growing applied abilities. However, the gain of distance getting to know is dearer efficient and much less time-ingesting than school room training. Moreover, online training is increasing at a faster fee. Online better schooling courses nearly tripling between 1995 and 2003, and nearly 100% of public institutions document online preparation as a critical part of their long-term plan. Despite the positive financial blessings of online schooling, there remain steady criticisms. A few criticisms are the shortage of certified professors, enough net connection, and college-scheduled internet outages. Advocates of distance mastering consider that it's far more profitable to look at online vices face-to-face education. Regardless, online guidance is extra useful for many because of the bendy packages presented, potentially lower fees, and multiplied self-route. The Literature evaluation of numerous peer-reviewed journals discusses the disadvantages and blessings of online training vs. lecture room education. Similarly, there are debates on the advantages and pitfalls of which technique is extra green. A few pros of getting to know are:

Pros

• Get right of entry to. Possibly the maximum precious advantage of e-gaining knowledge is that it gives access to a much broader target audience. Through cloud computing and the net, corporations can offer training tools to people every time, anywhere. These blessings huge, multinational companies with personnel in each continent due to the fact now there's a manner to provide them all of the same education, translated if necessary, and in their very own time zones. Even if the business enterprise is in the handsiest one-time sector, the benefit of getting admission through e-learning can exchange the way employees are trained and the manner employers manipulate their progress.

• Low fee. some other key advantage to e-learning—and one that finance departments anywhere can rejoice over—is its relatively low value. E-gaining knowledge doesn't require paying a teacher, businesses don't need to discover and pay for an area to maintain the education, and they don't have to shop for any new gadget or books. Any organization can find the right e-getting to know the strategy to fit its finances, relying on its strategic dreams and its personnel's desires. this is particularly authentic for organizations with hundreds or lots of employees that want to study identical talents or regulations, as scalability significantly reduces the fee consistent with the character.

• Ease of use. Given how a lot the average character makes use of era on each daily basis, and primarily based on our familiarity with software program packages, e-gaining knowledge of ease of use can be a big gain. By way of deciding on a consumer-friendly platform, companies can count on their employees being able to navigate their way around and learn how to use it fast. Of direction, no longer every e-learning platform is person-friendly, and not every employee is tech-savvy, however, normally groups can attain the blessings of getting a tech coaching device that maximum employees will sense secure the usage of.

• Tailoring. In phrases of access, value, function, and pretty much whatever else you could consider, e-getting to know can be tailor-made to your business wishes. Whether you need education for five employees or five thousand, e-getting to know gear can be custom designed to what works great on your company. They also can be tailored to your personnel's desires. If personnel sense like they realize positive topics thoroughly, they can skim over them and waste less time. That way they could deal with the subjects they want to honestly work on. Employees additionally get to study at their very own tempo, which's tremendous, thinking that most of them are balancing multiple responsibilities, workloads, and deadlines.

Cons

• One size doesn't fit all. One of the foremost risks of e-mastering is that it doesn't enchantment to all gaining knowledge of styles. At the same time as the general public admires the liberty and flexibility that e-getting to know offers, many pick the traditional study room technique to getting to know on a laptop. Some human beings would possibly opt to examine through an arms-on method and might discover e-getting to know a touch an excessive amount of like going thru the motions, rather than applying the training to real-life eventualities.

• Isolation. Studying through the internet on personal computers permits wider access, however, it can additionally easily result in isolation. Studying face-to-face manner employees can ask questions and feature them spoke back proper away, which isn't the case with e-mastering. Employees have the freedom to research on their very own time anywhere there, however, this will depart them with a feeling of isolation and absence of assist. The shortage of a physical lecture room and trainer can be irritating and demotivating.

• Tech troubles. Even though most of us are comfy navigating the internet and the pc global, no longer all of us are as tech-savvy. These employees may additionally discover the concept and/or execution of e-getting to know difficult to grasp. Even supposing the e-gaining knowledge of software program is consumer-friendly, the concept of the use of it may be daunting to some, in particular personnel who don't should use computers often on their jobs. Different capacity tech problems can consist of a gradual net connection, particular browser requirements, and terrible tool compatibility.

- Loss of manipulating. Through e-learning, employers are giving control to the employees to research their very own time and in their personal way. Because personnel can use e-studying gear at their very own tempo, there's a threat a few may fall behind or just go through the cloth without surely paying interest. This loss of manipulation over the studying procedure can lead a few to be wary of the use of e-studying for training purposes.

Loss of verbal interplay

One of the maximum hazards that all agree on is the dearth of verbal interaction "among instructor[s] and student[s]". Because of the reality that most online mastering applications can simplest provide a one-way communique, this drawback is inevitable! As stated in "top ten distance getting to know hazards", the lack of human contact, let alone personal touch with instructors, furnished in a traditional study room wherein "-way or face-to-face communication always proved it's critical" is the glaring truth. Further, Hinkle (2009) additionally believes that there is a massive reduction in the amount of interplay through distance gaining knowledge. To further discuss this, Kartha (2011) makes the readers privy to that e-learning does not provide newcomers any assist in improving their conversation abilities. Although some online courses enable their customers to communicate thru "discussion and network boards, this certainly differs from carrying a communication to a classmate sitting after you in person. Furthermore, Dogra (2011b) assumes that an e-mastering pupil may not be uncovered to sufficient multidimensional views of a certain subject or topic. She shows the problem of online getting to know by way of pronouncing that the chances of growth or getting to know of students who pursue full-time guides and are facilitated to talk about many factors of trouble, many troubles of one problem might be higher than folks that do not. What's more, in a class, a debate bobbing up does not always contain in what was taught. Rather, a huge variety of troubles about plans or expert lifestyles is likewise targeted.

This enables college students to develop their personality and teaches them how to cope with life "in the best way". To gain achievement in lifestyles, one desires not only bookish however additionally revel in and especially, expertise approximately "numerous lifestyles troubles in addition to situations". She summarizes that, in some instances, the sale of expert development received thru online mastering, therefore, might be restricted. Apparently, online learning means reading in isolation and without a hard and fast timetable and proper have a look at timings and it demands strong self-motivation and self-control to be an awesome learner. She warns that this type of mastering is absolutely no longer appropriate for college kids who need normal and immediate feedback from instructors. Pakhare (2008) expresses his agreement with Dogra's assertion and says that the absence of face-to-face communique outcomes inside the failure of receiving instantaneous feedbacks for college students' assignments and fieldwork research. They may not have their problems and questions of the closing lesson solved through professors or classmates as in traditional elegance, which could function as a barrier in one's learning. In case of receiving feedbacks, college students need to watch for the long term, until the teachers evaluate their work. Similarly, according to the item "pros and cons of distance learning", while instructional assets are supported in maximum traditional schools/universities which include libraries, stadiums, observe regions, and laboratories, online learning surroundings are a great deal extra challenging. It is pretty realistic whilst mentioning the impossibility of "losing a tutoring center or attending greater assist". Consequently, mastering technique, because of all of those elements, can be less powerful. Perhaps, it is the main contributor to lesser weightage to online studying. There is a not unusual belief amongst employers that students following e-getting to know class are a long way much less knowledgeable and more experienced than people with full-time training and worse in terms of mindset as well. A few employers even refuse to present online studying as a piece of acknowledgment. Of course, she says, this example will unique in case the one's students have sure years of revel in. however, most organizations nevertheless provide a desire to freshmen with traditional certificate or tiers.

Whilst strategically and well applied, e-gaining knowledge has the capacity to change the game for any organization's worker schooling. Have you adopted any e-studying tools for skill training and professional development? What were the benefits and downsides of your business? Traditional sorts of learning were developed new technologies. Therefore, increasingly humans are deciding to improve talents using online learning. The majority of people say it is useful while others argue that online education has risks as well. People are on the lookout for many new approaches to mastering. One of the maximum famous techniques is online mastering. Sadly, this way has no longer simplest blessings however and drawbacks. The online technique of schooling is tremendous for lots motives. To begin with, it's far completely convenient. A human can use a laptop to get admission to an internet connection everywhere, for instance, at domestic, outdoor, or even on a bus. This benefit is especially critical for folks that stay in remote and rural regions and cannot relocate or trip to high school. However, it is also useful for mothers and fathers who need to examine younger kids at home or any student who prefers to work in the comfort of their personal home or espresso. Moreover, online studying is inexpensive than traditional classroom academic or exchange courses. These courses are unpaid. Students can shop for money. As an instance, they should no longer pay for a course of costs. Alternatively, online gaining knowledge has poor elements. Initially, confined social interplay prevents examining how much time an individual wants. Usually, online applications supply humans with an opportunity of restraint to apply for their program. Later college students will pay money if they want to keep a route further. Furthermore, the handiest method of the communique of online studying is thru email, chat room, or dialogue corporations. Human beings cannot engage with others head to head. It's far the unnatural verbal exchange manner. Humans do not see and sense relationships with classmates and feedbacks. Today, the development of data technology brings human beings many beneficial programs that assist them to work more efficaciously, shop time, cash, and maximize productivity. Online studying (E-studying) is one every of many useful programs that gain many corporations. Consistent with the internet site talentlms.com, E-mastering is an online tool that "allows each student and business executives to learn everywhere and at any time. you can learn from virtually any place with a laptop or cellular device and net connection, which means you could study from domestic, on vacation, or in your damage." usually, you will be waking up, eating breakfast, going to high school, and finishing your route work without leaving the comfort of your home or maybe your pajamas. The concept of attending college online and at non-public comfort is a choice that many excessive schools and university students have trouble passing up. In these days' training system, college students have the choice to wait for school in a traditional lecture room putting or attend online within the comfort of their personal houses. Both alternatives have their benefits. But, in maximum instances, conventional classroom training better prepares students ok-12 for his or her futures by way of encouraging strength of mind and verbal exchange among instructors and friends. Online studying, additionally known as distance learning, is developing hastily in the USA. The 2012 survey of online studying determined that "the number of students taking as a minimum one online course has now handed 6.7 million". With 2014 online studying facts being launched on February 5th, it was predicted that the wide variety of college students has grown drastically in the past years and is only set to grow into 2015. A traditional classroom setting exposes college students to what it will be like of their destiny place of work. In a schoolroom, students are anticipated to speak head to head with their peers and instructors. On every occasion college students attend school in a conventional study room, they interact with their friends and learn what it's like to work amongst humans that they see and understand and are comfy around.

Online learning vs traditional getting to know

Online education has faced several unfair scrutinies due to the fact its inception. The great of learning thru an online medium has constantly been challenged, however, why? Information display that online inexperienced persons score better on standardized testing (online vs. conventional getting to know). furthermore, educators have rallied in the back of the net medium with seventy-seven percentage asserting that online mastering is simply as correct, if not better than traditional and sixty-seven percent of them consider that the use of online media is vital teaching equipment in helping the education system (on-line vs. conventional learning). The numbers display that the first-rate of online education is on par with conventional learning and the accreditation of the over - hundred and seventy-five online universities compare and approve their first-rate. Creation thru the advancements of generation many things have changed; as an instance, schooling is now not following a strictly in seat method/medium. This "new" way of gaining knowledge has opened many doorways for nontraditional college students (adults with present-day careers and duties or even enlisted military personnel). But, because of its group, there was many controversies' wondering if the great is on par with conventional gaining knowledge of. This will speak how useful online getting to know definitely is and display that the fine is identical to if no longer better, than conventional and the students get out of it simply as a lot. amongst schools with twelfth-grade students for the duration of the numerous faculty years, the common percentage of twelfth-grade college students who graduated with a high school diploma changed into eighty-nine percent for traditional public schools, ninety-one percentage for public constitution schools, and ninety-percent for non-public schools (Institute of instructional Sciences). Conventional on-campus lessons are those wherein a pupil earns a degree or a degree in a study room environment taught by way of a professor. Students are supplied with excessive amounts of social interplay with college students and faculty to prepare them for careers out of the doors of the classroom.

From the time children are enrolled in kindergarten as much as commencement, the familiarity of a lecture room atmosphere sets up a structural guide to assist them via their studies as well as offering college students a sense of the societal field. Traditional on-campus instructions are more useful to a pupil's schooling than online guides. Traditional classes provide unequaled face-to-face interaction with professors and classmates. In her article, "traditional vs online gaining knowledge of that is right for you", Janelle Pagnucco, a communications engineer at ECO Canada explains, "A classroom surroundings allows for the instant expression of opinions and mind via face-to-face interplay with classmates and the teacher. These conversations help reassure college students whether or not or now not they're headed inside the proper course and assist maintain the gaining knowledge of process shifting". Gaining knowledge is a countless process; it is in no way too overdue to pursue extra information. Training has constantly been a controversial topic around the sector because it could be carried out to humans in different age organizations. As human fulfillment in the era has substantially advanced, the get admission to schooling will become lots easier as nicely. Many humans believed that the traditional style of schooling, which is a face-to-face gaining knowledge of, can offer the most beneficial bring about terms of gaining knowledge of. College students attending faculty regularly based on an organized agenda can greatly avoid the laziness in mastering and beautify the activeness in college life. but, a few argue that getting to know online can reap even better grades than face-to-face studying while having a simpler time arrangement. Moreover, with the increasing frequency of hearing the time period of the line training, we, the learner, are being aware of an obvious growing fashion of online gaining knowledge of. For plenty of university students, they have very exclusive perspectives in the direction of online getting to know and conventional learning. It's very critical for college students, who're one step into maturity, and rookies to discover the simplest fashion of schooling so that it will be most beneficial in special guides. I need to discover whether or not online mastering ought to replace traditional mastering or now not. In step with the effect of E-mastering in clinical schooling through Jorge G. Ruiz MD et al, online training is essentially mastering via the net. It's past doubt that online studying calls for a few devices. Traditional kinds of e-studying can be taken as examples right here. First, pc-based training gives users with getting to know items along with audio, videos, animations, and application simulations through a CD-ROM or a mainframe and a local network, while some other kind, web-primarily based schooling, has its getting to know materials introduced over the internet. A computer-related to a community is a need to with both of them. In line with Hinkle (n.d.), this triggers off the era-associated trouble to individuals who "do not have prepared access" to this system, in other words, they are "ill-equipped" to use it. Besides, electricity cutoff, failure in the internet server on any hardware issue can also make intense impacts on the mastering method. Closing however no longer least, the technical requirements can also place fantastic stress on ones who're absolutely not computer-literate, which, in turn, would possibly result in strain and frustration.

Chapter Seven

Boarding Schools

In everyday lifestyles, we spend most people of our existence within the schooling gadget and barely are aware of it. From kindergarten to university, all of us take a seat down in a classroom by way of both a teacher and instructor constantly educating our minds of the simple abilities to analyze, writing, and mathematics. In life, the maximum vital years are excessive school and college years. These two elements play an indispensable part in how we had been before and the way we are currently, and from these two durations of time, we usually grow to be friendlier. College may be very vital and often we're sent to faculties that we don't approve of, specifically boarding faculties which have such a lot of stigmas attached. A boarding faculty is a faculty where college students move to school to study and live collectively with some or other college students in the course of the school months. This practice has been in many components of the arena for nicely over one thousand years as recorded in classical literature. In many countries, boarding faculties are impartial faculties. These boarding faculties are controlled via positive guidelines set with the aid of the department of kids, schools, and families collectively with the branch of fitness called the country-wide Boarding standards. Many children attend kingdom faculties. Very few families send their children to boarding colleges, most of which might be personal. In 1998 there had been seven hundred and seventy-two impartial boarding colleges in England and about one hundred thousand children everywhere in the United Kingdom attending boarding colleges. However, this exercise remains very common in positive elements of the arena. Parents regularly give several motives for sending their children to boarding faculties. The decision is said to be a manner in which the dad and mom try and perpetuate their social beliefs. This takes a look at units out to are seeking the motives why some parents ship their children to boarding schools. Especially, this research is targeted on sure immigrant families from the former British colony in West Africa (Nigeria) who're resident within the UK or stay abroad and have their youngsters in boarding colleges within the United Kingdom. In the colonial era of the British Empire, boarding faculties have become popular many of the directors who were abroad and sent their children back to Britain for education so that they imbibed the British culture. Additional time, the way of life of sending children to boarding colleges became associated with the higher magnificence. further, army boarding faculties came into lifestyles to cater for the kids of these inside the defense force whose careers frequently take them overseas if you want to supply the youngsters solid schooling wherein they're no longer uprooted on every occasion their dad and mom are transferred to stay in a foreign country. Additionally, in some societies, it has grown to be a way of life to ship youngsters to boarding school. a number of these motives given consist of the perception to imbibe the same culture that was imparted on those parents in their young people to their very own kids. However, the motives given can also genuinely disguise some other reasons for taken such decisions. A number of the actual reasons can be the dad and mom's notion that the children are disobedient, acting poorly academically, or in families in which the mother and father are divorced or separated. Different reasons regularly said via mother and father for sending their kids to boarding faculties also consist of discipline, therapeutic measures, and religion.

Why boarding colleges?

There are such a lot of motives why parents ship their kids to boarding school. It emerged that dad and mom agree with that because they attended secondary boarding faculties their youngsters must also comply with the same subculture. All of the mother and father interviewed beside one had attended boarding schools as kids. The dad and mom had a company notion that having attended boarding colleges helped them to develop independently. This similarly helps the theory that loads of the motives given by using the parents are socially built and social revel in are for this reason created and given meanings using people. They also said that boarding schools make children independent. Aside from making it a culture any other figure said that the cause he determined to ship his kids to boarding school turned into that, it presented him the excellent schooling. Boarding colleges help students to broaden independently; in reality, they provide some excellent training. A few dad and mom believe that attendance at boarding school allows the children with adulthood and mannerism. They consider that boarding faculty enables the kid to shape character and learn how to live with other people. They accept as true that if a child goes to boarding college he/she has a threat of having better final results in life. There are numerous reasons for parents' selections, but, one of the most crucial ones is that we believe that it's far inside the boarding faculty that you mature and you examine plenty of things which you need, the way you discover ways to stay with other humans and feature suitable mannerism. It's within the boarding residence you form your person, and the first-class comes out of you whilst you're far away from domestic. A number of the reasons given in the literature are that the children who're considered disobedient or underachieving are dispatched to boarding faculty.

Several motives had been given for choosing sure faculties. Similarity to previous colleges attended using his children overseas become given by using one of the members as a motive for sending his kids to a selected school. Also, a high educational rating was some other motive given by way of some parents for the choice of unique boarding schools. As mothers and fathers spend loads of money bringing their kids to boarding schools, they don't simply need any college. Other reasons include spiritual determinism, area, pastoral care, and precise wearing and track facilities. Many parents just like the fact that during boarding colleges, children are taught approximately Christian doctrines and the pinnacle of the faculty is a reverend. So that they agree with that the faculties will be a piece strict. parents respect the advantages of boarding college include established scholar improvement, self-actualization, independence, adulthood, educational achievement, well-adjusted boom, capacity to live with human beings of various backgrounds, motivation, and potential to plan and be better prepared. They grow, they mature, academically they arrive up tops in school, and they examine a lot in boarding faculty. Their lives are planned, tailor-made, and geared toward what they want to do. They see and study about position fashions and all that and on the cease of all of it you're satisfied with them and maximum of the time, they turn out to be what you want them to be. Despite all the positives, there are dangers associated with sending children to boarding faculty encompass bullying. Other risks blanketed problems of Gangs in college and children falling into the bad organization. When children are in boarding schools, alas, dad and mom lose the closeness with their youngsters and it could affect their relationship negatively. There are two styles of those who attain success in life. A few acquire their dreams in a single shot and some attain with stories of their past. The mindset of the person that achieves achievement with reviews is powerful. It's predicted that experiences at a boarding faculty need to train what students need to do to get the achievement. It's far continually hard for a student to pay attention to studies if he/she is staying away from home. The only one who overcomes the distractions and disturbances will constantly get fulfillment in lifestyles. One has to prioritize their needs in existence for you to attain their dreams. It ought to be understood that life isn't pretty much residing to the fullest at every instance, but it's all approximately making plans for our destiny and stepping on the right stones on the proper factor of time. It should be understood that to reap something larger, one has to dream massive and start running towards the aim. Many times we discover ourselves living lifestyles without desires until that point in time. Consequently, we're simply playing around, thinking that we have time on our aspect, however, that by myself isn't always live, in reality not. We ought to realize our flaws and start taking life significantly via solving a goal in our minds and visualize it turning into a reality. A few would possibly ask why all people would even begin to need to leave home for something like excessive college. Why could you leave your property, your buddies, your own family? Knowledgeable, clever college students at boarding college gained just agree with your faith; they might need you to explain it. This means that at boarding colleges you have a bigger pressure on you to examine more approximately the way to defend your religion in addition to justify its ideas. Essentially, at boarding faculty, you'll be uncovered to more religions and thoughts, which would force you to desert or fortify your faith.

Education at boarding faculties

For most people boarding faculties conjure up the mind of younger guys in army blue blazers with white shirts and a tie going to a stunning school with ivy-protected walls and the game of polo being played inside the distance. Oh, and bear in mind thoughts of dad and mom with fat wallets and a circle of the relative's trust fund. This is what Gordon Vink, the director of admissions at Mercersburg Academy in Pennsylvania, calls the "Holden Caufield-Catcher within the Rye syndrome", a book approximately the problems a boy faces at his prep boarding school. To a quantity the image holds real. Prep faculties provide collegiate kind atmospheres, have strict guidelines, and regularly teach generations of college students from equal households. The simplest definition of a boarding college is an area that mother and father pay for a pupil to live and cross to high school. The faculty's teachers, coaches, and administrators stay in dormitories with borders and act as their circle of relatives implementing the stern policies, making disciplinary choices, and overseeing conduct and academic performance. Boarding faculties may be one or all of the following: instructional boot camp, an area for dad and mom to place children they don't need round or don't have the time for, a haven from deteriorating public faculties, an important credential for children of the wealthy and famous, or a schooling ground for the day after today's leaders. These schools range from small unknown institutions to accept everybody, to the elite schools, which can be very selective and are a pipeline to Ivy-league faculties and fulfillment. Boarding schools are superior to public day schools. Proponents of boarding prep faculties declare the colleges offer unparalleled area, a more potent curriculum, great centers, a way to get into higher schools, an advanced mastering environment, magnificent greater-curricular alternatives, and allow college students to achieve a higher degree of overall performance. Warring parties argue that the astronomical price, anywhere from eight thousand greenbacks to twenty-five greenbacks consistent with the year for the maximum elite, is too high-priced. They also claim the guidelines are too extreme and suffocating, and that students revel in an abundance of strain.

The largest argument against boarding colleges is price. High school is a quintessential duration in the development of students, mainly for the guidance of the student's destiny where they're forced to join the real global. There are numerous distinct paths to pick out from while determining what kind of surroundings would be most beneficial for each person pupil. Some of those paths would encompass public, domestic, and boarding faculty. However, high college students who have the possibility to attend a boarding school benefit extra at some point of the high faculty years, compared to people who don't have the boarding experience till university. The discipline obtained, whilst at boarding school, aids within the child's capacity to deal with traumatic conditions instill the preference to advantage a better training and present a basis for acceleration. However, whilst attending a boarding school the students' mentors include educated specialists who might be more than successful to deal with any state of affairs that could stand up. With this steering, students gather the subject and expertise needed to take care of stressful conditions that are nearly assured to come back at some stage in one's lifestyles. In a ballot taken by way of The association of Boarding colleges, seventy percent of boarding faculty college students say that boarding faculty has helped them increase the strength of will, maturity, and independence. This isn't to aid the stereotype that most effective stricken children are sent to boarding packages, in truth inside the identical have a look at ninety-five percentage of boarding Faculty College students say their social lives do now not revolve around capsules and alcohol in comparison to the great difference in public school college students. This indicates the high-quality of existence to be anticipated in the boarding environment out of doors of the home. Inputting "boarding college extracurricular sports" into a search engine could yield a plethora of extracurricular picks and possibly some unrecognized, consisting of the "stroll about" software on the Baylor faculty in Chattanooga Tennessee. This after-school pastime takes a group of students on various activities along with paddle boarding, mountaineering, or kayaking. With this sort of good-sized array of paths, it is near impossible for a person to no longer find an interest they can turn out to be absolutely immersed in.

Boarding college life

The scholars at Boarding schools are usually the high-quality-behaved kids in a faculty environment. The schools commonly have the best children; they may be exceptional. Their record cards dispatched to their parents are said to be protected in high-quality remarks and first-rate marks. Many are having a quandary in deciding on the right school. Dad and mom are given a preference to choose between a boarding faculty and each day faculty for his or her children. Students can learn many essential abilities whilst read in a boarding school. Mother and father should ship their kids to a boarding college as it's the best way for children to learn how to stay independently, improve their educational overall performance and learn how to socialize. College students from boarding faculty stay without having much guidance from their mother and father. This encourages them to be unbiased. They should be hardworking and patient as they must do all the chores by themselves. There's no maid to scrub their garments or make breakfast for them. They end up mature once they learn how to make a selection logically without being influenced by using their emotion. They're those who determine what food they may be going to eat and which shipping they're going to apply. Additionally, they become involved with their fitness. As they may be stressed with the aid of plenty of homework, they should keep their thoughts sparkling and body wholesome. A boarding school is a network that usually affords a clean secured and healthful environment for students living on campus. But, everything created on the planet has a terrible and high-quality aspect of view. Properly start speaking approximately campus; the manner students stay in it, how hard for a number of them to simply accept it! And the way do they get used to it? Nicely talk approximately some blessings and disadvantages of living on campus. Then well move on and talk approximately the other manner for abroad students to stay "flats. A few parents would love to see their youngsters getting greater matured one of the approaches that dad and mom use to help their children to get matured and growing up is by using sending them to boarding faculties. Boarding school is not generally the proper solution to get the kid to be greater independent and mature, because once an infant finds his freedom he will become more careless. Supervision is one of the most vital things that a boarding school ought to and needs to provide around the school on the campus during training and all because the manager is the main determinant of the pupil at a boarding college. College students being prompted and boarding schools have a huge impact on a toddler beginning with the aid of the person he decides to start a friendship with "accompany". In the article, why boarding faculties produce horrific leaders by Nick Duffell, Duffell describes the linkage between the academic historical past of boarding college and the final results of being an insufficient leader. Many boarding college knowledgeable people move on to ivy-league colleges and a good-sized variety of them then pursue management positions in politics. Duffell is a psychotherapist that works with previous students of boarding colleges. He argues that attending boarding faculties turns kids into adults that hector and have toddler-like characteristics because boarding colleges pressure kids to act like adults too quickly. In addition to these surroundings that encourage pseudo-development, children additionally lack the capacity to be themselves or express how they feel approximately a situation.

The behavioral perspective of psychology may be defined as when your surroundings decide your conduct. This attitude pertains to the article because the boarding school environment shapes the conduct of the youngsters it produces.

As an example, the author discusses the former high minister of Britain David Cameron, and different British politicians with an educational background of attending boarding colleges. Because of this background of no longer being surrounded through lady developing up, this tends to increase sexist behavior and attitudes closer to girls via British politicians. Similarly, as soon as those graduates unavoidably are part of politics, they generally tend to exclude ladies.

Individualistic subculture can be described as a way of life that produces individuals who attend to themselves and their very own aspirations. Duffell argues that because kids didn't develop up in a family unit, they don't have an attitude that values the desires of humans apart from themselves. Duffell goes on to give an instance of boarding school-educated David Cameron doesn't price others' opinions and engages in hectoring instead of teamwork. Furthermore, Duffell believes this conduct is because of the boarding faculty tradition, which is an individualistic culture. In conclusion, psychotherapist Nick Duffell discusses and educates readers on the one-of-a-kind world of boarding colleges and counters the notion that this form of college generates able leaders. Duffell describes the behavior tendencies visible in boarding faculty college students and relates it to British politicians who were boarding school educated. Boarding colleges are the instructional institutes, in which candidates are living on the college premises for the whole consultation. Few people recall boarding schools to be the higher option for scholars, whereas others disagree with this opinion because of numerous reasons of their personal. I can examine each of these opinions, earlier than developing my standpoint in the following paragraphs. One school of notion argues that students should not be sent to boarding faculties as there they could encounter melancholy and homesickness. A maximum of the children spends their adolescence with their parents, siblings, and grandparents. And, whilst they may be suddenly left alone within the boarding colleges, they tend to get depressed and homesick, after they do not see any in their circle of relatives contributors close by. Next, because the youngsters live in schools day and night time, with their classmates and other seniors in addition to juniors, they end up victims of bullying. Alternatively, few humans don't forget boarding colleges to be the high-quality option for students. First of all, boarding colleges put together youngsters for his or her maturity. In such colleges, children grow to be extra responsible as they have to manipulate their time on their personal, easy after themselves, make their beds, and do different chores.

As a result, they come to be punctual and responsible. Next, due to the fact the children stay in boarding faculties, they spend greater time in the instructional environment, where they examine without distractions. Furthermore, they can seek advice from their instructors and clarify doubts every time they want. it's far important to recognize that beginning boarding school comes with a few stumbling blocks in the beginning, however, whilst the scholars collect their complete education from such faculties, they get greater groomed and grow to be informed individuals who can live to tell the tale in any state of affairs. For plenty of students, the concept of 'boarding faculty is a chance. It's wherein disobedient kids are dispatched to undergo bloodless showers, cruel schoolmasters, and awful school dinners, all in some remote exile far from their dad and mom. However, in reality, these stereotypes and myths do little to mirror the true nature of boarding faculties nowadays. College students who attend boarding school are normally achievement orientated with aspirations to attend university. These are groups wherein instructional enterprise is widely known with the aid of teachers and students alike. Not like at many public colleges, students who are clever, dedicated, and curious aren't alienated, however, the norm. Similarly to this, boarding college students also possibly symbolize a numerous range of backgrounds; informing communique and breadth of attitude in social spaces. Students are usually mastering other cultures and nations, and this exposure to range presents them with a more open, worldwide mindset. Boarding school elegance sizes tend to be very small, the average being simply twelve students. The gain of that is that instructors can offer individual interest and they're easily on hand to students with many boarding school instructors selecting to stay onsite at the faculty itself. With fewer students, teachers additionally have greater freedom to test and strive for new things. Humanities are frequently taught the usage of the Socratic approach which matches to open communication around a topic between students and their instructor. With the time to accomplish that and the self-belief that they'll be heard, students are advocated to talk up and actively participate in their studying. At boarding schools, round a clock mentorship manner that students are continuously encouraged to be the nice, they can be. Loose time is spent on homework, reading, sports activities, tune, and chores. College students learn how to be responsible for their personal washing, cleaning, and meals and time. They end up more independent and self-assured.

Consistent with a current study performed by way of the humanities & technological know-how group of Baltimore for The affiliation of Boarding colleges, (TABS), boarding college students are more likely than a personal day and public faculty college students to earn a sophisticated diploma and achieve quicker career development. Studies have additionally shown that boarding faculty college students feel more prepared for university and university than their peers. They may be additionally much more likely to earn advanced tiers like a grasp's or Ph.D. and enhance to more prominent roles in their careers and groups. Ana Luiza is from Brazil and these days graduated from EF Academy Oxford. Her feedback that, attending a boarding school is a totally extreme academic enjoy. The environment reminds you to look at and seeing all of us around you analyzing or writing essays encourages you to have a look at it too. This may make adapting to university life a lot simpler. Boarding schools today are environments that nurture dedicated and creative newcomers. The advantages cowl these areas discussed and greater: better college steerage, lifelong friendships, and pastoral care covered. College students who board will now not only flourish in school, however, they'll graduate with a bonus on the way to increase their whole existence. The controversy across the information of sending one's youngsters to boarding faculties is a vintage one, with no exact solution. As with every preference, there are pros and cons. What remember are your own reasons for selecting a boarding college education? There are numerous feasible motives for placing one's baby in a boarding college. Right here are a number of the most not unusual:

1) Family lifestyle: A circle of relatives can be sending their children to one unique college over numerous generations. For them, it's far a familiar and geared-up choice pushed through the company perception that boarding schools produce a higher character and offer superb schooling.

2) A manner to ensure a stable education for running dad and mom who have little time to spare for their children: The busy professional lives of cutting-edge parents mean a lack of fine time for children, which can be unfavorable to a baby's educational support. For dad and mom with

demanding careers, boarding schools are an ideal answer for his or her kids.

3) The urge to give kids a schooling gadget that provides values to existence: every other reason can be a choice to give kids a decent, wholesome training that provides values to their lives, improve relationships, and prepare them as responsible residents.

4) Sparing the kid from witnessing the ugliness of an ongoing marital feud: For dysfunctional households characterized by using fractured relationships, boarding faculties may be a feasible technique to store youngsters from a few emotional damage as a consequence of steady confrontations.

Interviews of numerous educational specialists and lecturers that specialize in boarding colleges reaffirmed that education in boarding faculties teaches college students about workouts in existence and the art of being prepared. inline with them, it presents a help structure and prepares students for the challenges they may face as adults. Boarding directors consider that boarding school schooling isn't just about teachers; it's additionally about individual building in youngsters through extracurricular sports. It imparts life capabilities and prepares children for leadership roles. Educators sell the reality that borders live out values like confidence, humility, resilience, braveness, kindness, determination, and difficult work which can be most effective stated in passing in normal study room teaching. Records show that 50% of the scholars in any boarding school are the most effective infant of dad and mom. In this manner, boarding faculties may additionally salvage such college students from developing up in seclusion and tedium. Robert Kennedy, a representative and a writer onboarding schools says a few of the many reasons to visit a boarding school are that those college students live in a "domestic far away from home", learn to be accountable, and develop in surroundings conducive to growth. An independently-run co-academic boarding faculty in Jordan, King's Academy, expresses that boarding faculties serve to optimize both educational getting to know and social development of students. collegebound.net, one of the United States' most relied on resources on higher education, says that one gain of boarding schools is that they represent a celebration of human diversity in which children live and analyze collectively. A boarding college in London for inner-town children guarantees that every baby is supported if you want to reach his or her full potential. This isn't pretty much-shifting kids from their domestic environments, however presenting a superb shape of schooling that is targeted, wealthy in curriculum, and uplifting. For deprived kids, boarding schools offer an opportunity to sense worth, value, and locate their manner into mainstream society with self-assurance. Switzerland is thought of for its top-notch boarding schools, typically because they're among the most steeply-priced in the globe. But, it isn't just the fee that makes these colleges stand out. On what makes her school exclusive from different boarding colleges, Sarah Frei, Head of advertising & verbal exchange at Brillantmont global faculty, said that it's miles a family-owned faculty with a smaller amount of students, permitting personalized interest.

Also, it's positioned in the center of the city in which college students get to revel in the town's animated lifestyles and practice their faiths in most of the city's nonsecular centers. Justin Usher, Head of Boarding, university du Léman, said "I sense boarding may be very a lot complimentary schooling. It's got nothing to do with hammering in exercises into college students' heads, however, at the same time, exercises are important. If you turn up overdue for meetings, if you spend your existence now not being prepared, commonly it becomes a bit of an issue for your life at a few stages. We intention to offer all-around schooling encompassing teachers, activities, social improvement, and pastoral wishes, all inside a supportive and near-knit network." Jacques Bonin, Director of Admissions, Le Rosey, said "We don't recognize on especially one factor. We take the man or women as he is with his capability and we broaden it." some critics of the boarding college system say that it's no longer for all and sundry, and that can be genuine. A border lives in very precise surroundings, which may create a first-rate disconnect with the arena outside. Developing an existence away from dad and mom may be hard at times. Children in boarding faculties might also emotionally float away from their dad and mom, and such children find it hard to reconcile with them once they're back domestic. Some other capability hassle is that during the horrific business enterprise, a border can easily fall into the traps of experimentation with tablets and alcohol. Additionally, a few boarding colleges are for either boys or women only, and this will cause a lack of studies with the opposite sex and create interpersonal problems in a while. Sooner or later, in most instances, boarding faculties are high-priced. Even though scholarships and different monetary resources are available in some instructional establishments, it could still be difficult for some families to have the funds for such training. within the final evaluation, the query of whether or not or not to ship children to boarding college is a character preference that needs to take into account a toddler's desires in addition to the house and monetary conditions of the own family. Something choice mother and father choose, it's going to affect the lives and careers of their children.

Records of Boarding schools

British boarding colleges have historically provided the version for boarding schools in Canada. Top the various antecedents is the King's College in Canterbury, England. It became founded in the months and, till the dissolution of the monasteries acts nearly a century later, it remained a cloistered religious institution. At King's, college students have been stored apart from society at big, had been told via clergy, and had been expected to commit themselves to religious contemplation. Really, there wasn't time for a whole lot else there had been chapel offerings each day similarly to mass and day-by-day prayers for the useless. King's was a grammar college in the literal which means of the time period. The primary consciousness of observation was Latin grammar, the language of the church. Even as there were a few other subjects on offer, all had been intended totally to put together college students for religious work, no longer innovative questioning or instructional engagement. There was a track for spiritual offerings, astronomy, and mathematics to set and interpret the church calendar, and law to put together students for administrative roles inside the church. Further, whilst Eton was based inside the fifteenth century by using Henry VI, it becomes a charity college intended to offer loose schooling to seventy boys. As Sir Henry Lyte wrote in his history of the faculty published in 1877, Eton reflected a renewed hobby inside the dissemination of knowledge, and that "a movement in popular schooling had set in." He writes that the muse of the college "is also important as marking a turning-point inside the battle among the ordinary and the secular clergy. Throughout the middle a while the monasteries had been the precept seats of schooling in England, however, their inefficiency had emerged as infamous." Lyte didn't see it, possibly, however it wasn't so much a query of nice that it changed into a converting view closer to the purpose of training. The monasteries produced spiritual leaders, even though the founders of Eton desired as an alternative to deliver the universities with "students from a wonderful grammar-faculty." the ones that, in turn, might increase to positions of leadership within business and the army rather than the church are noticeably taken into consideration. That said, life at the school, with the aid of today's standards, can appear strikingly monastic. College students have been roused at 5 a.m., chanted prayers whilst they dressed, and were at their classes using 6:00 a.m. they had two food every day besides Friday, once they weren't fed in any respect. Lessons ended at 8:00 p.m. when all students went to bed.

When William Shakespeare attended King's new school in Stratford, the faculty become open to all boys. There has been no training. The only requirement for admission become the capacity to examine and write. "Pupils sat on hardwood benches from six in the morning to five or six in the night," writes invoice Bryson, "with handiest two brief pauses for refreshment, six days a week. For tons of the year, they can hardly ever have seen daylight." The faculty become, for the time, one of the first-class within the US. There Shakespeare learned Latin grammar and rhetoric ("one of the principal texts of the day," writes Bryson, "taught pupils one hundred and fifty exclusive way of pronouncing 'thank you to your letter' in Latin") and little else. "something arithmetic, records, or geography Shakespeare knew, he almost definitely didn't analyze it at grammar school." but daunting the enjoy can also have been, the early boarding colleges met the needs for which they had been created, namely to train boys into positions of spiritual leadership within a society that become organized, socially and politically, around nonsecular lifestyles. As society modified, so did the schools. At the time of the Reformation, faculties were eliminated from the authority of the church, marking an abrupt exchange in how education was performed, and what it became meant to do.

The Reformation coincided with (if no longer directly caused by) a decline in feudalism and an upward thrust in nationalism, commonplace regulation, and revealed books. Grammar faculties quickly meditated all of that, adopting new curricula and adjusting admissions to produce the human sources wished in publish-Reformation England, one more and more organized across the needs of a marketplace economy. The result became the improvement within the sixteenth century of an educational curriculum based totally on humanism and a formulation of the liberal arts as we think about them nowadays. The intention of education become to prepare free people for active roles in civic life. Debate, crook regulation, good judgment, and rhetoric had been taught intensively for the primary time. Math and geometry were once taught for calendar making, we're now taught additionally for engineering and the preservation of civic works. That sort of curriculum; liberal arts training grounded in classical languages and literature endured throughout Europe and North the US nicely into the twentieth century. Even as there has been the latest proliferation of opportunity curricula, the inspiration of education of North the United States nevertheless reflects the improvements undertaken inside the sixteenth century. Often unwittingly, a number of the opportunity procedures do as well.

As Britain moved into the age of empire and enterprise, schools persevered to evolve. Via the 18th century in reaction to Britain's geographic and monetary increase students have been learning contemporary languages, political leadership, navy principle, and commerce. While Thomas Hughes wrote Tom Brown's faculty Days within the 1830s, he used Rugby school as the place, a college that his readers could have visible as strikingly modern-day. As he admitted at the time, Hughes created the characters of Tom and Dr. Arnold to illustrate a way to stay an amazing life and, through analogy, a way to build an exquisite nation. All of the conventional elements of the boarding college novel were there: students mentoring each different, a robust and empathetic instructor, and sports and, necessarily, bullying and corporal punishment. With the assist of friends and the recommendation of Dr. Arnold, Tom defeats the bully and becomes a mentor himself. He doesn't cheat on homework, he plays cricket, and life goes on. What could have struck early readers aren't the things that strike us these days. Corporal punishment, for example, could have regarded as acquainted and never precise to boarding faculty. What additionally would have struck them had been the instructional reforms that Dr. Arnold introduced to the school. What might have struck them were the academic reforms that Dr. Arnold added to the faculty.

Rugby wasn't the King's faculty, but something completely specific. Rugby becomes an instance of a modern-day faculty addressing the needs of students in a present-day international. Boys have been advocated to follow their dreams, to think and act like people, and to choose their personal route into spiritual, secular, or navy lifestyles. That becomes massive. College students, remarkably, were supplied with options, choice, and an unheard-of range of individual autonomy. Of course, there was additionally a dark facet. At the same time as Hughes worked to expose what boarding college might be, Dickens, as in Nicholas Nickleby, intended to reveal what it genuinely became, exposing the faults that he found there. Whilst writing the unconventional Dickens toured boarding faculties, an experience that informed the fictional Dotheboys Hall, the boarding faculty for undesirable youngsters that Nicholas attends. As merciless and abusive because the schoolmaster there may be, it seems that Dickens didn't must do a lot whilst growing the individual, Mr. Squeers, even right down to the wording of his business card, is a loyal portrait of a schoolmaster that Dickens had met. not long after that assembly, the grasp changed into sued for blinding considered one of his students thru physical abuse, malnourishment, and forget about. Notes from the court docket case describe the faculty, and the similarity among it and Dotheboys is putting. Each Hughes and Dickens was writing at a time of severe exchange, each in England and the world. Indeed, it was converting, in particular, that they have been writing approximately. There was an enormous upward thrust in literacy, literature, and clinical inquiry. Faculties had been turning into the extra secular. There has been a growing sense of how an individual may participate inside society, and a greater focus on the strength of impartial thinking. At some point in the 1800s, boarding schools cemented an association with the British ruling magnificence, trading the non-secular cognizance for a navy one. Sons of officers and administrators of the Empire attended boarding school at the same time as their dad and mom fulfilled political and military postings in distant places. The focus of training turned into international relations for the top lessons, and navy life for those of lesser stature. Rudyard Kipling turned into an example of the former. He attended United Offerings College even as his parents had been stationed in India, an enjoyment he wrote about inside the novel Stalky & Co. Like Kipling himself, Stalky became knowledgeable to emerge as a part of the imperial device. And he does. At the end of the eBook, sparkling from that schooling, he is proven leading troops in India. In existence, as in fiction, boarding faculties have been a part of the spine of the empire, educating its military officials, senior clerics, lawyers, and administrators. They used the manner that had been famous for the time. Ben MacIntyre writes that Durnford college "epitomized the extraordinary British faith in bad food, masses of Latin and beatings from an early age." on the school "there was no clean fruit, no bathrooms with doorways, no restraint on bullying, and no possibility of escape. Nowadays such an institution could be unlawful; in 1925 it become considered 'individual-forming.' "School practices meditated a popular notion in social Darwinism survival of the fittest and that academic, moral, and bodily energy had been received via undertaking and adversity. Strict field, soreness, even bullying turned into considered a vital revel in within the development of moral and physical development. Royals experienced these things, too, no longer simply students who came from terrible households or who attended sub-popular faculties. Fortuitously, over the path of the twentieth century, all of that would alternate.

Boarding in Canada

The oldest boarding college in Canada, King's Collegiate faculty (now King's-Edgehill college), in Windsor, Ontario, changed into founded with the aid of United Empire Loyalists in 1788. It became given royal assent using King George III the following year, the first example that honor became bestowed out of doors Britain. Starting with just twelve boys in a non-public home close to Windsor, Nova Scotia, and the school quickly set an educational widespread for the vicinity and, later, the USA. It keeps holding an area in the countrywide recognition nowadays. Because of the age and significance of the homes, King's College is a country-wide ancient site, a designation it has held due to the fact 1923. King's changed created a moment of heightened political anxiety within the wake of the American Revolution. Whilst there have been colleges in NY and New England, there had been none within the

British colonies that remained after American independence. The initial purpose of the school turned into to prevent younger guys from traveling abroad to get hold of schooling, guys that would be had to live to administer and defend the colonies. Even as the school remained small, its alumni took outstanding roles in military, criminal, religious, and political existence (along with the fathers of Confederation). King's set the tone for other boarding faculties that would be created inside the British Empire outside of the UK. They have been hooked up so that the kids of British ex-patriots should acquire authentically British training, as well as hold and augment the human sources required to keep the colonies. Schools all through the commonwealth have been organized in an identical way as their British counterparts and there had been homes and headmasters, bureaucracy and terms and reflected the values of Victorian England.

The instructional surroundings became an awful lot as we may think: highbrow, strict, and reflective of all of the magnificence distinctions of the age. Leadership changed into a critical subject matter, in component as it becomes of top interest to some of the political leaders who dispatched their kids to board. further, the advantages were unequivocal, merely having gone to boarding faculty, regardless of any instructional fulfillment there, became regularly considered an affordable prerequisite to positions of management in enterprise and political life. Most of the high-quality-acknowledged Canadian colleges were founded in the late nineteenth century; life there, as a minimum in the early days, become spartan and difficult in methods that no boarding college is today. At top Canada University, Frederick Hutt, a scholar inside the 1830s, wrote to his brother, "I hope you'll spend plenty of nuts and cakes as I will hardly ever subsist on what we get." Ted Rogers, the founding father of Rogers's conversation, went to the board whilst he became seven. Having had a nanny at home, he recalled that "I went from having any individual brushing my enamel for me to being caned if my teeth weren't clean sufficient. There's not anything incorrect with that, but it changed into a chunk of a surprise." He later described the school as his "a surrogate father" within the absence of his own father, who had passed away before his enrolment. There was a sturdy affiliation with the army, something that becomes nevertheless very prominent whilst Rogers arrived. The Cadet Corps of higher Canada university became began in 1869, and through its one hundred and twenty-seven months history, it remained a critical part of faculty existence. College students took element in everyday drills and exercises, including people with active rounds. Boys were predicted to be organized for deployment at any time, as every so often they had been. Throughout the Fenian Raids of 1866 UCC students had been mobilized to defend army homes and the port in Toronto. The cadet software changed into an expression of the spirit of volunteerism and the Victorian militia motion, and it maintained an ongoing affiliation with the national military. Between 1875 and 1937 UCC produced six commanding officials of The Queen's very Own Rifles. All through WWI, 1,089 volunteered for military providers, and a hundred and seventy-six gave their lives. In 1919, membership in the corps became compulsory for all students. None of this changed into unique to a specific UCC School, with boarding colleges and many public schools the following the match. Many cadet corps remained active into the nineteen sixties and seventies. In time, however, the cadet applications began to sense much less applicable, greater relics of an in advance time. Which certainly they have been, in particular, whilst actual rifles have been changed with wooden ones, or while actual training evolved right into a form of pantomime of army education, and when the connection with the navy became much less explicit. At UCC the corps changed into officially retired in 1987, one in every of final of its type in Canada. (Colleges, St. Andrews College, and Bishop's university school have lively cadet corps, although for the maximum component the applications have advanced, becoming extra akin to outdoor training applications than military).

Boarding colleges tend to have very exciting reputations. Due to books and movies, you can image an elitist cult, stricken teenagers, a spooky manor, or a few different odd experiences whilst you think about boarding school. With this effect in mind, the concept of sending your infant to boarding school can fast become difficult and downright scary. This decision would not need to overwhelm you, though. We talked with Lucy Pritzker, who works as an educational consultant and enables households to locate the appropriate schools and settings for his or her children, to recognize extra approximately the boarding school choice manner. There's No "proper" preference- "there may be no 'exceptional' faculty, but there's a faculty that is 'satisfactory' for your toddler," says Pritzker. "Simply due to the fact Aunt Sally's neighbor's son thrived at a specific faculty doesn't mean your baby will." there may be No "kind" of a pupil who's pleasant for Boarding faculties- while your kid is going to a boarding college, it doesn't suggest which you're transporting your youngster off, nor is it simplest for stricken kids. "Sure, there are schools for children, however, this is simplest one segment of the boarding college international," says Pritzker. "There are exceptional schools for all one-of-a-kind varieties of students." There are four special sorts of boarding colleges- Junior boarding colleges serve center college-aged youngsters and provide an established gaining knowledge of the environment. College prep colleges have what Pritzker describes as "rigorous academics" and assist your teenager to reach educational goals to guide their future. Opportunity faculties offer a college-prep curriculum with a twist. "Every school has an exceptional way of life and serves a spot population," says Pritzker. Lastly, healing schools have instructional additives, just like other colleges, but also offer remedy support with a scientific team of workers. Institution, man or woman, and own family therapy classes are constructed into the shape of this system. You don't need to be notable wealthy. "Especially, in essential cities, non-public faculties can value nearly as a lot as a boarding faculty," says Pritzker. "Many boarding faculties try to have socioeconomic diversity on their campuses and provide financial aid. There are also loans particularly for investment private faculty lessons." on the low stop, tuitions begin around $25,000, although a few (generally Christian) boarding schools can start even lower. For classic boarding faculties with a conventional school calendar, assume tuition to be everywhere from $25,000 to $50,000 (or more). Therapeutic schools can price around $100,000 for a twelve-month stint, although some run as little as $30,000. Pritzker advises finding out economically useful resource and fee alternatives. Many colleges have scholarships available, and, for a few therapeutic colleges, your coverage can assist cover expenses. It won't harm your own family's Bond. "Our society's intellectual health model is based on 'family maintenance. ' And for maximum, that means keeping the family collectively, regularly in any respect prices," says Pritzker. "But families I work with locate their own family is preserved because of boarding school. It offers them happy, thriving children who they can have a court with, either due to the fact their baby is now in a rigorously academic way of life that validates the child's desires, or because they're capable of play sports activities or carry out extra often or at a distinctive level than they may at domestic. Or, it's because their baby's healing wishes have become met in a way outpatient therapy couldn't cope with." Boarding College. "Many mother and father come to me due to the fact they recognize that their baby is a vivid and capable scholar, but not achieving academically or socially or both," says Pritzker. "Frequently these are college students who're unable to preserve up with the pace or the quantity of labor expected of their nearby faculty. They require a high level of assignment, but at a slower, extra comfy pace with a focus on effort rather than manufacturing. Those are children from excessive-forced faculties and households. after I work with this profile, I'm searching at colleges that are options to standard college-prep colleges, but which could nevertheless prepare their college students for four to twelvemonths schools and universities." if your teenager is struggling, boarding college may also be an amazing choice on your circle of relatives. "those are adolescents who, for a ramification of reasons; trauma, own family troubles, behavior problems, substance abuse—need a healing intervention and the 24/7 help of a therapeutic boarding college," says Pritzker. Ultimately, boarding school is probably simply the new setting your infant desires to be triumphant. "a third organization, whilst they're now not sad at domestic or faculty, are looking for a special experience, both children with mother and father who went to boarding school and want the equal experience, or a chance to be a part of a like-minded instructional and social peer organization, or a deeper possibility inside the arts or athletically," says Pritzker. Therapeutic Boarding colleges can be beneficial for your teen, even in case you don't suppose so. "Sometimes mother and father think that a toddler suffering at home simply needs a place to reinvent him or herself. And now and again, in particular, while a toddler's educational desires aren't being met, this could be real," says Pritzker.

"However, whilst a baby is using alcohol and different tablets and/or is indignant and defiant with authority figures, simply a trade of surroundings, with no therapeutic guide, is not going to help. The problems the kid struggled with at home will be repeated in boarding faculty. In those instances, I help my clients discover suitable healing boarding faculties." whilst in doubt, don't forget hiring a consultant "often, families use the net to do their boarding college seek, and speedily discover that there is an amazing amount of records. Hiring an educational consultant brings firsthand information to the hunt," says Pritzker. Academic experts visit colleges for insight into what sort of kid would do nicely there. Even as hiring one will add to the fee, it may be well worth it if you're at a loss as to which to ship your toddler. You can find out more about instructional experts and hiring one at the independent educational specialists association. Realize how boarding college differs from different faculties. Boarding colleges frequently offer greater educational aid than conventional colleges. With small classes (a few faculties even provide one-on-one teaching, whilst most school rooms average no more than twelve college students), have a look at corridor hours, get admission to teachers that live on campus and a fashionable push for resources, your infant can excel in the schoolroom and out. "Afternoon sports and extracurricular activities are just as important as the academic day," says Pritzker. Many college students come from all over the kingdom if no longer the arena so your kid may be uncovered to and work in various networks. Boarding faculty isn't always the last hotel. "Boarding school is an underutilized useful resource in this USA," says Pritzker. "I frequently listen to to to to the families I work with say that they want they could have found a tremendous boarding faculty faster." Enrolling a child in a boarding faculty isn't a mirrored image of an incapability to discern; it's really providing your child with sources they can get in a greater traditional faculty.

Chapter Eight

Adaptive Physical Education

What is adaptive physical education? Adaptive bodily schooling is bodily education that has been modified so that it's far as appropriate for the person with a disability as it is for a person without. Basically, making physical schooling available so that every student can participate irrespective of their skill level or capabilities is fairly encouraged. Adaptive physical training is something that should genuinely be always funded and is something I accept as true with is vital. As an aspiring bodily training teacher, I completely consider the benefits of Adaptive bodily schooling and it should be provided to every scholar. Of course, the current country of adapted bodily schooling has no longer been around for a long term. Over the years tailored bodily training programs, have been progressed. Early packages consisted of "medically inspired efforts towards remediation in their condition." a few years ago, students with disabilities had been no longer treated with the identical appreciation as they are nowadays. Through therapy, they would try to remedy the pupil's situations as opposed to working with them. The second one, half of the remaining century has seen a few foremost changes. People with disabilities are seen as having a "valuable but modified set of capabilities" which means that because a pupil is in a wheelchair does imply he cannot do something. The competencies he possesses and the matters he's able to do are useful to the class. Due to this alteration in perspective, physical education has required a one-of-a-kind method, which is a selfless provider. The formal definition of adaptive bodily schooling from the Adaptive physical schooling national requirements is "adapted physical education is physical education which has been tailored or changed so that it is as appropriate for the individual with a disability as it's far for someone without an incapacity." The motive of an adaptive physical schooling elegance is to work at the improvement of physical talents, essential motor abilities and patterns, throwing, catching, walking, walking, etc., abilities in aquatics, dance, and person and group video games and sports and to include intramural and lifetime sports. Those country-wide requirements are used "to make sure that physical schooling for children with disabilities is brought via a qualified tailored physical Educator. To meet this purpose a hard and fast of fifteen countrywide requirements representing the content a certified adapted bodily Educator ought to recognize to do their process become evolved".

The fifteen countrywide standards for an adaptive physical training magnificence are a human improvement, motor conduct, exercise science, history and philosophy, specific attributes of learners, curriculum idea and development, evaluation, instructional design and making plans, teaching, consolation, and staff development, student and software improvement, scholar and software assessment, persevering with education, ethics and ultimately communication. Those are essential to recognize due to the fact those are the requirements that a bodily schooling teacher is going to want to execute for an adaptive physical education class. As a bodily training teacher, I'm going to have so one can make modifications to the games or activities that are being played in the class so that everyone can take part. For instance, for students that having a seeing incapacity, there'll need to be changes made to the type of ball this is being used. Adaptive bodily education is also described as, "the art and science of growing, enforcing, and tracking a carefully designed physical training instructional program for a learner with a disability, primarily based on a complete evaluation, to offer the learner the abilities important for a lifetime of rich amusement, undertaking, and sports reviews to beautify bodily health and wellbeing" (apens.org). In easier phrases, it's simply bodily training this is adapted or changed to be suitable for someone with an incapacity, at the same time as nevertheless being suitable for a person without an incapacity. Instructors of all levels will run into this sooner or later in their teaching career regardless of what problem they teach. All college students are entitled to take part in bodily training. Adaptive bodily schooling allows for students with disabilities to take part in the bodily activity and get active. College students without disabilities additionally have the opportunity to benefit from adaptive bodily schooling. In a class where there are students with disabilities, other students have the chance to learn how to assist and lead activities. Adaptive bodily schooling can provide the scholars a chance to be the lecturers; they may be the ones who provide the instructions or exhibit a talent. Adaptive bodily education is bodily training that has been adapted or modified so that it's far as appropriate for the individual with a disability as it is for someone without an incapacity. It is an exceedingly beneficial magnificence in particular in the excessive school placing. Disabled kids can do sporting events they generally can't do, enjoy full health club lessons with non-disabled college students, and study new and useful fundamental abilities they will use for relaxation in their lives. To teach a class like this the trainer needs to learn the FAIR model, learn exclusive competencies to educate disabled kids and be able to assess all students who're involved inside the elegance.

The FAIR model is a gadget to arrange statistics in a way that you can design. If the various college students did now not pass the way, the instructor wanted them to then the teacher needs to take some time to modify the activity even greater to suit the students higher. This version is extremely essential while the teacher is attempting to discern out their college students. It helps the teachers have a plan for the magnificence so that they aren't stuck while it comes time to educate. For teachers to train this class they may be going to should develop other competencies than their fundamental bodily schooling instructor. There are six standards for an APE trainer. Those requirements include human improvement, motor conduct, exercising science, curriculum improvement, coaching, and communique. Human development is the basic understanding of how skills expand and progress and the way they follow people with disabilities. That is critical to know due to the reality there are disabled and non-disabled college students in this elegance. The Motor behavior preferred is having the information to reveal how motor talents broaden and being capable of maintaining in mind the effect of improvement put off for those that are disabled. This additionally is going along with the next trendy that's curriculum development. This is the understanding of ways every pupil has an extraordinary aim relying on their disability. Teachers should be aware at all times of their students and what's unique about them. Adapted bodily schooling (APE) is specially designed coaching in bodily education supposed to address the precise wishes of people. Even as the roots of tailored bodily education can be traced lower back to Swedish scientific gymnastics in the 1700s, tailored bodily training, as practiced these days, has been drastically formed using the mandates of the Individuals with Disabilities schooling Act (concept). This act, enacted in 1997, amended the education for All Handicapped Children Act, which became enacted in 1975 and stipulated that each one kid with disabilities specifically, idea defined special schooling as "particularly designed practice, for gratis to parents or guardians, to meet the precise desires of a child with an incapacity, including (A) guidance performed in the classroom, within the home, in hospitals, and institutions, and in different settings; and (B) instruction in physical training." The inclusion of bodily training in the definition of special training is widespread for two motives. First, it recognized bodily education as an immediate service that must be provided to all college students who qualify for special education offerings in place of associated offerings, including physical or occupational remedy, which might be required simplest when they're needed for a child to gain from a unique schooling provider. Second, it highlighted the significance of physical schooling for college students with disabilities.

The idea also described bodily education, mandated that everyone's unique schooling offerings are brought inside the least restrictive environment (LRE), and prescribed a management report known as an Individualized education program (IEP). bodily schooling turned into defined as "the development of (A) physical and motor health; (B) essential motor abilities and patterns; and (C) talents in aquatics, dance, and person and institution games and sports activities (together with intramural and lifetime sports activities." concept similarly delineated that "bodily training services, mainly designed if necessary, have to be made available to each handicapped child receiving a free suitable public training" and that "if specifically designed physical schooling is prescribed in a child's individualized education application, the general public company chargeable for the training of that toddler shall offer the provider immediately, or make preparations for it to be furnished via different public or non-public applications. "With recognize to LRE, concept said the subsequent: "To the most volume suitable, children with disabilities, consisting of the ones in public or personal institutions or different care facilities, are knowledgeable with children who do no longer have disabilities; and special lessons, separate schooling, or different removal of kids with disabilities from the everyday academic surroundings occurs best when the character and severity of the disability are such that education in normal classes cannot be accomplished satisfactorily. "To make certain that concept became implemented as intended, the act required that IEPs must be evolved and monitored for all students who qualify for special education. The IEP is advanced using a team and includes the scholar's gift degree of performance; annual dreams and quick-time period educational objectives; particular educational services so one can be provided and the extent to which the pupil will participate in regular schooling programs; any wished transition offerings; the projected dates for the initiation and duration of services; and objective standards and approaches for evaluating, as a minimum yearly, development at the stated desires and instructional objectives. Eventually, the concept mandated that qualified employees deliver unique schooling coaching. In this context, "certified" meant that a person has "met country academic company accepted or identified certification, licensing, registration, or other comparable necessities which apply to the place wherein she or he is providing special education or related services. "The criminal foundation for tailored physical training outcomes from the mandates that require that all students who qualify for special training need to acquire physical schooling. If specially designed bodily schooling is needed, then those services have to be stated in the IEP, introduced inside the LRE, and supplied via a qualified instructor.

It's far essential to be aware that whilst concept requires that each one college students who qualify for unique training have a right to adapted physical schooling if had to deal with their particular desires, adapted physical schooling is, can, and must be supplied to all students who've particular physical and motor desires that can't be adequately addressed in the ordinary physical schooling program. It isn't always uncommon, for instance, for lots of students to have brief orthopedic disabilities along with sprained ankles, broken limbs, or muscle traces at some stage in their faculty years. Short-term APE packages would be appropriate for those college students both to assist within the rehabilitation of their injuries and to decrease any health and/or ability deficits that could arise for the duration of their healing. different college students can also have mild physical or health impairments, which includes asthma or diabetes, that do not intrude with their academic overall performance enough to qualify them for special schooling but which might be extremely sufficient to warrant special resorts and concerns in physical schooling. Within the United States of America bodily schooling and maximum principal sport/pastime applications for children are college centered, therefore the emphasis on training within the phrases bodily training and tailored bodily education. In different countries, bodily schooling, recreation, and recreation are generally carried out independently or outdoor of the schools and sponsored by different corporations and corporations. In these settings, the term adapted bodily pastime may be used as opposed to adapted bodily education.

Although the idea has provided a legitimate legal basis for tailored physical training, there are nonetheless some troubles that need to be resolved throughout the career to make sure that the physical and motor needs of all college students with disabilities are correctly addressed. Two primary troubles relate to who's certified to provide APE services and how selections are made regarding the proper bodily training placement for college students with disabilities. While concept special that physical training offerings, particularly designed if important, should be made to be had to each baby with a disability receiving free suitable education, it stopped quick of defining who become certified to provide these services. Idea said that it changed into the obligation of the states to establish teacher certification requirements. Unlike different unique schooling regions (e.g., instructors of individuals with intellectual retardation or gaining knowledge of disabilities), maximum states did not have in vicinity described certification requirements for teachers of tailored physical schooling. Given the monetary constraints placed on colleges through the mandates of the idea, most states were reluctant to location additional demands on their faculties by using forcing them to lease APE experts. As a result, via 1991 best fourteen states had truly defined an endorsement or certification in tailored physical training.

The life of a mandate that required that services be supplied however that did now not define who became qualified to provide those services created a quandary for both teachers and college students. in many cases, regular physical educators with little or no schooling related to people with disabilities and/or therapists with no training in physical schooling have been assigned the obligation of addressing the bodily training needs of students with disabilities. When you consider that those teachers do no longer have the prerequisite competencies to deal with the wishes of these college students, these needs are in large part going unaddressed. To respond to this situation, the country-wide Consortium for physical schooling and activity for people with Disabilities (NCPERID) created country-wide standards and a voluntary country-wide certification examination for adapted bodily schooling.

The adapted bodily education countrywide requirements (APENS) delineate the content material that tailored physical educators ought to know throughout fifteen standards. The national exam has been administered yearly because 1997 at more than eighty take a look at websites in the USA. while the creation of the Adaptive physical schooling country-wide standards and the countrywide certification examination were sizeable steps closer to addressing the issue of who's qualified to educate APE, a lot greater work still needs to be carried out. The NCPERID is working with a small wide variety of states on developing a method through which states can adopt the NCPERID APE standards and APE countrywide certification examination as to their nation credential. it's far was hoping that a uniform certification much like the APENS examination will be adopted by way of all states with the aid of 2010, and this trouble can be resolved. The reason for defining bodily schooling as an immediate carrier, especially designed if essential, in idea, became to ensure that the physical and motor development wishes of these students had been now not overlooked or sacrificed at the cost of addressing other educational needs. This emphasis was warranted given the great studies documenting marked bodily and motor development delays and extended health risks (e.g., coronary heart ailment and weight problems) in lots of children with disabilities. There may be also a wealth of studies that have shown that well-designed and carried out bodily schooling applications can reduce both bodily and motor delays and many health dangers in students with disabilities.

At the same time as the rationale of the law changed into clean, the way it has been applied has been much less than ultimate. What has come about in many colleges is that most people, if now not all, of the scholars with disabilities are being dumped into normal bodily education classes. The justification for this practice can be linked to several sub troubles. First, like many other problems in the schools, maximum faculties have been not provided with sufficient assets to put into effect the mandates of concept. Given the need to conform to prison mandates and constrained resources, many schools have been forced to look for methods to fulfill the letter of the law using their present resources. Particular mandates fashioned this conduct. First, a part of the LRE mandate stated that students with disabilities be educated inside the ordinary education environments to the maximum extent suitable. Second, the IEP mandates required handiest that in particular designed services be described and monitored inside the IEP. Many schools, therefore, deduced that if they put all the students with disabilities in ordinary physical training, then they would be addressing a part of the LRE mandate and on the equal time avoiding the additional time, attempt, and expenses associated with actually creating specially designed bodily training programs. Fiscally this solution was very attractive for the reason that most colleges lacked qualified employees who were educated to assess the physical and motor wishes of college students with disabilities and who may want to make appropriate choices concerning what will be the maximum suitable (LRE) physical education surroundings wherein to address their wishes. Preferably, this exercise could have been diagnosed and stopped throughout the early years of implementing the regulation thru the required kingdom and federal monitoring methods.

Unluckily, it changed into no longer for several reasons. One of the motives became that the IEP document turned into used as the primary tracking record. Due to the fact bodily schooling become now not recognized as a needed specially designed service, it turned into now not monitored. inside the rare cases in which mother and father understood their rights and demanded particularly designed physical schooling to satisfy the specific desires of their infant, colleges tended to address these requests on a personal basis and subcontract to have these services delivered. The approach to stopping the practice of placing all students with special needs in everyday physical training should be multifaceted. The ideal solution would be certainly for faculties to rent qualified tailored physical educators as supposed through the regulation. This solution, but, isn't as easy as it may initially seem. First, schools might need to apprehend that their current bodily training placement practices had been wrong and then be prompted to make a trade.

In many colleges, those practices have long gone on unquestioned for more than two decades. In addition, there are not any new economic sources to lease the extra instructors needed to accurate this problem. To reap additional public monies to fund those positions, colleges ought to explain why these new teachers had been needed and why they had not provided those suitable services inside the beyond. Resolving the trouble of irrelevant placement of students with disabilities into normal bodily education is critical now not only for the students with disabilities but also for the regular training students and the everyday physical education instructors. studies within the subject have time and again proven that many normal bodily educators experience unpreparedness to deal with the needs of students with disabilities and that seeking to accommodate the desires of these students hurts all of the students in their training. Spotting the quandary schools face in resolving this hassle, the difficulty is being addressed at ranges. The primary degree is to train colleges and national departments of training about this problem and propose that they expand both lengthy and brief-term answers. An example of a protracted-time period solution could be to require colleges to lease licensed tailored bodily educators as replacements whilst present bodily educators retire or leave for different positions. An instance of a short-time period answer would be to use in-service education applications for school directors and everyday bodily educators. Those programs would focus on teaching them what's suitable physical education and then offering them a number of the essential talents had to provide a continuum of opportunity placements in bodily training as meant via the LRE requirements. The second stage is to teach parents thru the various parent advocacy groups concerning their rights and what needs to be concerned in making the correct placement selection in terms of physical education. This data might permit dad and mom to make greater informed choices and to endorse appropriate physical education offerings for their kids.

Song and studying with incapacity

People with gaining knowledge of disabilities enjoy many intellectual, emotional, bodily, and mentally demanding situations. Wherein this occurs, music can play an important role in enhancing the attention, social functioning, shallowness, and memory of college students with studying disabilities. The Salamanca assertion and Framework for action on special desires education is one of the frameworks that urges the global representatives to transport to the idea of inclusive training that tends to profess that no person will stay unwanted from the academic institutions because of their caste, creed, color as well as vulnerabilities. It, in addition, states that children with disabilities or significant educational needs and capabilities have to have got right of entry to normal schooling and baby-focused pedagogy. As a way of addressing this, a few researchers have promoted using music and music schooling to enhance the instructional experiences of college students with gaining knowledge of disabilities. One of the fundamental arguments is that song facilitates college students with studying disabilities. Even as researchers recognize that each gaining knowledge of disability (those being, attention-deficit/hyperactivity disease, and autism) may be specific and that this could have an effect on the approaches in which they're educated, they agree that track can help enhance their self-assurance and their stories inside the college machine. Despite these discussions, there are few studies in Trinidad and Tobago that explore the demanding situations going through special educators, the specific strategies which might be used to educate individuals with studying disabilities, and the possible effect of tune at the getting to know studies of those youngsters inside the classroom. Given such, the researcher tends to attend to several key ideas as (i) what are the challenges widely wide-spread in those areas to educate the inexperienced persons of learning disabilities, (ii) How tune affects the getting to know of these cookies, and (iii) how this method signifies enhancing coaching and mastering in lecture rooms. thus, this research tends to (i) examine demanding situations the teachers face in teaching college students with studying disabilities, (ii) discover the viable consequences of the song as teaching and gaining knowledge of tool in such lecture rooms, and (iii) make pointers for improving coaching and getting to know stories within faculties that cater to the wishes of students with gaining knowledge of disabilities.

The term getting to know Disabilities (LD) may be defined in lots of ways. Donchin & Coles (1988) as an instance defined it as a fabrication of center elegance households supposed to awareness interest on unique studying desires in their children while not having to label them mentally retarded or emotionally disabled. Donchin & Coles (1988) further substantiated his view by mentioning that during a few elements of the world, the LD category became utilized in diverse approaches to provoke or maintain a form of racial segregation (1988). The category provided the kids of middle-class households a diploma of safety from probable outcomes of low achievement because it upheld their highbrow normalcy and the normalcy in their domestic backgrounds. It additionally advised hope for a remedy and for his or her potential eventually to obtain higher popularity occupations than different low achievers. In this situation, race and class served therefore as criteria for labeling, treating, or responding to kids with LD. these days the perception of studying disabilities is not connected with racial segregation however is now commonly regularly occurring as a general time period that refers to a heterogeneous group of disorders manifested using giant difficulties in the acquisition and use of listening, talking, analyzing, writing, reasoning or mathematical capabilities. These issues are intrinsic to the person and presumed to be due to significant frightened gadget dysfunction. But, even though a studying disability may additionally arise concomitantly with different handicapping situations or environmental influences it is not the direct result of these conditions or impacts. The time period studying disabilities is defined to include deficits in visible, spatial, auditory, and motor functioning that creates a discrepancy between general capacity and success. The phenomena related to getting to know disabilities embody a wide range of developmental, cognitive, and behavioral troubles that are manifested in unique however recognizable patterns. A great deal of this however creates a deficit knowledge of kids with studying disabilities. However, some researchers strengthen the notion that getting to know a disability isn't always a hassle with intelligence or motivation. If a person's highbrow capacity is under regular, then his/her studying hassle isn't always said to stem from gaining knowledge of incapacity. Those are processing issues that arise for reasons apart from diminished cognitive ability. In truth, researchers argue that maximum kids with learning disabilities enjoy neurologically-based processing problems. Those processing issues can intervene with studying primary skills along with reading, writing, and/or math. They also can interfere with better level abilities together with employer, time making plans, abstract reasoning, long or quick-term memory, and interest. It is critical to understand that learning disabilities can have an effect on an individual's existence beyond teachers and may affect relationships with family, buddies, and in the workplace (LDA). Instead of this, they argue that their brains are absolutely stressed out in a different way. This distinction impacts how they receive and manner facts. This perspective consequently pushes the belief that each infant is precise, it is only when a character tempo, pattern, fashion, or overall performance hinders a baby in carrying out developmental obligations that the kid's variant pattern will become a dysfunctional one. The extent to which a difference turns into a true incapacity depends on internal factors, which include the child's compensatory strategies and the impact of other developmental dysfunctions, and on outside variables, inclusive of the significance of the duties affected by the stress of expectation, and available supportive structures. A few researchers additionally draw at the truth that the term gaining knowledge of disability is so standard in its conceptualization that many rent it as synonymous with getting to know troubles, school failure, and the like. In fact, frequently times, it refers to a particular diagnostic category. The class of studying disability has been referred to as the maximum heterogeneous of any special schooling classification. An exam of the definition shows that this heterogeneity refers greater to the extensive variety of academic deficits located inside the population than it does to the cultural and linguistic range. The term "children with precise getting to know disabilities" applies to those youngsters who have a disease on one or greater of the fundamental psychological approaches involved in understanding or the use of language, spoken or written, which may additionally appear itself in an imperfect ability to listen, talk, read, write, spell or do mathematical calculations. Additionally, people with gaining knowledge of disabilities are frequently considered as "bizarre", "exceptional", and "incapable" people. Their bodily and useful impairments might be partly accountable for them being conceived via a few as 'deviant'. This will bring about them being rejected through their network, society as a whole, and even spouse and children and fitness services. Conformity to societal guidelines is of paramount importance to the very life of humans. Lawlessness and non-conformity are comparable to the destruction of human lifestyles. Bodily incapacity is taken into consideration via many a sociologist as a shape of deviance. In this manner, incapacity has often been taken into consideration as deviance in reality as it does no longer meet society's expectancies. The idea of social role valorization (SRV) may be introduced as a manner of assist. SRV is particularly relevant to instructions of human beings in society: folks who are already societally devalued, and those who are at heightened danger of becoming devalued. As a consequence, SRV is in the main a reaction to the traditionally popular phenomenon of social devaluation, and specifically societal devaluation. This allows to empower them and to facilitate their integration into society as valued people. Paramount in this paper is the desire to illustrate that musical activities may be one of the interventions, which could beautify the best of life for people with getting to know disabilities.

Measuring gaining knowledge of Disabilities
Numerous strategies may be used to measure mastering disabilities, along with; (i)Screening programs, (ii) reaction Intervention, (iii) comprehensive assessment, and (iv) character schooling Programme. Screening is stepped one

inside the procedure of collecting applicable records approximately a man or woman with a suspected learning disability. Screening does now not determine whether or not the man or woman has a studying disability. It could include observations, informal interviews, the usage of a written tool, and/or an overview of scientific, college, or work histories. Screening is a manner for an endorsement to higher determine the chance of the suspected studying disability, and to help the man or woman determine if he or she wishes to maintain an LD diagnosis.

Response Intervention (RI) is the call given to the system used to assist pick out youngsters with getting to know Disabilities. Response intervention generally includes the following:

• Tracking all students' development carefully to identify viable learning issues

• Offering a toddler identified as having troubles with help on special degrees or levels

• Moving this teenager through the ranges as appropriate, increasing instructional help if the child does not show development.

Complete checks, a technique used to measure studying disabilities, evaluate and become aware of a scholar's strengths and needs (countrywide Joint Committee mastering Disabilities 1990). Comprehensive assessments can:

• Become aware of whether a child has a mastering disability

• Determine an infant's eligibility below federal law for unique schooling offerings

• Help construct an individualized schooling plan (IEP) that outlines supports for a teen who qualifies for unique schooling services

• Set up a benchmark for measuring the child's academic progress

A man or woman schooling program (IEP) is now and then developed to assist define someone's learning strengths and weaknesses. It spells out your child's getting to know needs, the offerings the faculty will provide, and how progress can be measured. Numerous people, consisting of parents, are involved in growing the report. The complete manner can be a remarkable way to type out an infant's strengths and weaknesses. Working at the IEP can help in figuring out methods to assist him to succeed in school.

Responding to mastering disabilities

Educators and researchers are starting to pay greater attention to the perception that some students have issues gaining knowledge of abilities and ideas taught inside the study room. It's essential for college personnel and mother and father to work collectively to become aware of issues once they stand up and to cope with them both at college and home. Instructors ought to deal with this task in their lecture rooms as properly. Not best will these students call for more trainer time and persistence; they'll also require specialized educational strategies in a structured environment that helps and complements their learning potential. Many of those young youngsters warfare to communicate their wants and needs, to freely flow their body to get entry to and engage their world, and to research summary concepts and thoughts. The depth of their desires method that delays are in all likelihood to have a pervasive impact on the kid's development and are possibly to retain to affect the family and the child nicely beyond the early adolescence years. When instructors use a needs-primarily based approach to support the gaining knowledge of young children with multiple disabilities, it is possible to become aware of the person supports every infant wishes to have greater get entry to and engagement across environments. In addition, teachers must additionally make sure that the recognized practices are people who we've got the greatest self-belief at this point that they will cause nice impacts for the child. it's far crucial to keep in mind that studying disabled college students are not college students who are incapacitated or not able to learn; rather, they need differentiated guidance tailor-made to their distinctive getting to know capabilities. Differentiated training is a versatile method of coaching in which an instructor plans and consists of out numerous techniques to address content, getting to know approaches, learning style, practical procedures, presentation strategies, and evaluation gear. When instructors differentiate guidance, they offer college students the structures to maximize strengths, work around weaknesses, and enjoy timely remediation. This permits college students to take advantage of powerful learning strategies as they start to apprehend their own private learning patterns, hobbies, desires, and interact with their learning. As a result, pupil motivation will increase. An important aspect of powerful collaborative instructional programming is the involvement of a circle of relatives' individuals or the forming of partnerships with households and running collaboratively with them. Given that households recognize their infant the exceptional, they have the records needed to manual the group inside the improvement of a powerful and individualized academic software. Disability labels can be stigmatizing and perpetuate fake stereotypes where college students who're disabled aren't as successful as their peers. In general, it's far appropriate to reference the incapacity simplest while it's miles pertinent to the situation. But, the mastering disabilities affiliation of the US (2014), confirms that we can educate children with gaining knowledge of disabilities to "discover ways to research". The social constructivist attitude informs this method. This angle speaks to the social and cultural context of newcomers' lives. therefore, so that it will help college students in their development, it's miles important to exchange the learning context in the sort of manner that it'll correspond to distinctive getting to know abilities and desires of college students. A few intervention practices encompass direct practice, using sequential established multi-sensory processes, imparting printouts and visual aids inside the classroom. These are also be supported via the usage of scaffolding as an approach to build the gaining knowledge of college students with gaining knowledge of disabilities. In this situation, it begins out with the instructor the usage of closely mediated coaching, referred to as explicit instruction, after which they slowly begin to allow the scholars to collect the ability, moving closer to the intention of scholar mediated education. Achievement for the student with studying disabilities requires a focus on character achievement, character progress, and character gaining knowledge. This calls for particular, directed, individualized, extensive remedial preparation for students who are suffering.

Music therapy

Music gives a form of repayment for people with language impairments in addition to a way of facilitating language improvement. Song therapy is taken into consideration as a related provider modality in special schooling. Research in neurological functioning supports the association between song and cognitive improvement. Song organizes sounds and silences in a drift of time. It creates expectancies and is then happy. It increases a query and solves it. Tune focuses on accuracy and attention. Gaining knowledge of a way to play a tool can enhance interest, attention, impulse manipulates, social functioning, self-esteem, self-expression, motivation, and memory. Music creates physiological responses, which are related to emotional reactions. Song explains the tension release sequence related to emotional arousal. The rate and intensity of the musical beat create special emotions in each kind of song. The opportunity to play an instrument may be used as a reinforcer for undertaking behaviors. Tune also can foster superb attitudes. Psychological and neuro-clinical research demonstrates that musical training in children is associated with the heightening of sound sensitivity as well as enhancement in verbal competencies and fashionable reasoning abilities. Studies in the area of auditory cognitive neuroscience have begun revealing the practical and structural brain plasticity underlying these results. Paying attention to tune calls for sure perceptual abilities including pitch discrimination, auditory memory, and selective interest so one can understand the temporal and harmonic shape of the tune as well as its effective components and engages a disbursed network of mind systems.

However, the extent to which the depth and duration of instrumental training or other factors along with a circle of relatives history, extracurricular activities, interest, motivation, or academic techniques contribute to the advantages for mind improvement is still no longer clear. Song education correlates with plastic adjustments in auditory, motor, and sensorimotor integration regions. The strength of song to behave therapeutically has lengthy been identified. Therapy can contain being attentive to or actively making songs. Increasingly it can contain each. Passive music intervention in song therapy also influences how children with studying incapacity interact inside the schoolroom. Song listening that's an approach in which a character is taking note of stay or recorded music, is considered passive because no tune engagement or active participation is involved. Though some differentiate therapeutic song listening alone as a remedy that's separate and apart from clinical music remedy, music listening is indexed as one of the many strategies used in music therapy. From a neuroscience angle, passive and energetic song sports differ inside the elements of the mind that they spark off. Being attentive to track engages subcortical and cortical areas of the mind, together with the amygdala, medial geniculate body inside the thalamus, and the left and right number one auditory cortex. some others take a look at demonstrated that the anterior medial frontal cortex, advanced temporal sulcus, and temporal poles are engaged when a character/individual listens to tune because she or he can be trying to perceive the song maker's purpose. In music listening, the man or woman's desire for song kind also impacts the brain areas which might be activated. For instance, exceptional components of the brain are activated when the track is self-decided on as opposed to while it's miles chosen via the researchers. Emotional information in individuals with autism is related to their capability to communicate socially and is frequently considered one in every of numerous characteristics which are underdeveloped in this population. In a have a look at done in 1999, younger kids with autism had been able to understand emotional expression in song at an equal degree to kids without autism. Moreover, studies indicate that track can assist youngsters with autism in growing their attention and awareness, as well as to bring vital information, and make their studying surroundings more fun. Primarily based on those papers, a take a look at turned into carried out at the consequences of history tune and song texts on emotional expertise. The researcher observed that a number of the control conditions and experimental conditions of having heritage music that represented emotion or having verbal commands simplest, the historical past tune become most effective in enhancing emotional know-how. As stated before, the expanded emotional expertise ought to assist individuals with autism enhance their social interactions with others.

Tune and mastering

The empirical literature on the subject determined that track was and has been used to treat numerous mental fitness troubles. Following similar research, it became later identified that song improves health by way of focusing on the distinctive bodily, mental, and emotional factors of people. Song tends to be one of the pinnacle motivators for youngsters with special wishes. It employs using fascinating instruments to set off an infant to make requests, i.e. maintaining out a drum and watching for them to talk. Using unique instruments to inspire the development of motor abilities are simply examples of the way this may be achieved. Music is a smooth, amusing, and motivating manner to connect to children and encourage them to broaden new abilities. Brown (2012), however, indicates that track has the power to power away from the feelings of fear and tension whilst going through the unknown on my own. If used in such a way, then tune has the capacity to promote innovative and crucial thinking amongst college students inside the schoolroom. This has been well documented inside the literature. In reality, Nabhan and Bitar (2018) discovered that that mastering track facilitates studying other topics and complements capabilities that youngsters necessarily use in different regions. In this example, it involves greater than the voice or arms gambling a device. in which a child gaining knowledge of about tune has to tap into more than one ability sets, frequently simultaneously, then it song enables with language, cognitive and social improvement, this will be assisted by way of linking familiar songs to new information can also assist imprint information on younger minds. It's been proven that high faculty song college students have higher grade point averages than non- tune college students within the equal faculty. This equal take a look at also observed that 16% of the song students had a 4.0 ordinary grade factor common and most effective 5% of the non-music college students had a four.0 common grade factor average. An observation of graduates of the New York metropolis college of appearing Arts discovered that 90% of the cross on to university. Involvement in excessive school tune applications facilitates students to expand the talents important for a ramification of occupations. A Stanford study also confirmed that track engages areas of the brain that are concerned with paying interest, making predictions, and updating activities in our reminiscence. By using so doing, musical revel in strengthens most of the identical aspects of mind characteristic which might be impaired.

Demanding situations of the use of track as a learning tool

A mission to coaching track to kids with getting to know disabilities is the reality that every infant learns differently .identifying an infant's getting to know style or degree of intelligence (auditory or kinesthetic) is a helpful device when coaching track. while it's been decided how a toddler learns excellent, steps may be taken to ensure that form of getting to know is bolstered inside the study room and all through home examination. However, very little research furnished a comprehensive view of a few disability classes together with autism, mental retardation or cognitive delays, attention deficit issues (ADHD), studying disabilities, and bodily and other fitness impairments (POHI). A prime thing that turned into discovered was the cognitive and behavioral challenges of coaching students with studying disabilities. Specifically, the study highlighted the assignment around preserving the attention span of students and of controlling or guiding how their explicit their personal know-how of their sexuality. In terms of the previous, this turned into mainly obtrusive at some point of the observations and interviews with the academics. In my commentary, the researcher recorded that: An eight to twelve months-antique autistic girl turned into very energetic, in and out of the schoolroom, getting her to live nonetheless to talk to her was near not possible but she, in the end, gave me precisely minutes of interest in which I used to be able to get her to signal her name, she managed to sign the primary letters and mumble some stuff earlier than she ran off." the academics' responses to the interview questions supplied some perception in this. In that admire, trainer A said that: Having unique disabilities can be hard due to the fact each toddler's stage of development is distinctive, and the trainer has to work doubly difficult to put together for them and ensure that each baby is reached at their various stages. Using having a short attention span, instructors may also need to repeat themselves for the sake of a toddler who has lost interest at some stage in the lesson. In speaking to the equal issue, she additionally shared that a number of these disabilities often go omitted in the classroom. She said consequently that "every so often they seem ordinary but we are forgetting that they've one or more than one disabilities". The difficulty in this case for teacher A is that "we genuinely don't recognize what we're dealing with, a way to deal with it". She insisted that whilst we "are doing our satisfactory, we are treating with something that we aren't exposed to." trainer B additionally said that there are students with special disabilities and having a differentiated lesson is usually difficult. She stated that: I have skilled being with a pupil who's deaf but is aware of whilst he's doing right, knows when he's doing incorrect and would climb the walls, lie down inside the cabinet, lie down under the table, hit the scholars, lie down in a corner at the back of the pc desk and all of that is occurring while looking to get a lesson done and the project of having him settle occasionally is non-existent.

As a way of summarizing her stories round this, she also shared that: They revel in (as a unique education trainer) has opened my eyes because I have been in primary, secondary and now special schooling and it is a whole distinction, things that we take as a right, so tying a shoelace, buttoning a button, saying precise morning, all the ones things have modified for me. If I have a scholar that has by no means been capable to talk and say a phrase, it's a massive factor, so being a unique educator has made me respect the lifestyles that we enjoy generally and facilitates me to higher recognize and take time to deal with special students at their level understanding that I'm able to rush the curriculum with them, knowing that if I'm running on the letter "A" for the whole term I must prepare the assets for that and assembly their specific need and watching them grow and taking part in it. The academics also spoke to the challenges around college students' expression in their sexuality inside the lecture room. In both instances, they called for extra interventions and training of these college students on the way to recognize their frame and relate to others of the alternative sex. In that regard, teacher B indicated that "those kids' sexual urges are more advanced than the common man and that is a challenge due to the fact you have to always be at the lookout for touching in numerous parts and you have to be alert and aware". whilst she did now not elaborate too much on this factor, she insisted however that addressing those challenges requires wanted intervention and the adoption of unique strategies in and outdoor of the schoolroom.

Musical intervention and pupil participation

One of the most invisible locating of the examination became the extent to which using music as a mastering and teaching device affected the extent of scholar player. In truth, from the interviews, it seemed that the use of tune as an intervention tool solicited the willingness of the students to take part in classroom activities and the engagement of students into the lesson. This was clean at some stage in the shipping and execution of the instructions on June fourth, in which the scholars had to pick out and healthy letters to an image. In reviewing the method of the instructor, the researcher mentioned that the researchers required that the scholars fit the letters of the alphabet with photos that had been positioned before them. So one can help the scholars, the researcher cited that the lecturers also sang the alphabet with a specific rhythm to stimulate the scholars. In talking to using track trainer B said the subsequent: I exploit music every day due to the scholars I have in my magnificence, to learn the alphabet, to learn the syllables of their call and that kind of aspect, so let's say your name is Paulena, I'll make a clapping out of it Paul-ena Paul-ena. One unique student, she doesn't have an awful lot speech, however the ABC song that became played every day, she's able to say it how she can, in her very own way and to better apprehend the students.

In observing this lesson, the researcher mentioned that the students right now sang alongside; without the encouragement of the academics. In searching at the responses from teachers, the researcher additionally discovered that this response was due to the unique integration of the rhythmic factor of the lesson. In truth, instructor B indicated that "I recognize that song is a way to the touch them, get them to study, to open up greater than the everyday chalk and speak." Likewise, teacher A's in reaction to the identical query indicated "music is a medium that most individuals will gravitate to". Even as instructor A cautioned that this will affect both college students in the mainstream classrooms and people in unique colleges, she insisted that this become mainly a success for students with learning disabilities. In reality, each teacher recommended that the use of songs inside the lecture room has left a nice effect on the scholars. In truth, she advised that the incorporation of tune, not best solicited their participation, but that this participation also extended their mastering of the principles or the work. In that regard, teacher A additionally stated that: Participation in my classroom via tune has positively impacted the learning for those students in that the repetition, once you play or provide them the ones beats they'll quickly get that, what you put obtainable; what you want them to present you returned, so it's like a give and take. You play with them thru tune and that they study even better. In that regard, trainer A elaborated that using the tune "holds the interest of college students." She is careworn that "the day will run smoother if you start a lesson with the track; it would surely seize them". She cautioned that "their attention span isn't always as large as, you will start with this and after the song, you drop the little sensible and concept a part of it and to being incorporated to educate that difficulty area". Trainer A introduced that this interest in mastering prolonged while instructors used different ways which include visible and acting arts, physical education, wearing and outside activities, and gardening. Teacher B speculated on the purpose of why the song elevated the engagement of college students. In that regard, teacher B stated that the use of tune as a coaching tool helps to build the memory and enthusiasm of college students; a response that added of their study room gaining knowledge of. thus, she stated that "what changed into recognizing is that it builds memory, even whilst you assume that they may not be paying attention, the use of music makes them learn". Given the above, trainer B brought that "song has to be utilized in coaching the whole lot because it may be incorporated into any issue". She is also unique tin hat instructors can incorporate this into the "set induction of the lesson".

Musical interventions and behavioral demanding situations

While the usage of track in the lecture room improved their participation, it became also clear that it intensified the demanding situations of dealing with students who had different levels of getting to know disabilities. On June fifth, the present-day researcher referred to that "as soon as the song teacher arrived, they began to leap, and scream and it took approximately ten minutes to calm them". On June sixth, the modern-day researcher made the following observation changed into made: It becomes easily recognized that each baby desires to be concerned if one infant realizes that they are being unnoticed, that's when they turn out to be difficult and display symptoms of wanting the teacher's interest. It was clear that within the study room placing they're very restless and mischievous in place of music time after they get very excited. Once the tune trainer arrived, they started to leap, and scream and it took about ten minutes to calm them. Upon final touch of the found lesson, it changed into noted that considered one of my hearing impaired cases played the drum and there has been an apparent distinction in his behavior when he became assigned the drum; he became almost wild with pleasure, as opposed to his mischievous classroom behavior. The teacher turned into displaying him how to beat the drum and his pleasure changed into so much, he did his personal issue, she needed to calm him before she may want to hold. After approximately five minutes she becomes capable of settling him and among the others and carries on with her elegance. The other one changed into very reserved at song time however very attentive and alert, I used to be of the assumption that he didn't need to play the pan, however, I couldn't confirm my suspicion. He confirmed exhilaration, but he changed into bent on being sly and mischievous so from time to time he could forestall and beat any other pupil's pan, or drum. When he realized that he become being observed, he would smile and do what he knew he should be doing. In this case, the remark was that using the track as a teaching device triggered a very different behavior for those youngsters. In this case, their elevated participation additionally required the use of extra control techniques for the lecturers. Once this came about, then instructors resorted to other psychological and educational measures to manipulate/calm their college students.

The calming technique concerned sternly addressing the

magnificence collectively or calling the child/children who seemed disruptive. It could even involve a little "palms up, out, up out and down." to get them to settle themselves and get quiet. As soon as calm, the lesson commenced." The lesson plans show that interplay is in truth common, extra so amongst teacher and infant, as the instructor needs to be repetitive and makes use of quite a few reinforcing techniques within the class setting. That is proven by way of the usage of the word repetition after each section in the lesson plan. The lesson plans also display that repetition is the custom within the classroom and the statement confirms it. Repetition guarantees that the kid is getting to know and retaining what is being taught. The need for high-quality reinforcement for learning additionally required using more than one strategy. Therefore, instructors additionally repeated a concept in more than one instance to make certain that the kids are paying interest and they recognize. Once in a while, it concerned the trainer calling on a selected child to copy what become stated, which is added to ensure that the kid is centered and is familiar with what is being taught. From observation I cited that the trainer can also even say "repeat after me" and allow the magnificence to copy an assertion or word at the same time as she teaches, this too ensures retention and alertness. In all instances, this required that teachers use their instructor schooling abilities and adopt school room control strategies that also aided gaining knowledge of inside the schoolroom. instructor A insisted that this turned into particularly vital in view that "it isn't usually clean to get these kids to pay the interest due to the fact they naturally have a short interest span." instructor B shared her personal enjoyment of trying a couple of strategies (reading, writing, homework) and of no longer succeeding with those. She called for greater attention to the techniques used given the various demanding situations around coaching youngsters with disabilities. She also stressed the subsequent: praise, praise, and results! As a good deal as they have got disabilities, they understand the consequences of being rewarded and not rewarded. Many have used that lot and it seems to work. The song is one of my biggest strategies in seeking to keep the kids calm, a generation so if it is you perform this particular project, you're allowed ten minutes or fifteen minutes of track time or any shape of a generation that you like, and it works. She additionally said that the usage of manipulative becomes a critical aspect of having college students worried about their mastering techniques and preserving their interest span. She stated that "now not all my students' function, so you should get them into it, the usage of manipulative or locating out where their interest lies so one can get them to the characteristic".

Need for Social aid

Instructors additionally insisted that coaching kids with studying disabilities remained an assignment and that transferring forward required extra sorts of social assist to cope with some of the more than one demanding situation (cognitive and behavioral) that impacts those students. In handling those demanding situations, the lecturers insisted that addressing those required sorts of social assist that prolonged beyond the teaching of these college students. Trainer A suggested the want to increase better family members with the students. She stated the subsequent: I try to expand a dating; a real sturdy dating with those students, because a number of them you understand their backgrounds and also you try to touch absolutely everyone, you try and attain out to all people of their little very own manner which will sense relaxed, come to you and speak to you as a friend because, at the give up of the day, most humans just need any person to have a listening ear. also what I have started, I want them to experience a part of something subject is, so in the grammar, I might come to them one morning and say "hello what y'all did over the weekend and I would jot it down, however, they say it, I'll write it after which we will cross and edit it, so that is my story for the week, all people placed up their tale, from there we'll grab the vocabulary, all of the situation areas so they'll feel aside, this is all about me, wow. That's what I've begun now and then you definitely see that they're absolutely interested in learning. Every other project both instructors shared was the task of a lack of guidance from dad and mom. Teacher A said that this is especially important given the want to maintain the interest and learning potential of those college students. She shared the subsequent: I'm not bashing dad and mom or anything like that, I'm no longer, however occasionally parents don't make the effort out to sit and concentrate and understand their special wishes toddler, you special, o.k. you sit down in a nook, go and watch television, but running with them you recognize that they've stories similar to every other baby and now and then they'll now not be capable of express themselves at home so having that one on one relationship with them makes them sense at ease, make them feel every day. Being a part of the entirety, the sporting occasions, the tune festivals, those various things, build their vanity and self-confidence and it is going a protracted manner. Using pointing out the above, the instructor expressed grave problems over different social and psychological troubles that students with learning disabilities face. A part of addressing these problems she said blanketed the need for a holistic technique wherein multiple partners were concerned.

Thus, instructor B said that: The college wishes to have the team, the group that works with the students, the physiotherapist, the occupational therapist, the social worker, the steering officer, we need that crew if we don't have that team of individuals we're failing due to the fact we have college students who need speech remedy that I may not be able to provide or leave out might not be capable of providing however you would possibly have the social employee, coming in as soon as each term. This does nothing for the scholars! It's useless, so having that help, actual aid, now not just, very well the ministry coming, let's faux, no longer that form of help, we need the actual help due to the fact listening and going around to conferences or whatever it's far. She, therefore, referred to as for an extra holistic method that protected an extra high-quality and inclusive mindset toward kids with learning disabilities. In speaking to this, she shared the experience of listening to a person push aside the possibility of working with these kids based on the stereotypes that they had approximately them. She shared the following: I do not forget going to 1 of those young people programs. I spoke to the person in fee and that I added myself. I defined that I am looking to get the scholars into the program and he became inclined but when he went to his superior, his superior shut it down pronouncing "how ought to you say yes and bring the ones unique youngsters here, who do you anticipate to assist them? And I was appalled because these are our kingdom's children. even though they'll not be capable of write CXC or NCSE they might be precise in woodwork, they are probably appropriate in music, they might be able to make a drum or something else and it became, in reality, disappointing to peer that the entire college was close down because human beings didn't recognize what it meant to have a disability. It's virtually coronary heart-breaking." Given such, she insisted that the problem extended past the study room. She referred to as for greater interventions that addressed these issues and promoted a more inclusive and embracing method to students with studying disabilities. In responding to this comment, trainer A also alluded to the reality of aid for kids with unique needs. She responded with the following: For me, I can relate to this, it touches domestic, due to the fact I'm a figure of an infant with special desires, so I'm residing it, I see that matters take lengthy in the machine, you need to actually knock on doors and you're shut out in case you don't really persist, so a number of the mother and father that I know of these children on the faculty, they're now not exposed, they don't truly know wherein to visit because if I wasn't at this school, I wouldn't have been uncovered to most of this stuff and genuinely say wow, if I don't get this, I will cross here, ok, because I went to a workshop and the query that I'd have asked, y'all are speaking about early intervention, in which are we able to move for early intervention? And that I was given the politically accurate answer, but afterward the individual came to me and stated there's none so within the occasion that these youngsters are simply left behind, what's the following pass? Who can the figure go to?"

"Given the above, each instructor called for education of teachers who engage with children with getting to know disabilities. Teacher A said that "everybody must be trained; do a nationwide sensitization of special needs and address how they are handled after they depart college. She insisted that the intervention needs to address the problems that they face each inside and outside of the school machine if an exchange is to be found out. Instructor B also had similar sentiments. She said that: I apprehend that human beings don't understand what special desires are, they don't understand what it approaches to have a disability or even when the officers from the ministry of training or whoever come to visit, we put on a façade for them to sing the students sing and dance however they don't simply apprehend what it's miles to come back take a seat in a lecture room and reality work and notice the scholars at their worst and see the scholars at their fine. So my recommendation is to have all and sundry skilled, do a national sensitization of special desires, and being accepting due to the fact when college students leave the faculty what are they going to do? Work in a resort? Work a little CEPEP? That's now not precise enough, they may be higher than that. She also referred to as for greater specialized training that addressed the challenges of coaching and gaining knowledge for college kids with disabilities. She insisted that: All teachers; all team of workers of special schools learn and now not simply trained in special schooling, but one teacher can move and do hearing impairment, one trainer should do autism, one teacher ought to do getting to know disabilities, one teacher ought to do intellectual disabilities so that we've got an extensive sort of information so that the understanding base would be high-quality. these children may not be capable of writing the examinations that would allow them to feature in a normal job placing doing clerical work, however, their talent set is unlimited, they just need the possibility. From the quotes, it may be interpreted that the special training department lacks a guide. Support from parents, assistance from numerous departments within the schooling department, and preferred help from the department itself. It's very feasible that if most of these entities come together and work collectively for the betterment of the school and its kids, matters will be plenty better.

Chapter Nine

The Importance of Grouping

Grouping is a set of related humans performing collectively, specifically within a bigger corporation. Capability grouping is a not unusual practice in today's classrooms, which involves using intelligence checks to location people ensure academic groups with others who have equal competencies. Sorts of potential grouping encompass among-elegance and inside-magnificence grouping, which offer each blessing and stumbling blocks in a study room putting. Whilst a school or trainer businesses students "primarily based on their capability or achievement," the college is practicing among-class capacity grouping. In lots of instances, among-elegance ability grouping is utilized in an excessive college putting as a manner to institution students with comparable goals and skills. This shape of grouping is used in fundamental colleges in which a classroom instructor divides the scholars into two or three corporations based totally on student potential. This sort of grouping is much less debatable than between-magnificence grouping however that can be due to less research. In this form of grouping, a teacher may additionally divide kids into businesses depending on the challenge count number. This makes it less complicated for the teacher to teach however may also have detrimental results on the overall schoolroom. Inside-class capability grouping like among-class benefits the ones within the better group, leaving those college students at the back of conflict if they do no longer achieve the right guide. This could create tension amongst students in addition to an inner struggle inside those that are positioned on a slower tempo. Although among-magnificence and within-elegance ability grouping have many benefits, a trainer desires to understand that many damaging reactions can rise especially for those college students placed in a set that isn't always working at a faster pace. With the many types of intelligence tests, also come many theories. Two theorists which have outlined their own understandings of intelligence consist of Robert Sternberg and Howard Gardner, every theorist presenting a very exclusive view of intelligence. Robert Sternberg states that "intelligence comes in three most important bureaucracy: analytical, creative, and practical". Analytical includes the capabilities of evaluation and reading, innovation involves advent and creativeness to create an outcome. Capability grouping is an extensively unfold practice used amongst many educators today. Among-magnificence grouping is by way of ways one of the most normally used forms of capacity grouping. "The purpose of grouping is for each magnificence to engage students who're homogeneous in standardized intelligence or achievement check ratings".

In this form of grouping, the faculties separate their college students into special lessons or publications. "Among-elegance potential grouping is where students spend a maximum of the day in potential organizations and use the equal or comparable curriculum substantially adjusted to their potential degrees. This impacts their success degree and in turn impacts their vanity. Such consequences reason the students to become bored in faculty, and in the long run, many of those students begin to drop out. Although there are certain benefits to between-elegance potential grouping, they may be outweighed by the terrible consequences this kind of grouping can produce. in the long run, the point of interest has to not be on how to label college students, however alternatively, at the quality of the training, the scholars can acquire whilst work with friends in precise concern areas. Regrouping is any other sort of potential grouping. Students of equal age, potential, and grade, however from special school rooms, are added collectively for a particular concern together with studying or math. In line with their desires, activities, and character desires, the scholars are grouped and then regrouped again. There are common regrouping strategies: teacher-led businesses and student-led organizations. Instructor-led groups are effective in introducing material, summing up the realization made by using the companies and meeting the common needs of the organizations. Those corporations commonly encompass entire magnificence, small group, and man or woman instruction. Complete class preparation permits the teacher to introduce new material to the whole elegance. It also allows students to apply their earlier understanding to shape new acquisitions. "Small organizations can offer opportunities for operating with college students who have common desires, inclusive of reinforcement or enrichment". Institution work is a mode of getting to know I've struggled with for much of my coaching career. The idea of college students operating together to learn is precious for many motives, however, growing a group hobby wherein all college students are engaged within the collective work can be difficult. Currently, I attempted a group essay writing interest that now not simplest worried every scholar inside the mission but also created situations for rich student discussion that ended in some real boom in their writing abilities. The significance of group Work in present-day companies it can be argued that so one can achieve success, modern-day agencies need to actively develop strong and cohesive work corporations. Why? Is it actual that there is no room for the individualist in these days' business enterprise? The fast progression and development in the records and conversation era have led to modern employers locating new approaches to work. One of these innovative methods is the use of workgroups. More organizations are actually turning international than ever, which means that they depend on dispensed groups to perform certain responsibilities. For the truth that the task must be finished via a collection way, it needs employees with one-of-a-kind capabilities. Consequently, managers must discover workers who can satisfy the requirement of the project and ensure the right schooling is given to them.

According to Belbin, he diagnosed nine roles and argued that all the roles should be fulfilled for a collection to be powerful. However now not all work institutions are composed of 9 participants which means that some members may additionally soak up a couple of roles. Although all the nine roles won't be vital in a collection which means it could be a waste of time for managers to try to have nine contributors with all the roles. In addition, managers need to be careful while placing one-of-a-kind humans in a collection due to the fact conflicts can get up so that they have to make certain that the group member's traits complement every other. Richard Hackman suggested that various factors could affect a group's cohesiveness. The time given to finish the mission and form of leadership fashion can determine how individuals within the organization engage with each other. The group participants must speak with one another so duplication of labor does no longer occur and vital statistics circulate on time. Resources ought to accept on time so that the institution does now not enjoy any postpone, which may additionally affect their project.

Cindy explained the significance of group work in schooling; she stated, "When I was in excessive faculty, and one in all my teachers might ask us to form companies to be able to do something, I would commonly roll my eyes. Sarcastically enough, a number of the nice work that I placed fourth and found out from was accomplished in a collection work placing. Via working with my peers towards a common stop, I got things executed a whole lot quicker and thoroughly than I ever did by myself. I chose to research institution work for this essay because in my restricted enjoy as a trainer, children worker, and pupil, institution work proves to be the best teaching technique; whilst it's miles completed effectively,"

However for students to become authors and creators and speakers in the schoolroom shows new roles for them and different teachers. College students need to speak. Studies indicate that each instructor commonly takes up seventy to ninety% of class time. John S. Mayher figured out the facts although every student was capable to speak in elegance; inside a forty-five-minute duration, if each member of a thirty-student elegance talked for one and a half minutes a period that would be seven and a half minutes per week. That rarely seems enough time to pretty makes a contribution to one's very own ideas to a class. By developing their oral language competencies in the classroom, college students will expand a capability for universal understanding and alertness of and in getting to know each in all regions. The best manner of growing oral language abilities and getting enough time to place them into practice is by way of the use of organizational work. Coming to recognize is an active procedure wherein the learner should be engaged in acts of discovery and inquiry, and, as Vygotsky has shown, this procedure always takes vicinity within a particular social/cultural context, with language internalized from and fashioned by way of that context. Most real global gaining knowledge of takes place in interaction with others, however, maximum lecture rooms isolate learners from that type of interplay. The institution inside the classroom mirrors the way most people examine out of doors the lecture room.

Organization work calls for students to ask questions and explain their factors of view to others. This not most effectively assists college students to grow the opportunities to use their know-how but additionally complements their interest and capability of getting to know. Moreover, it allows them to accept distinctive opinions, extends their insights, and promotes the sustainability and development of wondering. It helps to enhance studying efficiency. That could consult with every member of the organization to actively participate within the gaining knowledge of method and activities; every member must have high-quality enthusiasm, and learn from duties shared by everybody. Also, it is endorsed that every member must brainstorm, and express their factor of views. Absolutely everyone is likewise encouraged to proportion their efforts and do their nice with the strength created, so the hassle can be solved. Organization work can enhance the cooperative feelings among college students, and develop college students' interpersonal skills. organization work is a system of replacing data and expertise among college students, which refers back to the development of directing the emotion and senses using speaking and helping others, and especially know-how the lifestyle differences which refers to one-of-a-kind backgrounds. It has to be found out that to take care and assist each other via spotting their merits and also be tolerant of their shortcomings. Moreover, it is endorsed to pay attention with an open mind to research from others and listen to their points of view. This could permit every member to integrate themselves right into a collective group and beautify their collective recognition. It additionally assists college students to increase their self-getting to know the potential. Organization work involves students participating in place of being bystanders. It encourages the student who has mastered certain knowledge and abilities to transfer and educate others who do not have themselves. Students who seek excellent performance in group work have to carefully research the class material and examine thru the text e-book studying its content. Some contents might not be available in modern-day textbooks, so it encourages students to locate information by way of searching on the net and also makes a few notes. Those projects improve scholar studying so that it promotes their self-mastering competencies. Group work broadens the mastering space for college kids. It's a manner that transfers the character competition to a collaborative institution attempt.

Group work is a cooperative studying among students via trade with the purpose to achieve complementary strengths to promote knowledge of production, fully arouse the student's subjective attention, and explore their issue of customized mastering, and growing college students' creativity and innovation. Also, it makes college students examine in an open ecosystem, and carry out lively exchanges of facts and knowledge; as a consequence enhancing self-confidence, selling for the excellent practice of possibilities. Further to growing students' sense of opposition, the collective values and spirit of cooperation so establish a corresponding development for exclusive students. "An organization is a social association which pursues collective goals, controls its very own overall performance and has a boundary separate from its surroundings" (ACCA). Businesses are vital in each business enterprise. The effectiveness of agencies influences the overall performance in addition to getting work done; companies provide social pleasure to their contributors. a set accommodates of or greater interacting and interdependent individuals who understand that they're contributors of a group and with a reason of achieving common goals. There are formal and casual organizations in an organization. Formal groups are in the main closed businesses. Their membership is tight and described. There's no flexibility however there are rules and harmony of reason which each member should try to adhere to. The team spirit and cooperation among the members of a closed organization removes creative differences making sure effectiveness. An example of this sort of organization is a work team. A work team is a set of individuals with complementary competencies, decided on from a group to obtain a deliberate goal. other than the workgroup are different varieties of formal corporations; the command group which is the traditional workgroup as visible inside the organizational chart of an organization wherein there's a manager with subordinates who are answerable to him, the pass-functional crew is introduced together due to their expertise and capabilities. The self-controlled crews are an unbiased group and task force is a form of the formal group set up for a particular project and dissolved as quickly as the venture is achieved. The distinction between group and team is that group is any series of humans with a commonplace purpose whereas team is associated "with sports, implies choice, similar competencies, cohesiveness, exercise, education, and leadership". A casual group is of a social nature. Such businesses are more for the advantage of their participants than for the business enterprise to which they belong. An example of an informal institution is the workplace hiking membership.

Handiest workgroups build shared values and techniques of working to satisfy the agency's goals and needs of its members. In assessment, a useless workgroup may be a soreness for its individuals and useless for the agency. Informal groups are open organizations; members should alternate their membership at any time as they move up the ladder of leadership. There are extraordinary reasons why individuals be a part of businesses in agencies. Becoming a member of an informal institution may want to most of the time be spontaneous than joining a formal institution. human beings be a part of organizations including alternate unions to guard their employment rights, guide groups for emotional assist, to help them carry out difficult tasks in other words to assist them to grow. Formal companies are basically formed via managers for technical, governing, and normative motives. Technically, inside the sense that, to increase output, it'll be clean for the manager to delegate obligations and process management. It isn't below all situations that the institution work always is the nice and powerful. as an instance, someday we can see this kind of state of affairs takes place: when the scholars within the institution all through cooperative studying or reporting exchanges, they both say nothing or have no consensus agreement but handiest shape their subjective factors of view. The primary cause this situation occurs is that students either do no longer examine in intensity or apprehend the magnificence fabric very well or haven't any case coaching. Consequently, students must take a look at it in advance and recognize the importance and highlights from the route. In addition, group work needs to have some exciting content material, feasibility, and open inquiry through determining the center of content material and time wishes for cooperative institution studying. We need to not ignore and avoid the person's duty to assume independently within the cooperative institution studying. In general, organization work within the lecture room is based totally on the process of this structure this is 1). responsibilities lead the manner, 2). the individual independent learning, 3).institution studying, 4).institution exchanges, 5).collective assessment. In other phrases, for brand spanking new knowledge, new information, and college students need to assume independently, so the intensity of questioning, high quality, and originality may be developed. via, institution gaining knowledge of, man or woman opinions can be launched, so anybody in the organization has a hazard to share the ideas and outcome of the dialogue; then the institution will summarize every one of the records and contents, and report to the whole magnificence via deciding on a collection consultant. Ultimately, the group outcome can be regarded beneath assessment of the magnificence and via the trainer. The teachers are being empowered, reacquainted with the desires of the organization and the enterprise, via the introduction of workgroups, intend to lessen conflicts, motivation issues, and variations inside the place of work. There are distinct degrees within the formation of corporations as developed through Tuckman's version; the primary degree is the forming level. At this preliminary stage, the institution is cautiously coming collectively, At the second degree that's the storming degree, there may be a struggle in the organization as contributors get familiar but locate it difficult to lose their individuality, at the 0.33 stage, the norming degree, the contributors are becoming comfortable to do the undertaking for which they were accumulated and they're turning into a knit organization and on the fourth and very last level, the appearing stage, the individual roles are cleared and shared. Maximum of the blessings of groups in agencies are in selection-making. Institution choices offer extra whole information than personal choice. As the announcing goes "heads are better than one".

Groups are made from a diversity of human beings and they create their experience and perspectives to the decision technique which a character cannot offer. For instance, organization choice turned into a major tool inside the genesis of Zima, a clean malt beverage product marketed using Coors to the technology. There are more options to answers generated because of the divers' club of a group specifically while the organization is made of humans with unique specialties. It's pretty clean for the organization to just accept the decision because they've participated in achieving such a choice and consequently they may assist convince their colleagues to just accept the decision. Organization decisions are considered more legitimate than the ones made through people for the reason that character has not consulted another to arrive at the decision made. People are benefitted by way of group decisions as they are shielded from character duties, there may be a splendid opportunity to analyze and decorate self by way of interacting with distinctive forms of humans with divergent specialties. Individuals gain in more methods than notable. Even though the outcome of a challenge is a group's final results, the names of group individuals go down in records. In keeping with some pupils, character motivation is based totally on cognitive and behavioral strategies. Self-efficacy is a belief in a single's abilities to prepare and execute the path of motion required to produce given attainments. In teams, character goal-striving captures participants' allocation of personal effort closer to institution desires which might also involve effort directed at appearing their personal position within the organization in addition to supporting others perform their roles. Person performance and group motivation promote crew effectiveness. Due to the interdependent nature of person roles in agencies, participants are likely to be greater efficient regarding their roles once they trust that their institution is highly able to act its collective venture. People look at group buddies as critical means for his or her success in a piece team therefore group efficacy is an important supply of self-efficacy.

There are hazards of institution selections to each organization and the character. those are; deciding by the group is time-consuming and can incur some costs since the organization has to be accrued in contrast to the individual choice, In a group, a few individuals have extra capabilities and competencies than others, this could suggest that some members dominate others in decision making due to the possession of these skills, there is also the pressure to agree to whatever choice arrived at by the organization even though it might not be perfect to the character, therefore there's the stress to conform to the way of institution wondering; Naylor. Organization assume is a phenomenon wherein contributors of a set withhold something views they will have with the intention to provide the appearance of settlement. Apart from the above-mentioned blessings and disadvantages of corporations to each man or woman and the business enterprise, there are elements which hamper organization performance in maximum if not all companies. These are: the scale of a workgroup undermines its overall performance because there's no limit to the membership of a workgroup. The number of participants depends on the number of duties and their related elements that need to be completed at any factor in time. the size of a workgroup now not most effective impacts the organization's overall performance, it reduces lively participation of individuals while the institution club exceeds five or seven, participants come to be authoritarian, participation is inhibited, there's a want for guidelines and rules in large organizations. choices take longer to reach than in smaller businesses, activity delight and productiveness reduces and there are chances of social loafing or free-driving springing up as co-ordination turns into tough in large businesses. Cohesiveness is another issue that could affect an institution's overall performance. Cohesiveness is a measure of ways a lot of members of a collection are interested in and want to remain with a set". Small size organizations tend to be greater together than large organizations. The institution is normally made of people whose talents supplement each other, they have a commonplace cause and they locate pride in each different organization. There are several other elements as cited by Slobodnik and Slobodnik which adversely have an effect on workgroup overall performance, these are; some individuals might also falsely supply assent to a suggestion or a choice, there may be unresolved overt warfare which could reason a few contributors to leave, there might be underground conflicts occurring giving upward push to distrust, there can be contributors who may also locate it tough to attain closure in controversy, there are individuals who're inflexible in approaches of doing things, therefore, they play the same role at each meeting and individuals no longer having equal possibility at participating in responsibilities will reason a waste of sources.

Take for instance the running Room (OR) of an enterprise that includes NHS, the place of a human thing includes understanding and talents which affects the technical performance of the running Room workgroup. Such elements are related to the powerful communique, institution formation and renovation, management and choice-making, control of assets, workload prioritization, distribution, and coping with stress. The fact that the human elements of institution performance in the OR have been left out for one of these long time because of the narrow-minded awareness on technical problems indicates an extensive imbalance while the truth that seventy to eighty percent of anesthetic and surgical mishaps are caused by human thing issues regarding interpersonal interactions among OR workgroup. By carrying out a scientific observation of the OR workgroup it became apparent to encompass all OR personnel informal training which could address the problems in interpersonal troubles. "The factors which make a system prone to accidents are the complexity of interactions and tightness of coupling". The use of a structured approach to consist of each person operating in OR environment took under consideration the person, organizational, physical, and social context of all or workgroup. In keeping with this method, interactive processes and overall consequences depend on organizational, environmental, and man or woman elements. in this study, the maximum vital final results factors are affected person protection and quality of remedy however whilst assets are limited coupled with "other variables which motive rationing of healthcare, operational integrity end up crucial together with efficient operation, excessive productivity and advanced process delight and running morale". a few enterprises manage those issues higher than others .this could depend upon the subculture of such agency, which is the way it thinks, shows attention, shows a reminiscence and capacity to create and to solve issues. What subculture is to a business enterprise, the persona is to a man or woman? It's far the subculture of an enterprise that determines what duties are done, how they react to failure and mishaps. The exercise of powerful workgroup coordination, communication, decision making, vigilance, and tracking collectively with technical challenge overall performance ought to improve to an extraordinary extent the opportunity of optimum operational integrity regarding patient protection and productiveness. This will no longer most effective increase morale and activity delight but also improve attitudes and organizational performance. Mentioned above are the different varieties of businesses, the tiers they undergo in the course of their development stage and some instances of studies executed about the effect companies have on individuals and groups usually. While groups are set up for inappropriate functions they can waste sources and can grow to be effective resistors to exchange and some individuals can also leave or come to be less fascinated and they will see managing with such trees as a waste of time.

Advantages of organization work

It's far often said that extra hands make for lighter work, heads are better than one, and the more the merrier. These adages talk to the capacity organizations have to be extra effective, creative, and motivated than people on their own. Group projects can assist college students to develop a host of abilities which are an increasing number of essential in the expert global. Tremendous group reviews, furthermore, have been shown to make contributions to pupil studying, retention, and average college success. Properly established, organization projects can strengthen talents that apply to both group and person work, along with the potential to:

- Destroy complex duties into components and steps
- Plan and manage time
- Refine know-how through dialogue and clarification
- Give and get hold of comments on performance
- Venture assumptions
- Increase more potent communication abilities.

Organization initiatives also can assist college students to expand skills unique to collaborative efforts, allowing college students to...

- Tackle extra complicated issues than they could on their own.
- Delegate roles and duties.
- Proportion numerous views.
- Pool understanding and competencies.
- Keep each other (and be held) responsible.
- Obtain social help and encouragement to take dangers.
- Increase new strategies to resolving differences.
- Establish a shared identity with other organization contributors.
- Discover powerful peers to emulate.
- Develop their own voice and perspectives about peers.

Even as the capacity getting to know benefits of group work are significant, certainly assigning group work isn't any assure that those desires could be finished. In reality, organization tasks can – and frequently do – backfire badly when they may be now not designed, supervised, and assessed in a way that promotes significant teamwork and deep collaboration.

Faculty can regularly assign extra complicated, real

problems to agencies of students than they might to individuals. Organization work additionally introduces greater unpredictability in coaching, because groups may additionally technique duties and solve problems in novel, interesting ways. This may be clean for instructors. Moreover, institution assignments may be beneficial whilst there are a constrained wide variety of viable project topics to distribute among college students. And they can lessen the number of final products teachers have to grade. Regardless of the benefits in phrases of teaching, instructors must take care best to assign group work duties that clearly satisfy the gaining knowledge of objectives of the route and lend themselves to collaboration. Instructors ought to additionally be aware that institution initiatives can upload work for faculty at different points within the semester and introduce its very own grading complexities.

Potential grouping according to W.E.B Du Bois is that schooling is the entire device of human training within and without the schoolhouse partitions, which molds and develops guys. Grouping students via their instructional capacity has emerged as quite a trend within the USA. The upward push of this movement has constructed some questions from mother and father and educators. some of those questions consist of: is it hurting or assisting the scholars, what is the difference between simple and excessive school grouping, what do educators need to realize, and need to mother and father be more worried? Academic grouping allows students to learn extra at their own pace, and there are numerous reasons why it must be stored in our faculty machine. Instructors have a harder time coaching college students who're on specific tiers. The divergence within the study room can purpose students to experience just like the trainer isn't showing them enough quantity of attention. While we institution college students it grants the teacher greater time to easily help anybody straight away. In elementary school students are grouped by way of their analyzing or math skills. This approach lets the trainer assist every student in their weaker fields. Every other grouping approach is to the institution the scholars by way of common interest. The grouping isn't the motive of the scholars' transcendence, but what takes place in the corporation's units the scholars on their route to fulfillment. Kids experience more comfortable with classmates who are on the equal instructional degree as they are. The mutual feeling enables the kids to do the quality they could, and now not sense as they need to do higher than one another. Even though grouping isn't always tested to help shallowness, it may boost a few scholar's self-assurance.

Grouping in excessive school isn't always that special in comparison to basic college. In 9th-grade, college students select the route to their degree, either advanced or popular. In superior class college students research at a quicker pace. The instructions in advance are greater like college preparatory training, while, preferred are simple. Fashionable lessons are for those people who decide to move straight into the personnel and instructors in excessive college have a less difficult time teaching college students in divided training. One of the most difficult demanding situations facing teachers is the issue of differentiation. Matching the studying issue of texts and curriculum coverage with scholar talent and expertise is complicated and its benefits may be diffused, T. Shanahan. What approximately move-grade or pass-magnificence grouping? A new shape of the Joplin Plan is referred to as achievement and has been properly a success. The simple idea that these getting-to-know schemes attempt is to assist meet each scholar's instructional level. For example, a second-grade level student can read on a fourth-grade level. The student in the instance could pass classes for studying, however, be on a regular second-grade stage in every different magnificence. Move grade grouping is a top-notch learning method and may assist students of all age businesses to discover ways to the nice in their capability.

Within elegance ability grouping and as a future educator, capacity grouping is greater than possibly going to be part of my lecture room. I suppose it may and might be a treasured device inefficiently coaching all college students of various skills. Potential grouping is a significantly debated area in the area of schooling. Warring parties to the practice accept as true with potential grouping is averse to mastering and scholar vanity, but ability grouping, mainly inside-elegance potential grouping, may be very powerful in teaching kids. The students are capable of research at a tempo this is appropriate to their personal skills and instructors are capable of construct classes that might be particularly geared closer to every level. Within-magnificence capacity grouping necessitates flexibility and common interactions among students and instructors to decide whether or not or not the kid is in the proper group. In potential grouping, the excessive achievers benefit from having to compete with each other. The low achievers in a group of children of comparable level sense greater comfortable and are, therefore, greater willing to take part. Kids have to no longer be positioned into companies in every situation place, however, instead of in some areas wherein grouping has verified useful. "Low-reaching students seem to examine extra in heterogeneous math training, even as excessive and common attaining students suffer success losses—and their combined losses outweigh the low achievers' gains" (Loveless, internet). Regrouping for mathematics and studying has established power. The students are in heterogeneous companies for the maximum of the day, however then are grouped in step with a stage for those subjects. "Results indicate that regrouping for studying or mathematics can improve pupil fulfillment.

The difficulty of potential grouping has induced controversy within the education network. A few schooling students say that capacity grouping. A study with the aid of Dallas independent school District discovered that ability grouping now not simplest helped the pinnacle corporations of college students, however, the entire spectrum of college students found out extra than combined-potential classrooms. This isn't always an exercise that blessings best the white, wealthy, or smart, but an exercise that allows the complete pupil body. Joann DiGennaro reminded us that mixed capacity groups hurt nearly everybody involved because the pinnacle college students are bored and unchallenged and the lowest college students are left at the back. Potential grouping ensures that each pupil in every school is challenged but organized, and forestalls each person from being left at the back of or in advance. It's far the responsibility of the education to meet the desires of each student, and capability grouping is a medium to ensure that the aim is met. With the aid of no longer grouping through ability, most of the students' desires are met no longer appropriately. The idea and belief of potential grouping are that businesses are shaped and then college students haven't any ability to alternate companies. However, the truth is that the companies can exchange and that the tests used to assign organizations are truthful. Garelick factors out that in his schooling the ability to structure practice allowed for a sense of fluidity to ensure the students had been correctly placed. Garelick states that no longer capability grouping has attempted to "dispose of the fulfillment gap via getting rid of success". By using empowering 'Americans' brightest minds, America can remedy its demanding situations and troubles within the modern global. By reaching the brightest students with capability grouping, every scholar advantages academically. The Yankee education cannot forgo the clever words of Spock on celebrity Trek, "The wishes of the many outweigh the needs of the few or the only". The "wishes of the various" are met in the potential grouping, and all students could be challenged to their complete capacity. In combined ability lessons handiest the center organization of college students wishes might be met. Ability grouping doesn't harm any scholar, nor does it discriminate a racial or socioeconomic elegance. It's far imperative that the United States colleges' capacity group their classes, and have American students higher compete with different college students around the sector.

Chapter Ten

Cross-Cultural Differences in Cognition

Communique is the replacing of facts via speaking, writing, and signals.

It performs an essential to our development; it's miles the dissemination of ideas, and information to folks. Cognition is our intellectual procedure wherein we gather information and knowledge, and that is done through our thoughts, our reports, and our senses. Cultural differences contain what humans' agree with how they behave, the language they speak, and their practices based on their ethnicity. Move-cultural variations in cognition may be very effective to sure operations conducted through persons; but, it could also restrict us based totally on our attitude. Have you ever notion approximately the importance of cognition, and the position wherein it performs in our lives? According to dictionary.com, cognition is the mental system that includes how we study and understanding matters. But, the approaches wherein we understand and interpret things are partially a result of cultural influences. In Plato's look at the thoughts, it suggests that humans apprehend through first of all identifying the basic ideas which can be buried deep inside of them, which means that the knowledge human beings' gain from their culture will decide how they study. Within the communities and the arena at large, many different cultures are responsible for the manner we suppose and behave. Aristotle, B.F. Skinner and John Locke also believed that people collect their know-how via their observations of the arena around them. As said within the articles, cognition differentiates throughout cultures, therefore, there are many exclusive effects to how individuals understand and express their views. At some point of improvement, the shape and feature of the mind are stimulated by way of the surroundings that is stimulated by way of tradition.

Lifestyle additionally impacts the things human beings see, how they are visible, and those options. Cross-cultural variations are related to the distinctive backgrounds, values, and beliefs of every way of life. Consequently, due to the differences inside cultures, there can be misunderstandings among men and women who spend time working together. A have a look at turned into performed and it was found that even when human beings are presented with identical information at an identical time, the records are processed differently because of cultural variations. Every other look at that became achieved found out that humans are accurate at mind-analyzing individuals in their personal tradition.

In keeping with who men and women associate themselves with, tradition-brain interactions amongst humans can create confusion whether or not it is private or political. Because of cultural variations, it is sometimes hard to understand human beings from within different cultures, and this may create misunderstandings and conflicts amongst people. however, when folks are exposed to other cultures, they have got the opportunity to examine and recognize different cultures and the brain can turn out to be extra culturally tuned, and that is very crucial as it can affect our relationships, our profession, and our health. No matter our ethnicity, age, perception, and cultural historical past, all of us need to rely upon our cognitive procedure to expand and characteristic nicely in our distinct stages of life. In the course of history, tradition has been a power in the manner human beings think and behave and learn. It's far apparent that cultural variations impact human beings' cognitive technique, however, despite the way people perceive matters are in keeping with lifestyle and there are many differences, there are also a few similarities, and how information is being processed appears to be the same among cultures. In keeping with Vygotsky, human cognition develops in a unique cultural context, which is the collected pattern of symbolic and non-symbolic tool that is used all through historic existence. Whorf (1956) also contends that the precise language people of various ways of life talk influences their thought strategies. In terms of the articles, cultural variations in cognition are seen even in each child and adult resulting in a few cultures being unbiased and others interdependent. as a result of cultural differences, verbal exchange is damaged all the way down to a first-rate quantity, relationships are affected negatively, social interplay turns into nearly not possible, work productiveness is unsatisfactory, and resolving problems and reasoning are unachievable. Therefore, it's critical to learn and apprehend the distinctive cultures so that cultural obstacle can be removed to a degree. although prior theories suggest that development is more or much less time-honored throughout cultures, there is growing evidence of cross-cultural differences in adults found that Western and eastern cultures appear to differ within the diploma to which they emphasize decontextualized as opposed to contextualized interpretations of gadgets; where westerners exhibited objected centered attention while Easterners exhibited extra relational targeted attention. Western and Japanese cultures appear to vary inside the diploma to which they emphasize decontextualized as opposed to contextualized interpretations of items. the important thing results broadly speaking on studies of Western kids however the usage of a ramification of experimental obligations recommend an early emphasis on items and their personal properties and sensitivity to relational shape that emerges and becomes greater sturdy at some stage in the late preschool length. It has been hypothesized that there's a shift in the course of the preschool years from extra object-based comparisons to extra relational comparisons.

Relational match-to-preferred venture in two situations, with easy or richly specific items, eastern youngsters had been typically better than U.S. kids in making relational matches with both the simple and complicated gadgets. In test two, however, within the visible seek mission U.S. children outperformed their Japanese counterparts. Modern locating indicates that there exists a bias for item-targeted evaluation by way of Western youngsters and for extra relational-targeted comparisons through Jap children. 0.33, the modern results show, for the primary time, an advantage for Western preschool children in visual search tasks; Western kids determined the target in a scene more hastily than did eastern kids, suggesting that they have been higher able to hold a targeted seek of the goal item. Fourth, the effects recommend that the relational shape incoherent scenes slow item seek times for eastern youngsters relative to U.S. kids to advocate that family members and objects compete, such that children display more advanced relational reasoning while gadgets are summary and simple and display much less advanced relational reasoning whilst gadgets are wealthy and exact. Average, then, the pattern suggests a cross-cultural double dissociation in relational-centered as opposed to item-targeted responsibilities. Researchers have discovered that there's a go subculture distinction in cognition about encoding items in an imagined social context. An observation became completed on East Asian members and American participants and the researchers determined that Japanese individuals remembered greater heritage information and their reminiscence for objects was greater impacted by using the alternate inside the background, in assessment to American participants. In some other study, which turned into an eye-tracking look to check the encoding of objects, Chua and associates observed that American individuals' awareness greater on items while Chinese language people validated eye actions to their history. Similarly to this, East Asian researchers attended to take a look at the field wherein they incorporated objectives and background comparison to Canadian participants. In phrases of cognition differences among East Asians and Canadians, researchers found out that East Asians may be extra engaged in processing context when it is required to make significant item context affiliation which allows their reminiscence for contextual information. Yang and associates tested cultural differences and age-associated failure in memory for objects and their imagined social encoding contexts through the use of an intentional context memory paradigm.

Inside the observation, context becomes defined as an imagined social state of affairs wherein stimuli have been offered to members for his or her evaluation. The look at seeks to give the outcomes of the difference in cognition of East Asian and Canadian. The research query seeks to find out "Do Chinese language and Canadian individuals vary in rating items in an imagined social context at encoding. Secondly "Are cultural variations in encoding overall performance seen in younger person preserved in older adults? And thirdly, "Do cultural variations in encoding, if any, relating to the cultural results or recognition of encoding context? For the sample populace of this have a look at, the researcher used seventy-two Canadians of European descent dwelling in Toronto and seventy-two local Chinese languages residing in Beijing. Test required contributors to finished two blocks of context memory project, referred to as relational and impartial. In sum, the observation determined that there is a clear cultural distinction in the encoding of socially significant item-context associations. The Chinese language contributors supplied higher ratings, took longer to rate, and suggested more vibrant imagery of encoding contexts than the Canadian counterparts. Also, the consequences endorse that the previously mentioned context memory gain in Chinese can also have its starting place in the production of elaborative and meaningful object-context institutions at encoding. Earlier theories/research did suggest that there may be a cross-cultural distinction in cognition in terms of encoding objects in an imagined social context. In reality, Western and Japanese cultures tend to have interaction elaborative encoding to form the higher first-class association between items and imagined social context, relative to the Canadian. They're additionally extra touchy to the context variance than Canadian participants at encoding. However, those cultural versions tend to be preserved in older adults. Additionally, older adults' context reputation may be more heavily contingent on the effort invested for the duration of encoding. However, teens may be capable of retrieve even those item-context pairs encoded with low effort. Cultural psychologists have determined one-of-a-kind patterns of wondering and notion in one-of-a-kind societies, with some cultures demonstrating a more analytic pattern and others an extra holistic sample. Cultures additionally range of their social orientations; independence vs. interdependence. Those who appoint independent social orientation tend to emphasize self-path, autonomy, and self-expression while people who hire interdependent social orientation tend to emphasize concord, relatedness, and connection. Independently-orientated cultures tend to view the self as bounded and break free others, whereas interdependently-orientated cultures tend to view the self as interconnected with an emphasis positioned on relationships. In independently-orientated cultural contexts, happiness is most customarily skilled as a socially disengaging emotion, while in interdependently-orientated cultural contexts, happiness is most usually experienced as a socially attractive emotion.

In cultures that have an unbiased social orientation, people are more inspired to enhance their individuality on the price of others but this isn't practiced in interdependently orientated cultures. Diverse studies have proven that the covariation between social orientation and cognitive style even occurs out of doors of North the US and East Asia. It's also present in societies that can be a part of the EU cultural way of life. It may therefore be concluded that the cultures which vary in social orientation all differ in which cognitive style is worried. For instance, East Europeans and individuals differ along those dimensions. Russians are extra interdependent than Americans and they're more holistic in phrases of categorization, attribution, visual interest, and reasoning approximately exchange. Similarly, Croats are more interdependent than individuals, and that they show greater holistic styles of cognition in phrases of categorization and visible interest. Recent evidence additionally indicates that comparable variations exist within Europe. Moreover, Russians, who are more interdependent than Germans additionally show greater contextual patterns of visual attention. The troubles in the articles used have been truly stated. despite using unique articles, the content becomes found to be cohesive thrusting displaying how variations in lifestyle do in fact have an impact on cognition. There have been some minor problems which include the contributors used and the dearth of literature overview based totally on the questions beneath investigation. More or additional literature could have allowed readers to thoroughly observe other pieces of studies found on the subject in addition to how these studies have been performed. Moreover, it would have constructed up correct justification as to why this precise topic became important to research. Most significantly, the overall tone of the articles displayed an independent and scientific mindset testifying to its soundness and popular credibility. There are numerous splendid pass cultural variations in cognition this changed into obtrusive within the articles. One line of evidence comes from the fact that priming independence results in analytic cognition, while priming interdependence ends in holistic cognition. Whilst combined, these findings endorse that social orientation does in reality motivate cultural variations in cognition. Moreover, evidence for cultural differences within the specificity of memory for visual records changed into additionally observed. People have a tendency to exhibited extra accuracy in exams of unique reminiscence whilst compared to East Asians no matter appearing further when trendy memory become assessed. As a result reminiscence specificity did now not appear to affect the general recognition of photographs, which would advocate that difference lies inside the fine, however no longer the quantity, of visible information remembered. It became additionally located which are clean cultural variations inside the encoding of socially or experientially meaningful item-context institutions. Chinese language contributors supplied better ratings, took longer to price, and suggested more bright imagery of encoding contexts whilst as compared to Canadian counterparts. Moreover, the effects propose that the formerly pronounced context memory gain in Chinese can also have its beginning within the production of elaborative and significant item-context associations at encoding.

Innovative education
The primary idea of progressive training has similar

qualities in all settings like: 'Emphasis on mastering by means of doing palms-on initiatives, expeditionary studying, experiential learning, integrated curriculum targeted on thematic units, Integration of entrepreneurship in to education, strong emphasis on problem fixing and critical wondering, organization work and improvement of social capabilities, understanding and motion because the desires of mastering as opposed to rote expertise, Collaborative and cooperative studying tasks, training for social responsibility and democracy, especially personalized schooling accounting for each character's personal dreams, Integration of network carrier and carrier-learning tasks into the each day curriculum, selection of problem content material by looking forward to ask what skills can be needed in destiny society, De-emphasis on textbooks in favor of varied gaining knowledge of sources, Emphasis on lifelong gaining knowledge of and social competencies, assessment by using evaluation of toddler's tasks and productions'. The hard part of this learning is the evaluation. In conventional schools, the evaluation is straightforward and finished using pre-designed assessments. On this approach, accumulating the facts, assessing the performance and the outcomes, need to be analytic. 'mixed with simulations and gamification, experiential training merchandise come to be a powerhouse of information, which can be used to supply assessments effects as it should be throughout cognitive getting to know, abilities have an effect on and goal consequences. The analytics engines in these exercise record, examine, and provide an in-depth file at the contributors' interaction in the course of the gaining knowledge of.' Experimental getting to know offers lots of methods to motivate college students to contain in the studying technique. Use of 'generation and simulations with experiential learning, institutes are making this concept to be had each time and anywhere, across a couple of gadgets. This has brought the concepts of a flipped school room, wherein the learning is going to the scholars and not the alternative manner'.

Instructors should position high-quality emphasis on getting to know through motion: hands-on projects, expeditionary learning, and experimental gaining knowledge to deal with the numerous cultures. For the matters we must examine earlier than we can do them, we study using doing them, Aristotle, The Nicomachean Ethics. Mastering through doing is an arms-on technique to gaining knowledge. The crucial exercise is the direct interplay with the surroundings to its' complete attractiveness and learning. I believe that the school should represent gift existence-existence as real and critical to the child as that which he incorporates on within the home, in the community, or on the playground, John Dewey (My Pedagogic Creed). The teachers were to present actual-life problems to the children and then manual the scholars to resolve the hassle by using supplying them with a hands-on activity to study the answer. Cooking and stitching turned into studying at faculty and be ordinary. Analyzing, writing, and math changed into to be trained within the day-by-day route of those exercises. Constructing, cooking, and sewing had these education additives in it and these sports also represented ordinary life for the students, Peggy Hickman.

In expeditionary learning, college students find out about a subject with the aid of running for an extended length to analyze and reply to a complicated question, venture, or problem. Experimental mastering based on non-public revel in and defines as studying through the mirrored image on doing". And mirrored image is the awareness of one's questioning process and its visibility to others. Its assessment satisfies the question like "why" and "how" of the getting to know, and continue with the result. And it additionally facilitates strengthening the capacity to analyze. Principal to this is the main of the mirrored image as metacognition, where college students are aware of and may describe their thinking in a manner that allows them to close the space between what they recognize and what they want to analyze. Reflective beginners assimilate new mastering, relate it to what they already understand, adapt it for their purposes, and translate thought into movement. Over time, they broaden their creativity, their capability to think significantly about records and ideas, and their metacognitive capacity (this is, their capacity to reflect on consideration on their questioning), effective Pedagogy, the brand new Zealand Curriculum. This exercise has plenty of advantages in particular nowadays, as the eye span decreased and hobby in education distract other entertainments. Experimental learning grows pupil's interest, it keeps them encouraged and satisfies their curious minds. They use essential thinking, hassle-fixing, and selection-making abilities to gather a final result. This technique gives the actual lifestyles enjoy, in which they face many demanding situations and do mistakes. However, it offers the opportunity to input the response and study the actual situations, e.g., cooking instructions.

Allow them to explore the ingredients, attempt new thoughts and learn. However, the provided surroundings need to be safe, blanketed, and right monitored. It facilitates to keep data, idea, and the idea approximately the subject. It permits their mind to procedure it for a lifetime. Management guru Henry Mintzberg pointed out long in the past that, management, like swimming, can't be learned through studying about it. It develops the confidence to manipulate, deal with, resolve troubles, and train them to get along with others nicely. As their studying surprisingly specializes in the institution activities, so collaboration helps to acquire the 'ownership of the final results'.

Included curriculum focused on thematic gadgets

A thematic unit is an effective curriculum method to resource in the improvement of mind and openness the horizon of standards, thoughts, and thoughts of college students, instructor and mother, and father. On this technique, the curriculum is designed and organized in keeping with the principal topic, in mind. 'In other words, it is a sequence of instructions that integrate topics across the curriculum, which includes math, analyzing, social research, technological know-how, language arts, and many others. That each one tie into the principle subject of the unit'. All of the activities deliberate and designed in keeping with the thematic idea. And that theme is going for weeks in exercise with the aid of the trainer and students within the school room. Many special subjects can be part of the practice like all unique United States of America, animals, unique vacations, culture, traditions, earth, sun device, and many others. The thematic unit will increase the pupil's hobby inside the research, they gain better know-how and connections among the subject and real-life practices. It covers lots of subjects and subjects so, keeps the student engaged. And teachers can compact the curriculum and plan plenty of evaluation strategies. The guideline observed to put together the lesson entails 1)' theme based on not unusual core schooling based totally on scholar hobby. 2) Topic must be grade-suitable. 3) Objective to grasp for the duration of gaining knowledge of. 4) Planned the cloth used for the subject matter. 5) Choice of the activities outdoor the curriculum. 6) Create the dialogue; include a query and answers to stimulate college students' questioning manner. 7) Don't forget the version in books to correlate with the activities and most important theme of the unit. Inside the final, an assessment will provide facts concerning conceiving the data of the unit. This student must be a monitor at some stage in the practice. Thematic devices create a remarkable curriculum and it's very challenging for the trainer in particular. It makes instructors reconsider approximately the subject and work on it, so college students get the clean imagination and prescient of the entire unit. I practiced it in my elegance; absolute confidence, it takes masses of time and guidance to put in force in the lecture room. However, its final results changed into gratifying. The involvement, participation, and pleasure of college students, clean the imagination and prescient of the entire practiced unit.

Integration of entrepreneurship into training

Integrating entrepreneurship method,' making college

students greater creative, possibility oriented, proactive and innovative, adhering to a wide definition of entrepreneurship applicable to all walks in existence'. College students ought to teach their potential and willingly create fees and recognition for other human beings. This idea is the middle of entrepreneurship and is likewise a competence that every one human being wants to become the society, regardless of any type of variations. This technique 'aids students to assume out of the field and nurture unconventional abilities and capabilities. It creates possibilities, guarantees social justice, instills self-belief, and stimulates the economy. Entrepreneurship schooling is a lifelong mastering procedure, beginning as early as essential college and progressing via all degrees of schooling, inclusive of grownup education. Introducing younger children to entrepreneurship develops their initiative and facilitates them to be more innovative and self-assured in something they undertake and to act in a socially responsible way. There are numerous ways entrepreneurship instructions can be incorporated into the faculty curriculum.' enterprise, language artwork, wondering talents, Imagining, and questioning skills could be part of the curriculum. They could exercise reputable interviews with marketers and reliable letters. They could learn about the products and the process of their production or innovation. They could even use their innovative capabilities to provide a product or concept regarding the audience's interest or provide the controversy or change on the present product. They can research their competing merchandise and advantage statistics, in this manner they can study their competitors' strengths and weaknesses. It'll inspire them and grow their thinking capabilities to work on their venture in a better way within the constrained sources. This exercise opens the door of their creativeness, sharing the concept with the organization can assist to increase many possibilities in distinct attitude. This exercise is being used in lots of institutions and it allows to develop of self-assurance in college students and openness in their minds. It is noticeably endorsed to be implemented within classrooms to assist in 'coaching entrepreneurship talents through faculty is a technique so that students be left loose to find many approaches to be innovative thru it. Teachers must also be supplied recommendations to control college students and help them to foster a pleasing environment for college students to develop.'

The robust emphasis on problem fixing and critical questioning

Important questioning originates with the sensing of a problem. It's far a first-class of concept running to resolve the trouble and to attain a tentative conclusion that's supported with the aid of all to be had information. It's a system of problem-fixing requiring the use of innovative insight, highbrow honesty, and sound judgment. it is the idea of the method of medical inquiry. Citizens must learn how to think severely approximately the issues as it is the need to improve the excellent of their learning and desires of training. The curriculum concerned in this setting requires an instructor's demonstration on improving the improvement of vital questioning talents. It could be finished by way of modeling questioning out loud, thinking concerning the topic, developing surroundings to recognize the challenge, provide records and motivates them to analyze and check out, and growing the techniques to utilize various equipment to boom critical wondering. Surroundings ought to be superb and encouraging to achieve the required cause. College students' characteristics and development within the getting to know system may be decided as a readiness to the openness to assume severely. This means almost, maximum of the college gadget. It ought to be practiced with the coaching of questions to open their minds, like; describe what you spot/examine in this web page. What are the 'hidden' messages? What's lacking from this picture/reading? What are my ideals approximately this? Why do you accept this as true? Whose hobbies are being served who is advantaged? Whose pursuits aren't served who's deprived? What needs to trade and how will you make contributions to this variation? Then proceed with diverse activities, so they can see the challenge with unique views.

Institution work and improvement of social competencies

Coming into the school brings lots of challenges especially for individuals who lack social skills. Dedication of college students' interaction with peers in organization work is the underlying assumption. 'It's far typically concept that scholars can cooperate, speak, problem remedy and work together effectively with their friends inside a set. Frequently, educators consider that students know the way to interact accurately to fulfill their needs; that they recognize a way to ask for clarification whilst pressured, the way to take turns, and the way to give an explanation for their wondering and concentrate while others are talking. Then, toward the cease of their educational revel in, they go away with the give up of their instructional experience, they depart with the expectation of being capable of characteristic and correctly make contributions to latest society. Lack of social talents creates life-long issues. To solve this trouble, instructors can play an important function in knowledge the behaviors and needs of college students. And plan the institution activities, so the scholar receives more interaction with peers. For this purpose, proper trainer's education is required as properly so she/he can understand the benefits and advantages of organization gaining knowledge of. And she or he correctly implements Johnson's five elements of cooperative learning: 1. wonderful interdependence: students work towards a common intention. They fail or be successful together as a whole institution 2. Person accountability: each student inside the organization is classed individually. College students analyze together so they perform higher for my part. 3. Face-to-face interaction: students promote every different gaining knowledge of by way of helping, assisting, encouraging, and praising every different effort to reap. 4. Social skills: interpersonal and small organization capabilities which include leadership, choice-making, trust-building, communique, and struggle-management, want to gain knowledge of. 5. Institution processing: group members speak about the effectiveness of the group. What went nicely, what desires the improvement, and the way nicely they maintained an effective running courting.

Group sports and social interaction play an essential role in the fulfillment of a pupil's existence. It develops and complements their social competencies. They discover ways to clear up troubles, talk, learns to apply diverse instructional gear, and practice the numerous strategies to address the conditions. Get them geared up for actual-lifestyles reports and issues. At some stage in my teaching practice, college students are required to work with peers for different activities and assignments. To increase the benefit of getting to know, additionally, they requested to question, answer, share their thoughts, and mingle in any such way to get rid of their hesitation and increase their self-assurance. They advocated asking for help to solve the confusion. College students' learning will be maximized via the teaching of social competencies in the study room. College students will experience security and assurance in sharing their minds and soliciting for assist while vital. They may be better ready with social abilities as a way to help them engage as it should be and effectively with others in all conditions. These action studies helped discover scholar perceptions and views on social interplay for the duration of cooperative organization work. It also helped me advantage better expertise in which social interplay breakdown may arise inside a set. This led to my teaching of social abilities inside the school room and helped improve pupil interaction and cooperation within cooperative organization work'.

Knowledge and movement as the goals of mastering in place of rote know-how

Rote knowledge is a traditional way of studying. On this technique, college students repeat the textual content to reminiscences to its means and context as well. But the proper know-how is not in cooperation with this approach and college students couldn't relate it with their stored knowledge or don't even endorsed to research approximately the subject to get the right knowledge. The evaluation for this sort of studying is based on pre-designed tests. But on the other hand, if the pupil is aware of the idea and features a clean photograph of the difficulty, they can relate to shopping facts in the brain. They don't want to memorize the textual content or given records. Our brain works in one way that it chained one's statistics to some other and this system allows us to develop new thoughts and thoughts. It keeps the gaining knowledge of procedure and boom the information. The one way of this form of gaining knowledge of which I exploit in my exercise is visualizing. By watching, records keep for a long term in line with the research. And this method worked for my students nearly all the time. In this exercise, the exam gadget also doesn't require evaluating the development. College student's average overall performance is good sufficient to look at the outcomes. Getting to know needs to be a transformative method via which college students can transform themselves and rework their environment. For that to take place, children should be a vital part of their gaining knowledge of technique. The studying must recognition on the youngsters. This means the getting to know the system is constructed at the precedent information of the students and their lifestyle, vision and revel in. So in that method, students aren't considering as an empty bag to be area however as half-full glass. In that feel, while a subject is below take a look at the idea of the students on the problem is first taken into movement and discussion is undertaken to cope with cautiously their false impression or idea. Well-known pedagogical conceptions characterizing progressivism: the combination of getting to know, their scenario, and socializing dreams. training is a manner of non-stop boom that ought to continue in an incorporated manner, given the holistic nature of the model manner; dreams or desires also are critical conditions for learning; consequently, reactions are high-quality discovered in situations in which they are useful, or related to real-lifestyles conditions; in the end, the edition is each an individualizing and socializing technique, related to mutual modifications among individual desires and social establishments, the purpose of schooling being the improvement of an included social character. The essence of pedagogical progressivism is, in our opinion, expressed through Dewey (1920) through the concept that evolution exhibits intelligence because of the inner organizing issue of the experiment.

Therefore, Dewey explains, with 1st Baron Verulam and his successors, a reversal which reasons heralding modernity, motive "and its bodyguard of general notions" acting from then on as "the conservative element, the enslaving component of the spirit." Enjoy is releasing energy. Experience method the new, which takes us far from adhering to the past, and well-known shows new facts and truths. Religion in revel in does no longer produce devotion to custom, but dedication to development. What matters to the functionalist psychology at stake is, as Dewey likes to mention, the continuous reconstruction of the experience - translated pedagogically by using the students' confrontation with tricky conditions - and this reconstruction is suspended from an operating intelligence developed all through the subject's interactions with the environment. The idea of revel in, concerning a steady change in troubles and views, is then inseparable from that of development, accordingly giving it's deep that means to the concept of progressivism in education. academic progressivism is adverse, for the theoretical reasons said, to the transmission through a third party, without distinguishing among mechanistic transmission coaching, basically concerning memorization, and rational or explicit, attractive to knowledge. A question of precedence among "logical" and "mental" is performed out right here. Very normally, for psychology rooted in naturalism, good judgment is suspended from the psychological, even as in evaluation, for "rationalist" psychology, common sense leads to the mental, which we suggest increasing inside the destiny for the next technology. Progressivism is a commonplace reaction of the traditional instructional device. Conventional training encourages the kind of shipping that is teacher-targeted and it's miles based on how teachers deliver information to college students thru a specific text-primarily based curriculum. It is targeted on simple schooling of core subjects to create stability as a way to be of exquisite advantage. The transport of guidance to college students is important and determines positive or bad outcomes. Conventional faculties also cognizance of supplying simple instructional practices to enhance mastering. These days, instructional picks are many and many dad and mom are curiosity is growing among men and women of every age. But, many humans are familiar with the conventional type of study room. Even though this form of the model is criticized heavily by way of many due to its risks, it does have some blessings and extraordinary benefits.

The cultural shaping of cognitive phenomena

The idea that way of life profoundly affects the contents of notion thru shared knowledge structures has been an imperative subject in modern cognitive anthropology. Psychology has provided a hard and fast of concepts that are beneficial for describing these understanding systems. Schema, as an example, refers to expertise structures that govern thought with the aid of selective interest, retention, and use of statistics about a specific component of the sector. Built into a schema is the specification of how its parts relate to each other and the entire. as an instance, the schema for "going to the museum" can also consist of the following interconnected behaviors, "ready in line, shopping for tickets, preserving silent, admiring items, now not touching gadgets," and so forth. Schemas may be approximately people, items, situations, events, and sequences of activities. Drawing on this concept, the cognitive anthropologist has brought the concept of cultural schemas, styles of basic schemas that make up the means machine of a cultural organization. Those cultural schemas which are intersubjectively shared in a set are called cultural fashions. Cultural models govern the methods by way of which humans interpret their experiences and manual motion in a wide variety of existing domain names. A specifically critical kind of cultural model is a script. A script is an occasion schema that stipulates the individuals who appropriately take part inside the event, the social roles they play, the items they use, the series of actions they interact in. It is easy to peer why scripts are crucial to the supply-and-take of ordinary cultural existence, consisting of the functioning of establishments, the performance of rituals, and playing games. As Katherine Nelson keeps, "without shared scripts, every social act could want negotiating afresh". The schema notion enables us to prepare and explain how it is that the contents of human minds can vary as extensively across cultures as it obviously does, but does subculture have an effect on the very idea processes via which humans cognize the world? Some early anthropologists and psychologists held the view that extraordinary peoples indeed purpose differently. Wilhelm Wundt, in providing cultural psychology to complement experimental psychology, sincerely idea so while he wrote, "All phenomena with which the intellectual sciences deal are, certainly, creations of the social community". The French sociologist Levy-Bruhl believed there has been a characteristic "primitive" notion that did no longer understand the world in phrases of causal sequences and tended to merge emotion and cognition. Levy-Bruhl did not regard primitive notion as inferior but simply as distinct – and not unique in an essential pragmatic sense: "…of their ordinary interest, when they're now not being influenced (misled) through their collective representations, 'they' think the same as 'we' would, drawing the same conclusions from the identical types of proof". The Linguistic Relativity speculation. In George Orwell's novel 1984, the police state introduces a brand new synthetic language, Newspeak, designed to deter people from thinking positive kinds of thoughts that can be deemed to be dangerous.

Can this fictional attempt at idea manage to achieve real existence? One of the most well-known early concerns of the notion that culture influences idea is embodied within the linguistic relativity or Sapir-Whorf hypothesis, the competition that the precise language humans communicate affects idea. no matter the long-standing interest that this speculation has generated inside the social sciences sustained empirical research on it has been infrequent, and most of the beyond effects were inconclusive. Lately, but, there has been a new surge of systematic, compelling research that supports the linguistic relativity hypothesis. In an early try and address the linguistic relativity hypothesis, Berlin and Kay (1969) examined color classification throughout cultures. They found that coloration names are assigned in phrases of an orderly hierarchy. In the few cultures where there are most effective shade names, those are black and white. If a third color is delivered, it's pink. The subsequent tree color terms are probably to be yellow, blue, and inexperienced, and many others. Berlin and Kay also concluded that, even though obstacles of coloration terms vary across cultures and languages, the focus of every simple color (e.g., the most prototypical purple in an array of reds) is basically the same. The work of Berlin and Kay has been interpreted to indicate that there is a well-known, physiological basis to color type. The pioneering work supported Berlin and Kay's analysis. Running with Dani tribesmen in New Guinea whose language has the most effective two fundamental shade terms, Heider and Olivier confirmed Dani and English speakers coloration chips and then tested for recognition of the chips a few seconds later. the usage of this system, color memory become largely impartial of coloration vocabulary and consistent with the suggestion of Berlin and Kay, focal shades confirmed higher reminiscence than non-focal hues for both English speakers (individuals) and the Dani. This work has been commonly taken as clean evidence towards the linguistic relativity hypothesis. But, it has been criticized on methodological grounds for its narrow scope, and the loss of next studies confirming the findings of the authentic research with other responsibilities or linguistic corporations. Currently, idea-upsetting new research has emerged that questions the findings of Heider and Olivier (1972), and offers new proof for the have an effect of linguistic color phrases on shade perception and memory. Roberson, Davies, and Davidoff (sought to replicate and increase the unique studies of Heider and Olivier (1972) with the Berinmo of Papua New Guinea, a hunter-gatherer folks that speak a language that has the handiest 5 color phrases.

In a sequence of experiments, they discovered convergent lines of proof for linguistic relativity in coloration notion and memory. (1) Berinmo styles of naming and reminiscence have been statistically greater much like each other than Berinmo memory become to English reminiscence patterns; (2) whilst the discriminability benefit of focal colorings turned into eliminated, the memory benefit of focal shades relative to non-focal ones disappeared for both English speakers and Berinmo speakers; (three) class learning for focal as opposed to non-focal shades did now not vary. Accordingly, there has been no evidence that the Berinmo have an underlying cognitive employer of coloration that favors the foci of the eight English simple chromatic coloration classes (with the viable exception of focal red). (four) common, Berinmo audio system' performance in coloration categorization turned into drastically poorer than that of English speakers, replicating Heider & Olivier's (1972) locating with the Dani. However, Roberson et al. (2000) had been in a position to reveal that Berinmo and English-audio system did not range in a similar visual-spatial reminiscence venture that did not contain the coloration area. This shows that the poorer reminiscence performance of the Dani and the Berinmo will be defined by using the poorer coloration vocabularies of Dani and Berinmo, in preference to unfamiliarity with a proper check scenario or lack of formal schooling. Moreover, Roberson et al. (2000) determined that evidence for the effect of coloration terms on color categorization can be discovered even in Heider & Olivier's (1972) facts. An ambitious attempt to examine the linguistic relativity speculation in range marking has been completed by using Lucy and his colleagues. Following an early take a look at Carroll and Casagrande (1958), they tested the extent to which linguistic variations in a wide variety marking affect concept. Yucatec Maya and plenty of different languages (e.g., Chinese language, Japanese) range from English in a wide variety of marking styles. English numerals immediately regulate their related noun (e.g., one candle). Yucatec numerals are always followed through a numeral classifier that describes the fabric of the counted object (e.g., one lengthy thin wax). Does this result in exceptional styles of categorizing objects? In non-verbal category tasks, members have been presented with a triad of items that differed on cloth or shape (e.g., candle, stick, wax). Consistent with the lexical structures of those two languages, the Yucatec audio system showed a desire for fabric-based total classification, while English speakers showed a desire for shape-based total classification. Some other line of studies specializes in linguistic versions inside the coding of the spatial regions. Speakers of English and different Indo-European languages want the usage of body coordinates to represent the vicinity of gadgets (e.g., "the person is on the right of the house"). In assessment, Guugu Yiimithirr (an Australian language) favors constant cardinal course terms ("the person is west of the house"). Is this difference in linguistic convention implicated in cognition? The researchers created non-linguistic tasks that measured overall performance in finding items and manipulated the sensitivity of the 2 spatial referents eight structures to rotation. As predicted, the audio system of Guugu Yiimithirr was unaffected using rotation manipulation in finding objects accurately. English speakers, in contrast, have been thrown off by the equal rotation manipulation, being less accurate in locating the objects.

A famous experimental attempt to test linguistic relativity speculation is Alfred Bloom's (1981) work on counterfactual or hypothetical reasoning. Bloom noticed that the English language has a specific linguistic device to code counterfactuals (the subjunctive mode—e.g., "If I had been rich, I would journey the arena"). not so in the Chinese language, which as an alternative expresses counterfactual which means by way of relying on context, combined with the use of if-then statements. In a sequence of studies, Bloom gave English and Chinese language speakers, in addition to Chinese English bilinguals, controlled counterfactual memories and determined that Chinese speakers did more poorly in counterfactual reasoning than English speakers. However, scientists have criticized Bloom's work, raising questions on the accuracy of the Chinese language translations of the stories. Moreover, there may be no doubt that the Chinese language can counterfactual reasoning in ordinary existence. The Chinese honestly should think, "If I have been most effective five minutes early, I might now not have ignored the education!" The query then is whether or not or not the lack of an easy linguistic device to mark counterfactuals in the Chinese language renders counterfactual reasoning less likely. As we can see later, there's a case to be made that Chinese are certainly less probably to interact in hypothetical or counterfactual reasoning than Westerners, although for motives which could have extra to do by and large with cultural factors instead of differences in grammatical classes. To summarize, after a preliminary duration of combined findings, growing new evidence supports the Sapir-Whorf competition that linguistic differences affect the notion. Stable evidence has been determined for the cognitive effect of linguistic differences in variety marking, the coding of the spatial region, and even color categorization. The work supporting linguistic relativity has profound implications for psychology, and extra special, for the cultural mediation of thought. To the extent that societies have diverged in their linguistic conventions, so could cognitive methods, to a few degrees. Truly, however, extra research is needed to have a look at the pervasiveness of the influence of language on ideas. Furthermore, the tools of experimental psychology may be profitably used to look at in extra element the cognitive strategies that mediate the linguistic control of thought. Eventually, it is critical to differentiate linguistic consequences from different cultural outcomes on ideas, for example, results because of social practices, epistemic ideals, or know-how in a domain. Those questions are mainly tough to untangle due to the fact non-linguistic cultural styles and linguistic conventions that correlate with the equal cognitive orientations tend to co-arise in societies.

Sizable early studies program to promote the concept that tradition basically shapes concept is that of the influential Russian faculty of Lev Vygotsky (1978) and Alexander Luria (1971), and their friends in the West, which includes, in particular, Michael Cole and his colleagues. The Russian college continues to influence an extensive range of contemporary studies on the way of life and cognition which we can talk about. The Russian school stands as a stark contrast to the triumphing assumption of experimental psychology that there are unitary, unchanging, customary cognitive methods that perform throughout contexts, cultures, and historical durations. At the heart of the Russian college is the concept that cognitive strategies emerge from practical activity that is culturally restrained and traditionally growing. Cognitive procedures perform in sync with tools or artifacts in everyday sensible sports. Equipment can be symbolic, as within the case of languages, numeric structures, and guidelines for games; as well as material, as within the case of axes, needles, and bowls. Human cognition has coevolved with device use for most of the new human evolutionary records. As a result, cognitive structures end up people engage with tools in everyday sensible interest, inclusive of while hunting, playing, weaving, or talking. This Vygotskian notion that cognition is embedded in sensible interest has endorsed a circle of relatives of modern-day studies packages that are typically called located cognition. Researchers on this way of life eleven check out how the cognitive activity is intimately tied to the unique social context in which it evidently takes place. that is performed by way of inspecting how cognitive pastime interacts with device use; how it embodies the values and assumptions of a community of freshmen; and how its miles formed through social interactions, together with between figure and infant, teacher and scholar. The methodological preference is to take a look at understanding acquisition in its normal naturalistic setting, along with studies of mathematical wondering amongst sweet-promoting Brazilian kids, or arithmetic among tailors in West Africa (Lave, 1977). Research has additionally tested cognitive techniques in social features which can be sufficiently complex, inclusive of navigating ships, that the cognitive implementation of the venture by using a single person becomes not possible. This necessitates a sensitive manner of joint social coordination in context so that cognition will become "allotted" throughout individual minds and artifacts. According to the Russian college, human cognition develops in a species-precise medium, that of lifestyle, which is the gathered sample of tool-use in the course of the historical existence of a set. The numerous social activities that a child engages in interact with primitive cognitive systems. The kid step by step internalizes those social sports and develops ever extra complicated cognitive structures. The cultural version in cognition emerges because of the unique ancient tendencies of societies, leading to different social activities and gear, which then lead to distinct idea processes which can be congruent with the specific ancient trajectories of societies. thus Luria envisioned an ancient technology of psychology: "psychological tactics and most of all, better, particularly human, types of mental hobby…ought to be understood as a social phenomenon in starting place, mediated of their shape, and consciously and willfully directed in their functioning psychological procedures are of ancient individual and psychology should be understood as historic technological know-how.

The purpose of this challenge turned into having a look at the effects of huge social and economic reforms in faraway areas of important Asia on the logical reasoning of Uzbek peasants. Luria and co-workers presented simple syllogisms in a quasi-experimental layout to four organizations of individuals who have been at unique stages of modernization: Non-literate women in remote villages who did not participate in formal monetary practices; non-literate men who had been engaged in traditional farming; younger activists concerned in collective farming (some of whom have been minimally literate); and women attending instructor education schools. If logical reasoning is a familiar belonging of the thoughts this is impervious to historical changes, then no differences in logical reasoning could be located amongst those 4 organizations. But, to the extent that cognitive systems are converted with the aid of historic trade in socio-monetary and academic conditions, greater publicity to modernization would result in greater reliance on formal common sense. Luria and his colleagues located marked variants in logical reasoning. The most powerful effects emerged for syllogisms with contents unfamiliar to the villagers. Villagers living traditional lives had the most trouble with problems that did no longer agree to their normal revel in, suggesting that their responses had been pushed by measuring, know-how-primarily based approach to reasoning. In a few severe cases, this sample had brought about the refusal of a few individuals to have interaction in the logical reasoning venture at all, for the reason that the contents of the problems had been unusual, making the hassle in principle unanswerable. For example, considered one of Luria's unfamiliar troubles was, "inside some distance north all bears are white. Novaya Zemlya is within the ways north. What hues are the bears there?" To which one player responded, "However I don't understand what form of bears are there. I've not been there and I don't understand. Look, why don't you ask antique guy twelve times, he turned into there and he is aware of it, he will tell you." In contrast, the equally surprising problems posed no trouble to those who had some publicity to training.

Culture and the brain

While you study an image at the computer display at right, in which do your eyes linger longest? Particularly, the answer to that question might range depending upon where you have been raised. individuals stare extra fixedly at the educate in the center, even as Chinese permit their eyes to roam extra across the whole photo, in accordance to research by way of psychologist Richard Nisbett, Ph.D. That distinction reflects an extra widespread divide between the ways that Westerners and East Asians view the world around them, says Nisbett, who heads the subculture and Cognition program at the University of Michigan. He and his colleagues discover how human beings' cultural backgrounds affect their maximum basic cognitive methods: categorization, mastering, causal reasoning, or even attention and notion. The researchers have located growing proof that East Asians, whose greater collectivist way of life promotes group harmony and contextual know-how of conditions, suppose more holistically. They take note of all the elements of a scene, to context, and the relationships among gadgets. Western lifestyle, in assessment, emphasizes non-public autonomy and formal common sense, and so Westerners are more analytic and be aware of specific gadgets and categories. The concept that culture can form the way humans suppose at these deep ranges is a departure for psychology, which as a subject historically assumed that basic cognitive approaches are commonplace, in keeping with Nisbett. But it is an idea that has gained traction during the last decade or two.

Now, Nisbett and others are investigating the cognitive effects of the extra diffused cultural variations between, as an instance, one-of-a-kind areas of East Asia. They hope that this new research will also assist explain for extra exactly how and why the way of life and cognition have interaction.

Train spotting

In a recent observation, Nisbett and graduate scholar Hannah Faye Chua used a monitoring tool to display the attention movements of twenty-five American and twenty-seven Chinese language members-all graduate college students at Michigan-even as the students stared for 3 seconds at photographs of items in opposition to complicated backgrounds. The thirty-six pictures protected, amongst others, the education proven above, a tiger in a wooded area and an airplane with mountains in the historical past.

The researchers discovered that the people targeted at the foreground item one hundred and eighteen milliseconds faster, on average, than the Chinese contributors did, after which persisted to observe the focal object longer. The Chinese tended to move their eyes from side to side more among the principal item and the background and checked out the historical past for longer than the individuals did. In 2001 take a look at, as an example, Nisbett after which graduate scholar Takahiko Masuda, Ph.D., confirmed Jap and American individual's lively underwater vignettes that blanketed focal objects-three massive fish-and background items like rocks, seaweed, and water bubbles. When they asked participants to describe the scenes, Americans have been much more likely to begin using recalling the focal fish, while Japanese were more likely to describe the whole scene, saying something like "it was a lake or pond." Later, the Japanese contributors additionally recalled extra information about the heritage gadgets than the individuals did. "Individuals right now zoomed in on the gadgets," Nisbett says. "The Japanese paid more attention to context. "Cognitive variations between Westerners and Asians display up in other areas as properly. for example, in tests of categorization, Americans are much more likely to institution items based on how nicely the objects match into categories through kind-so, say, a cow and a fowl would possibly pass collectively due to the fact they may be both animals. Asians, in evaluation, are much more likely to organization gadgets based totally on relationships-so a cow and grass might cross together due to the fact a cow eats grass.

Any other distinction among Westerners and Asians regards the fundamental attribution errors-a mainstay psychological concept for the remaining thirty years that, it seems, might not be so fundamental in any case. The concept posits that humans generally overemphasize persona-related causes for others' behavior, whilst underemphasizing or ignoring contextual elements. So, as an example, a person may additionally believe he tripped and fell due to a crack in the sidewalk, however, expect that a person else fell due to clumsiness. But, it turns out, maximum East Asians do now not fall prey to this mistake-they're more likely to recollect contextual elements while seeking to explain different human beings' behavior. In 1994 take a look at, as an instance, psychologist Kaiping Peng, Ph.D., analyzed American and Chinese language newspaper bills of recent murders. He found that American reporters emphasized the personal attributes of the murderers, whilst Chinese reporters focused extra on situational elements.

Frontier spirit

Even though such research provides convincing proof of cognitive variations between Asians and Westerners, says Nisbett, they don't explain why those variations arise. "We announce that these cognitive variations come from social variations," he says. "However it's a totally tenuous connection. There is no direct proof for it yet." To find that proof, psychologist Shinobu Kitayama, PhD-who co-chairs Michigan's lifestyle and cognition application with

Nisbett-is examining different cultures to decide how their special takes on collectivism, interdependence, and different social attributes affect cognition. Kitayama is analyzing the cognitive fashion of citizens of Hokkaido, Japan-what he calls Japan's "Wild West. Settlers from the relaxation of Japan arrived there inside the mid-nineteenth century to be searching for their fortune within the barren region. If this frontier spirit is related to a sort of American-style individualism, Kitayama reasoned, and then possibly Hokkaido Japanese might look greater like Americans than like other Jap in their cognitive approaches. In a have a look at these days time-honored for eBook within the journal of persona and Social Psychology, he and his colleagues observed that Hokkaido residents were almost as probably like individuals to commit the fundamental attribution mistakes. "The frontier doesn't simply exist anywhere anymore, Kitayama says, "but its delusion and discourse are still powerful." some other strand of evidence comes from Asian people, who often are raised with a few blends of Asian and Western cultural traditions.

"In research that looks at Asians, European individuals and Asian Americans, Asian individuals typically fall someplace in among the alternative," Nisbett says. Subsequently, Nisbett is beginning a chain of research so one can observe cognitive variations between human beings in cultures that are quite similar in lots of ways, but fluctuate in their diploma of collectivism.

Why it subjects

In an increasingly multicultural world, those tradition-prompted cognitive variations could have realistic implications, in step with the University of California, Santa Barbara, psychologist Heejung Kim, Ph.D. Kim, who is from South Korea, observed her research notion in her revel as a global graduate pupil within the United States. In her graduate seminar classes, her inclination became to listen quietly and absorb what changed into taking place around her-however she felt compelled to speak up. "After suffering for some time, I began to suppose that someone ought to question whether or not the system of talking is valuable for absolutely everyone," she says, "as it truly wasn't for me." She decided to test ECU-American and first-era Asian-American students by giving them complicated good judgment trouble to resolve. Manipulate-organization individuals solved the problem silently, whilst participants of the experimental group had to talk out loud and give an explanation for their reasoning as they labored. Kim located that EU Americans who talked out loud solved the hassle just as well as people who stayed silent, however being pressured to speak significantly undermined the Asian college students' overall performance. In well-known, Kim says, Asians may think and purpose in a less easily "verbalizable" way than Westerners. It is extra intuitive and less linear," she says. So if you have to talk aloud, EU Americans simply vocalize their mind, but Asian Americans-on top of fixing the trouble-ought to translate their thoughts into phrases. In trendy, Nisbett says, he expects that over the following couple of many years work via researchers like Kim-and different Asian and Asian-American psychologists-will profoundly affect the way psychologists reflect on consideration on which factors of thinking are standard and which are culture-precise.

They're going to be bringing very distinct methods of considering cognitive psychology, social psychology, developmental psychology," he says. "They may be going to alternate the sphere."